MW01166660

The

TWO
NATURES

The
TWO
NATURES

LEE LEE

XULON PRESS

Xulon Press
2301 Lucien Way #415
Maitland, FL 32751
407.339.4217
www.xulonpress.com

© 2019 by Lee Lee

All rights reserved solely by the author. The author guarantees all contents are original and do not infringe upon the legal rights of any other person or work. No part of this book may be reproduced in any form without the permission of the author. The views expressed in this book are not necessarily those of the publisher.

Unless otherwise indicated, Scripture quotations taken from the Holy Bible, New International Version (NIV). Copyright © 1973, 1978, 1984, 2011 by Biblica, Inc.™. Used by permission. All rights reserved.

Printed in the United States of America.

ISBN-13: 978-1-54567-214-3

Please read this book through thoroughly, so that you will not miss out on the sequence and the importance of the messages that the beloved Lord Jesus is sending to His Church, through this and the other books that are to follow. You will therefore not understand what He is saying to His church, by partially reading any of them.

THIS BOOK IS WRITTEN FOR AND DEDICATED TO

THE BRIDE OF THE LORD JESUS CHRIST

"NOW THIS IS ETERNAL LIFE:

THAT THEY MAY KNOW YOU, THE ONLY TRUE GOD,

AND JESUS CHRIST, WHOM YOU HAVE SENT."

JOHN 17:3 NIV

TABLE OF CONTENTS

TABLE OF CONTENTS

INTRODUCTION

T his is the sixth Book in the series *"GOD SPEAKS"* which comprises a total of fourteen Books. The Books are all of the Lord Jesus, written by Lee Lee – the servant of our Lord Jesus Christ. He was called, separated and taught by the Lord for His purpose of sending His Light into His Church through these 14 Books. These Books are to give truth/knowledge for cleansing and preparation of His Church in these the very last of days.

> Therefore, brothers, we have an obligation – but
> it is not to the sinful nature, to live according to it.
> [13]For if you live according to the sinful nature, you
> will die; but if by the Spirit you put to death the
> misdeeds of the body, you will live, Rom. 8:12-13

Have you ever wondered how some who are called Christians, could have done some of the outrageous things that they have done?

THE TWO NATURES

"How are such things possible?" Some have also asked: "Those who have done these terrible things, are they really Christians?" The answer is yes – at least some of them are. These things happen because ever since they came to the Lord Jesus, they have never sought to sincerely lay down their lives to Him, and so to be sanctified/cleansed from the ways of the sinful nature. They would then have begun to be united to their Lord, thereby becoming one in agreement and purpose with the Word and ways of the Lord Jesus, by taking on His divine nature. Instead, they continued to live according to their sinful nature, the result of which is this horrible disobedience to their Lord, and so they continue to do what they have been doing – committing outrageous acts/sinning.

Do not be deceived: God cannot be mocked. A man reaps what he sows. [8]The one who sows to please his sinful nature, from that nature will reap destruction; the one who sows to please the Spirit, from the Spirit will reap eternal life. [9]Let us not become weary in doing good, for at the proper time we will reap a harvest if we do not give up. Gal. 6:7-9

It is God's will that you should be sanctified: that you should avoid sexual immorality; [4]that each of you should learn to control his own body in a way

THE TWO NATURES

that is holy and honorable, ⁵not in passionate lust like the heathen, who do not know God; ⁶and that in this matter no one should wrong his brother or take advantage of him. The Lord will punish men for all such sins, as we have already told you and warned you. *⁷For God did not call us to be impure, but to live a holy life. ⁸Therefore, he who rejects this instruction does not reject man but God, who gives you his Holy Spirit.* 1 Thess. 4:3-8

May God himself, the God of peace, *sanctify you through and through*. May your whole spirit, soul and body be kept blameless at the coming of our Lord Jesus Christ. ²⁴The one who calls you is faithful and he will do it. 1 Thess. 5:23-24

This decision is solidly placed in our hands and in our hands alone. This is called freewill, because we are free to exercise it in any direction we choose, for God has made us free moral agents. So, if we choose to go in the direction of the divine nature, which we are invited to do, we are certainly free to do so. On the other hand, if we choose to continue in the way of the carnal sinful nature, we are also free to do so, even after we have received the Lord Jesus.

THE TWO NATURES

Some have also been hiding from and escaping God through the images and defenses they have projected to cover themselves with. This is just as our predecessors Adam and Eve did, as they covered themselves with leaves and hid from the Lord among the trees of the garden. This is really what most of us have been doing all our lives, even those of us who are in the church; although we tend not to want to know or believe that this is what we are doing.

THE TWO NATURES

FOREWORD

The Lord Jesus freed us from under the heavy hand of the enemy, and so enabled us to oppose and to deny our sinful nature through our flesh, and therefore satan, any further domination over our lives, by fully embracing the life that the Lord Jesus paid for and bought with His precious blood, and gave to us. However, we have yet to embrace it in its fullness, because we have not fully trusted our lives into the hands of the Lord Jesus, and therefore embraced His divine nature, and at the same time, learn to deny the sinful nature through the denial of our flesh.

> Then he said to them all: "If anyone would come after me, he must deny himself and take up his cross daily and follow me. 24For whoever wants to save his life will lose it, but whoever loses his life for me will save it. 25What good is it for a man to gain the

THE TWO NATURES

whole world, and yet lose or forfeit his very self?

Luke 9:23-25

We are no longer to live according to how we feel, or according to the thoughts that come to our minds, since the devil uses these avenues to deceive Christians, reason with them and lead them off, and at times lead them off through others. Rather, we are to walk according to the knowledge of God's Word, believing it and holding firmly to it.

> Get rid of the old yeast that you may be a new batch without yeast – as you really are. For Christ, our Passover lamb, has been sacrificed. 1 Cor. 5:7

This satanic sinful nature is the nature which we have inherited from our ancestors, Adam and Eve, and it can be clearly seen manifested in and through each and every one of us in its various forms. This is why our beloved Lord Jesus tells us that if we want to follow Him, we must deny ourselves. What our Lord is really saying to us is: we are to deny ourselves of the ways of that sinful satanic nature, for it dominates and influences every aspect of our lives – everything that we believe, desire, think, plan, choose and do, along with all our senses, our emotions, our feelings, etc. – all are under the control of the sinful nature. For these reasons the Lord Jesus calls us to walk by knowledge.

> Grace and peace be yours in abundance through *the knowledge of God and of Jesus our Lord.* [3]His divine power has given us everything we need for life and godliness through our knowledge of him who called us by his own glory and goodness. [4]Through these he has given us his very great and precious promises, so that through them *you may participate in the divine nature and escape the corruption in the world caused by evil desires.* [5]For this very reason, make every effort to add to your faith goodness; and to goodness, knowledge; [6]and to knowledge, self–control; and to self–control, perseverance; and to perseverance, godliness; [7]and to godliness, brotherly kindness; and to brotherly kindness, love. [8]For if you possess these qualities in increasing measure, they will keep you from being ineffective and unproductive in your knowledge of our Lord Jesus Christ. [9]But if anyone does not have them, he is nearsighted and blind, and has forgotten that he has been cleansed from his past sins. [10]Therefore, my brothers, be all the more eager

THE TWO NATURES

to make your calling and election sure. For if you
do these things, you will never fall, [11]and you will
receive a rich welcome into the eternal kingdom
of our Lord and Savior Jesus Christ. 2 Peter 1:2-11

Therefore, if we choose to walk with the Lord Jesus and refuse
to deny ourselves of the ways of the sinful nature, we will not be
able to walk uprightly with Him. For the ways of the sinful nature
are contrary to the ways of the Lord Jesus, and so it will rob us of
everything that is of the divine nature, which we are to be clothed
with through the sanctifying work of the Holy Spirit, when we
come to the Lord Jesus and continue in Him.

Therefore, brothers, we have an obligation – but
it is not to the sinful nature, to live according to it.
[13]For if you live according to the sinful nature, you
will die; but if by the Spirit you put to death the
misdeeds of the body, you will live, Rom. 8:12-13

THE TWO NATURES

CHAPTER 1

IS THE FLESH EVIL AS IS BELIEVED?

The flesh is not inherently evil in itself because God made it. He did not make it evil, nor did He make it with evil intent or for evil purposes, for God can do no evil. Rather, evil was added to it by the enemy, the devil, when he deceived Eve to believe, accept and act upon his lying, deceptive version of what God had commanded them. Instead of holding firmly to what God had actually told them, Adam and Eve, in disobedience to God's command, believed and accepted the devil's version and acted upon it, because they heard something in his version that sounded good to them when he said, "You will be like God, knowing good and evil." This got hold of their attention, and their interest perked up. They then chose to believe the devil's lies, and therefore came into agreement with him. By so doing, they were defeated, conquered, captured and corrupted by the enemy.

> The LORD God took the man and put him in the Garden of Eden to work it and take care of it. [16]And the LORD God commanded the man, "You are free to eat from any tree in the garden; [17]but you must not eat from the tree of the knowledge of good and evil, for when you eat of it you will surely die."
> Gen. 2:15-17

God was speaking here of a spiritual death that would take place the very day when they disobeyed His command and ate the fruit of the tree that He commanded them not to eat from. He was also speaking of the physical death that they and all of their descendants – mankind as a whole – would undergo as a result of their disobedience/sin. And indeed, upon eating from the tree of the knowledge of good and evil, they did die a spiritual death that very day, as God had told them they would. Physical death, as a result of their disobedience/sin, will from then on be a part of the human experience. All this, and so much more, are the consequences of the fall and sin.

> For the wages of sin is death, but the gift of God is eternal life in Christ Jesus our Lord. Rom. 6:23

THE TWO NATURES

God's command to Adam and Eve was very clear, but as we have learnt, when you turn a listening ear to what the devil has to say, you will be deceived every time and be led off, just as they were.

Now the serpent was more crafty than any of the wild animals the LORD God had made. He said to the woman, "Did God really say, `You must not eat from any tree in the garden'?" ²The woman said to the serpent, "We may eat fruit from the trees in the garden, ³but God did say, `You must not eat fruit from the tree that is in the middle of the garden, and you must not touch it, or you will die.' " ⁴"You will not surely die," the serpent said to the woman. ⁵"For God knows that when you eat of it your eyes will be opened, and you will be like God, knowing good and evil." ⁶When the woman saw that the fruit of the tree was good for food and pleasing to the eye, and also desirable for gaining wisdom, she took some and ate it. She also gave some to her husband, who was with her, and he ate it. Gen. 3:1-6

As we can see, the flesh is not in itself evil. Rather, evil was imposed upon it when Adam and Eve were deceived by the enemy and chose to be in agreement with, and therefore in submission to his lying version of what God had commanded them. What followed next was their deliberate act of disobedience to God, and so they were conquered by satan. This allowed him to place his evil nature in them, and now they were corrupted. They then became one in nature with the devil. This resulted in the fall. In this way, the devil's nature/ways became theirs, and as a result became our nature – known to us as the sinful nature.

This means that their nature, their senses and their beliefs were immediately transformed from good to evil upon their disobedience to God's Word, and their obedience to the devil's lies. The devil's nature and beliefs now became theirs and as a result ours, which the devil has held us captive to, and which we have lived by in agreement with him – sinning, resisting and opposing God since that day.

This is the reason why evil is attached to the flesh – Adam and Eve were deceived to disobey God's command to them, and were therefore corrupted by satan, who planted his evil nature in them. Consequently, from then on they will serve him instead of God. This is the death God had warned them about – their spiritual death, which means separation from God (sin will always separate us from God), and as a result physical death will now be a part of their experience. From that day to this, the devil has lorded it over us, and without God's protecting arm, His love for us and His mercy, we would all be destroyed by satan.

> You are doing the things your own father does." "We are not illegitimate children," they protested. "The only Father we have is God himself." [42]Jesus said to them, "If God were your Father, you would love me, for I came from God and now am here. I have not come on my own; but he sent me. [43]Why is my language not clear to you? Because you are unable to hear what I say. [44]You belong to your father, the devil, and you want to carry out your father's desire. He was a murderer from the beginning, not holding to the truth, for there is no truth in him. When he lies, he speaks his native language, for he is a liar and the father of lies. [45]Yet because I tell the truth, you do not believe me! John 8:41-45

The Lord Jesus called satan our father. What we are understanding here, is that through conquest, satan even took the place of being our father because of his nature in us; along with the authority and every other position that God had given to Adam, and made it all his. This is usually what happens when one king conquers another.

THE TWO NATURES

Dear children, do not let anyone lead you astray.
He who does what is right is righteous, just as he
is righteous. [8]He who does what is sinful is of the
devil, because the devil has been sinning from the
beginning. The reason the Son of God appeared was
to destroy the devil's work. [9]No one who is born
of God will continue to sin, because God's seed
remains in him; he cannot go on sinning, because
he has been born of God. [10]This is how we know
who the children of God are and who the children
of the devil are: Anyone who does not do what is
right is not a child of God; nor is anyone who does
not love his brother. 1 John 3:7-10

So instead of Adam being our father, satan took that place through
conquest and became our father. I know several souls who have
told me that they heard the devil tell them that they are his, and to
a point he is right, because his nature is in us. This further legitimizes his claim. This is why it is so important to know that satan
is defeated, and his power and claim over us has been broken by
the Lord Jesus on Calvary's Cross, so that we who have believed
in the Lord Jesus Christ no longer belong to satan; nor should we
be under his power or control any longer, or walk in fear of him
and obey him.

THE TWO NATURES

In him you were also circumcised, in the putting off of the sinful nature, not with a circumcision done by the hands of men but with the circumcision done by Christ, [12] having been buried with him in baptism and raised with him through your faith in the power of God, who raised him from the dead. [13]When you were dead in your sins and in the uncircumcision of your sinful nature, God made you alive with Christ. He forgave us all our sins, [14]having canceled the written code, with its regulations, that was against us and that stood opposed to us; he took it away, nailing it to the cross. [15]And having disarmed the powers and authorities, he made a public spectacle of them, triumphing over them by the cross. Col. 2:11-15

However, for those who do not believe, and therefore do not embrace the Lord Jesus, the devil continues to be their father, therefore opposition and denial of God, even of His very existence, His Word and His ways continue by many. Consequently, theories such as the big bang, evolution, etc., become their beliefs, and they are held prisoner to those beliefs by their father the devil, and so their opposition to God continues. These are also some of the reasons for the different religious cults around the world, and why

God is so opposed and rejected. The Word, ways and things of God are being put down, belittled, scoffed at, ridiculed and turned upside down. The Name of the Lord Jesus is being blasphemed and rejected by a hostile world. Christians in schools and in the military and elsewhere, cannot use or pray in the Name of the Lord Jesus. Pastors are being arrested in Britain for preaching the Word of God, because areas of it are seen as "hate speech," and in many countries the Gospel and the Bible are not permitted at all.

Yes, things have been turned upside down. The things of God have been placed underfoot, while at the same time the things of satan have been exalted all over the world, and are being fully embraced by a world that is deceived as Adam and Eve were. The examples are before us: Halloween, the demonic movies, the millions of books that are sold each year about wizards and witches – training children how to cast spells – their little minds being taken over by demons, and according to the world it's all in fun, while the devil is laughing and seeing us for who we are – fools – to be buying into all this satanic culture.

> We know that anyone born of God does not con-
> tinue to sin; the one who was born of God keeps
> him safe, and the evil one cannot harm him. [19]We
> know that we are children of God, and that the

THE TWO NATURES

whole world is under the control of the evil one. [20]We know also that the Son of God has come and has given us understanding, so that we may know him who is true. And we are in him who is true— even in his Son Jesus Christ. He is the true God and eternal life. [21]Dear children, keep yourselves from idols. 1 John 5:18-21

For he has rescued us from the dominion of dark- ness and brought us into the kingdom of the Son he loves, Col. 1:13

Since the children have flesh and blood, he too shared in their humanity so that by his death he might destroy him who holds the power of death – that is, the devil – [15]and free those who all their lives were held in slavery by their fear of death. [16]For surely it is not angels he helps, but Abraham's descendants. [17]For this reason he had to be made like his brothers in every way, in order that he might become a merciful and faithful high priest in service to God, and that he might make atonement for the sins of the people. [18]Because he himself suffered

THE TWO NATURES

> when he was tempted, he is able to help those who
> are being tempted. Heb. 2:14-18

If you do not believe this Scripture, satan will still hold you captive, deceiving you to believe that either he does not exist, or that there is no alternative to him. So, either way he is free to intimidate you and keep you in fear, believing that the Atoning Sacrifice of the Lord Jesus had no effect on him at all. If you believe this lie, he will indeed continue to keep you intimidated, and therefore doubting the Lord Jesus and your Salvation – that is, if you believe that satan exists. If you do not, he will continue to hold you to that deceit of believing that he does not exist; therefore all your problems are God sent.

> No one who lives in him keeps on sinning. No one
> who continues to sin has either seen him or known
> him. [7]Dear children, do not let anyone lead you
> astray. He who does what is right is righteous, just
> as he is righteous. [8]He who does what is sinful is of
> the devil, because the devil has been sinning from
> the beginning. The reason the Son of God appeared
> was to destroy the devil's work. [9]No one who is born
> of God will continue to sin, because God's seed
> remains in him; he cannot go on sinning, because he

THE TWO NATURES

has been born of God. [10]This is how we know who the children of God are and who the children of the devil are: Anyone who does not do what is right is not a child of God; nor is anyone who does not love his brother. [11]This is the message you heard from the beginning: We should love one another. [12]Do not be like Cain, who belonged to the evil one and murdered his brother. And why did he murder him? Because his own actions were evil and his brother's were righteous. 1 John 3:6-12

The nature that we know to be our nature, and by which we live, is the nature of satan, which we have inherited from our ancestors Adam and Eve. In its manifestation, we see the devil's beliefs and his exalted ways, in some cases in total opposition, hate, rejection and hostility towards God, as well as in the lies and deceit so many of us practice which are of that nature, for the Bible declares all men to be liars. Indeed they are, just like the father of the unregenerate, the devil. We see in this evil nature the same pride, by which he, the devil, wanted to exalt himself over the throne of God to be above God, as if that were possible. Thank God that this is not possible. We can see this same determination in many souls, even in the church, to be number one, the best, etc. These are the ways of the sinful nature – the ways of satan.

THE TWO NATURES

Jesus told them another parable: "The kingdom of heaven is like a man who sowed good seed in his field. ²⁵But while everyone was sleeping, his enemy came and sowed weeds among the wheat, and went away. ²⁶When the wheat sprouted and formed heads, then the weeds also appeared. ²⁷"The owner's servants came to him and said, 'Sir, didn't you sow good seed in your field? Where then did the weeds come from?' ²⁸"'An enemy did this,' he replied. "The servants asked him, 'Do you want us to go and pull them up?' ²⁹"'No,' he answered, 'because while you are pulling the weeds, you may root up the wheat with them. ³⁰Let both grow together until the harvest. At that time I will tell the harvesters: First collect the weeds and tie them in bundles to be burned; then gather the wheat and bring it into my barn.'" Matt. 13:24-30

We can also see this same nature revealing itself through our very lives, and through others around us in many different ways: from the outright rejection of God, to a partial rejection of Him, to a general, deceitful acknowledgement of God, which says, "Oh yes, we believe there is a God" – although they do not know Him and cannot relate to Him; to an outright false acceptance of God, even to the point of acting as if embracing Christianity, and for some, even becoming a "Christian." These souls are often the hardest workers in the church, faithful in their attendance, their service and their tithing, even more so than many of the genuine Christians. We see this same satanic nature manifesting itself around the world, through those many counterfeit religions, groups, cults, witchcraft, etc.

> He answered, "The one who sowed the good seed is the Son of Man. [38]The field is the world, and the good seed stands for the sons of the kingdom. The weeds are the sons of the evil one, [39]and the enemy who sows them is the devil. The harvest is the end of the age, and the harvesters are angels. [40]"As the weeds are pulled up and burned in the fire, so it will be at the end of the age. [41]The Son of Man will send out his angels, and they will weed out of his kingdom everything that causes sin and all who do evil. [42]They will throw them into the fiery furnace, where there will be weeping and gnashing of teeth. [43] Then the righteous will shine like the sun in the kingdom of their Father. He who has ears, let him hear. Matt. 13:37-43

THE TWO NATURES

Don't you know that when you offer yourselves to
someone to obey him as slaves, you are slaves to
the one whom you obey – whether you are slaves
to sin, which leads to death, or to obedience, which
leads to righteousness? Rom. 6:16

These are souls who are deceived to accept the ways of satan, and
are dedicated to serving him wholeheartedly – much more than
many who say they are serving the Lord. This knowledge makes
it even more imperative for each one of us who are Christians, to
believe with our whole heart in the Atoning Sacrifice of the Lord
Jesus on Calvary's Cross; to make it our daily reality, and therefore
walk according to it. We are to hold to it and proclaim it to be our
reality, knowing that satan was defeated by the death of the Lord
Jesus there on Calvary's Cross, and his power over us has been
broken, and we are now free to yield our lives to the Lord Jesus
and serve Him wholeheartedly, while denying the satanic sinful
nature and its ways.

It is for freedom that Christ has set us free. Stand
firm, then, and do not let yourselves be burdened
again by a yoke of slavery. Gal. 5:1

THE TWO NATURES

We are no longer to live according to how we feel, or according to the thoughts that come to our minds, since the devil uses these avenues to deceive Christians, reason with them and lead them off, and at times lead them off through others. Rather, we are to walk according to the knowledge of God's Word, believing it and holding firmly to it.

> Get rid of the old yeast that you may be a new batch without yeast – as you really are. For Christ, our Passover lamb, has been sacrificed. 1 Cor. 5:7

All this of course, is part of the game the enemy plays through the sinful nature to deceive, confuse and separate the real children of God from Him, in order to have his way with them. He also causes suspicion and doubt in their minds to separate them from their Lord Jesus, to then lead them off captive to do his will. These souls are led by their feelings since they do not believe God's Word as they should, and many who believe are not holding by faith to what they believe, and putting it into practice as they should.

> Those who oppose him he must gently instruct, in the hope that God will grant them repentance leading them to a knowledge of the truth, [26]and that they will come to their senses and escape from the

trap of the devil, who has taken them captive to do
his will. 2 Tim. 2:25-26

In this sinful nature, you can pretend to be whoever you choose
to be. You could choose to be the world's nicest and most wonderful person. There are those who present themselves as good
and upright: good citizens, good spouses, good family members,
good and faithful employees, good bosses, etc., and even good
Christians, while at the same time lifting up themselves in pride,
taking great pride in being "good," and believing it to their shame.

And no wonder, for Satan himself masquerades
as an angel of light. [15]It is not surprising, then, if
his servants masquerade as servants of righteousness. Their end will be what their actions deserve.
2 Cor. 11:14-15

Then, there are those who will actually live out the evil and wicked
side of that nature. They will actually take pride in carrying out the
most vile and despicable acts that can be imagined, and still hunger
to do more. There are those who are bold in carrying out their evil
acts, and there are those who are in fact, very timid. There are those
who are brave and those who are cowards, and on and on it goes.
There are also the spiritually false and the unspiritual, who are

dedicated to carry out the ways of the satanic nature to their fullest. Each one has their part to play according to satan's plan through the sinful nature, and it all has to do with rejecting God and His ways to have their own way, which is according to the devil's plan for their lives. However, it will be the devil who will be having his way through them, instead of them having their own way, as they are deceived to believe they are and will.

> But we ought always to thank God for you, brothers loved by the Lord, because from the beginning God chose you to be saved through the sanctifying work of the Spirit and through belief in the truth. [14]He called you to this through our gospel, that you might share in the glory of our Lord Jesus Christ. [15]So then, brothers, stand firm and hold to the teachings we passed on to you, whether by word of mouth or by letter. 2 Thess. 2:13-15

In this satanic nature or the sinful nature, as we know it to be, we also see manifested the same arrogance and impertinence which the devil demonstrated when he disarmed Adam, and took from him all that God had placed under Adam's care and authority. Some thousands of years later, he goes many steps further to tell the beloved Lord Jesus to worship him. In this regard, the devil offered the

Lord Jesus His own creation – the kingdoms of this world, which he, the devil, took possession of when he deceived Adam and Eve in the Garden of Eden and overcame them. Here, he is telling the Lord Jesus that these were given to him, and in this the devil manifested himself to be the liar and deceiver that he really is. he not only took possession of all that God had given to Adam, but also the authority that went along with it to rule over this earth – the animals, the fowl of the air, the fish of the sea, and indeed, over everything that is upon this earth. We can see all his other characteristics which are of the sinful nature in our souls, and they are clearly revealed through our flesh/bodies. These include: exalting ourselves over others, taking charge, exercising authority that is not given to us, etc.

> Jesus, full of the Holy Spirit, returned from the Jordan and was led by the Spirit in the desert, ²where for forty days he was tempted by the devil. He ate nothing during those days, and at the end of them he was hungry. ³The devil said to him, "If you are the Son of God, tell this stone to become bread." ⁴Jesus answered, "It is written: 'Man does not live on bread alone.' " ⁵The devil led him up to a high place and showed him in an instant all the kingdoms of the world. ⁶And he said to him, "I

THE TWO NATURES

will give you all their authority and splendor, for it
has been given to me, and I can give it to anyone I
want to. [7]So if you worship me, it will all be yours."
[8]Jesus answered, "It is written: 'Worship the Lord
your God and serve him only.' " Luke 4:1-8

Here, the devil was setting up the Lord Jesus by offering Him that
which he took from Adam through deceit and conquest – if He will
worship him. If it were possible for the Lord Jesus to have done
so, the devil would have conquered Him as he did Adam (that was
his plan). he would then become the owner of the earth, and he
also would have taken from the Lord Jesus, the earthly authority in
which the Lord Jesus walked while He was on this earth. Thanks to
God that He sent His Son, where none of satan's deceits and plans
could have tricked Him into submission, to then conqueror Him.
But, if He had sent another in the form of Adam, meaning one of
us, satan would definitely deceive him and conquer him, just as
he did Adam. Therefore, none of us would ever stand a chance
of being rescued/saved. Thank You, Father, for sending Your Son,
who could not be deceived, and so could not be conquered.

As for you, you were dead in your transgressions
and sins, [2]in which you used to live when you followed the ways of this world and of the ruler of the

THE TWO NATURES

kingdom of the air, the spirit who is now at work
in those who are disobedient. ³All of us also lived
among them at one time, gratifying the cravings
of our sinful nature and following its desires and
thoughts. Like the rest, we were by nature objects
of wrath. ⁴But because of his great love for us, God,
who is rich in mercy, ⁵made us alive with Christ
even when we were dead in transgressions – it is by
grace you have been saved. Eph. 2:1-5

This satanic sinful nature is the nature which we have inherited
from our ancestors, Adam and Eve, and it can be clearly seen manifested in and through each and every one of us in its various forms.
This is why our beloved Lord Jesus tells us that if we want to follow
Him, we must deny ourselves. What our Lord is really saying to us
is: we are to deny ourselves of the ways of that sinful satanic nature,
for it dominates and influences every aspect of our lives – everything that we believe, desire, think, plan, choose and do, along with
all our senses, our emotions, our feelings, etc. – all are under the
control of the sinful nature. For these reasons the Lord Jesus calls
us to walk by knowledge.

Grace and peace be yours in abundance through
the knowledge of God and of Jesus our Lord. ³His

THE TWO NATURES

divine power has given us everything we need for life and godliness through our knowledge of him who called us by his own glory and goodness. [4]Through these he has given us his very great and precious promises, so that through them you may participate in the divine nature and escape the corruption in the world caused by evil desires. [5]For this very reason, make every effort to add to your faith goodness; and to goodness, knowledge; [6]and to knowledge, self–control; and to self–control, perseverance; and to perseverance, godliness; [7]and to godliness, brotherly kindness; and to brotherly kindness, love. [8]For if you possess these qualities in increasing measure, they will keep you from being ineffective and unproductive in your knowledge of our Lord Jesus Christ. [9]But if anyone does not have them, he is nearsighted and blind, and has forgotten that he has been cleansed from his past sins. [10]Therefore, my brothers, be all the more eager to make your calling and election sure. For if you do these things, you will never fall, [11]and you will receive a rich welcome into the eternal kingdom of our Lord and Savior Jesus Christ. 2 Peter 1:2-11

THE TWO NATURES

Therefore, if we choose to walk with the Lord Jesus and refuse to deny ourselves of the ways of the sinful nature, we will not be able to walk uprightly with Him. For the ways of the sinful nature are contrary to the ways of the Lord Jesus, and so it will rob us of everything that is of the divine nature, which we are to be clothed with through the sanctifying work of the Holy Spirit, when we come to the Lord Jesus and continue in Him.

In Romans Chapter 8, we are told that if we live according to that sinful, satanic nature, we will die.

> Therefore, brothers, we have an obligation – but
> it is not to the sinful nature, to live according to it.
> [13]For if you live according to the sinful nature, you
> will die; but if by the Spirit you put to death the
> misdeeds of the body, you will live, Rom. 8:12-13

So then, unless we sincerely surrender our lives to the Lord Jesus, and seriously embrace His Word and hold to it, and therefore deny ourselves of the old way of living, which is according to the sinful nature, we cannot walk uprightly with the Lord Jesus. We must deny that old nature by first acknowledging that its ways are sinful, wrong, corrupt, evil, and that it is opposed to the ways of the Lord Jesus, and therefore come out of agreement with it. We can then come into full agreement with the Lord Jesus in His Word, and then begin to live in obedience to it in our daily, moment-by-moment experiences, by the grace given us. When we do not do this, we will simply continue to be controlled by the sinful nature, living according to its ways. We are either believing the Lord Jesus and are embracing His ways, or we are believing the ways of the sinful nature – the ways of the enemy, to which we were accustomed in the old life, where we embraced its ways completely and lived according to it. It is one or the other.

We can easily see manifested through the sinful nature, in and through the flesh, the devil's selfish and prideful ways – always wanting to be number one, the best, and always demanding to have first place. We can see his vindictiveness, hostility, wrath, anger, rage, bitterness, resentment, frustration, impatience, lies, deceit, dishonesty, greed, envy, jealousy, suspicion and maliciousness. We can also see the devil's conceited, judgmental and vain ways. We also see manifested, his lust, sexual selfishness and greed, immorality, perversion and depravity; his covetous ways; his robbing, stealing, murderous, self-seeking and self-serving ways; his greed for power, money, pleasure, etc.; his sneaky, suspicious, defensive and divisive ways; his justifications for all the evil that is practiced in that nature through the flesh, and his excuses of all kinds – blaming God and others to escape taking responsibility for his own

THE TWO NATURES

wicked ways and practices. We can see all these and more revealed in our souls and manifested through our flesh/body.

> But I am afraid that just as Eve was deceived by the serpent's cunning, your minds may somehow be led astray from your sincere and pure devotion to Christ. 2 Cor. 11:3

> This is good, and pleases God our Savior, [4]who wants all men to be saved and to come to a knowledge of the truth. 1 Tim. 2:3-4

We see too, the devil's serpent-like character revealed in the lies, deceit and accusations he spews out with so much venom; his foul and poisonous words used to curse, accuse, judge, argue with and attack others with the intent to destroy them, with a special emphasis against God's people. We also see his provoking fights and wars between people and countries, between languages, races and nationalities to have them destroy each other so that they will forever enrage, endanger and damage each other, their families, neighbors, communities and their countries. All these and more are the ways of satan, and we have inherited them all.

The thief comes only to steal and kill and destroy;
I have come that they may have life, and have it to
the full. John 10:10

I know your afflictions and your poverty – yet you
are rich! I know the slander of those who say they
are Jews and are not, but are a synagogue of Satan.
[10]Do not be afraid of what you are about to suffer.
I tell you, the devil will put some of you in prison
to test you, and you will suffer persecution for ten
days. Be faithful, even to the point of death, and I
will give you the crown of life. Rev. 2:9-10

To have and to enjoy to the full this wonderful life that our beloved
Lord Jesus brought, we must deny ourselves of the former way of
life, where for example there are alcohol and drugs, the invention
and use of which was inspired and is sustained by satan. These he
uses as instruments to seduce man into a drunken stupor, so that
in some cases he will abandon his own life, his family, and all his
responsibilities to his neighbor, his community and to be a responsible citizen of his country, and on it goes.

But I am afraid that just as Eve was deceived by
the serpent's cunning, your minds may somehow

be led astray from your sincere and pure devotion
to Christ. 2 Cor. 11:3

All these things are the work of satan. The enemy does this to
humiliate and degrade people, and to make them look and act like
fools. In their state of intoxication they endanger themselves and
others, and in so many cases, destroy lives, families, communities
and property. We are all duped in one way or another by the tricks
and intrigues of the devil. However, most of these, indeed if any,
are not acknowledged to be of him, for we are deceived by him not
to believe that it is he who has deceived us, and is tripping us up
to carry out his will in all these areas and more. Be assured, that
in all of these areas, Christians are not immune from his intrigues
and deceitful tricks.

I will not speak with you much longer, for the
prince of this world is coming. He has no hold on
me, John 14:30

The Spirit clearly says that in later times some will
abandon the faith and follow deceiving spirits and
things taught by demons. ²Such teachings come
through hypocritical liars, whose consciences have
been seared as with a hot iron. 1 Tim. 4:1-2

THE TWO NATURES

Finally, be strong in the Lord and in his mighty power. ¹¹Put on the full armor of God so that you can take your stand against the devil's schemes. ¹²For our struggle is not against flesh and blood, but against the rulers, against the authorities, against the powers of this dark world and against the spiritual forces of evil in the heavenly realms. Eph. 6:10-12

The devil's beliefs are also manifested in our desires and demands to have our own way, such as with wanting an easy and pleasurous life. When this is not attained or attainable, God is accused of being hard and unloving and not deserving of us. This and more is the true nature of the devil. He fills us with anticipations, expectations and even demands for a better and easier life, and in many cases, much beyond reason and beyond our means to attain it. In this way, he sets us up to judge and accuse God, and to see Him as hard, unloving and not being the inestimably good God that He is. Thereafter, he pushes us to accuse God of being unkind, unloving, hard, etc., for not fulfilling our greedy and selfish desires. All this is designed by the enemy to move us as far away as is possible from the Lord Jesus, and to keep us from ever going to Him.

The goal of this command is love, which comes from a pure heart and a good conscience and a

THE TWO NATURES

sincere faith. ⁶Some have wandered away from
these and turned to meaningless talk. 1 Tim. 1:5-6

Through these deceptions, the devil is then able to keep us separated from God, for as long as this is how we see God, we will not
go to Him. Rather, we will always be running from the Lord Jesus,
escaping Him and rejecting Him, while our mouths are proclaiming,
"Jesus, we love You." This is precisely what the devil seeks to
achieve, and he is successful in too many cases, while we are proclaiming to be the Lord's. This is prevalent in the church today.

but I know you. I know that you do not have the
love of God in your hearts. ⁴³I have come in my
Father's name, and you do not accept me; but if
someone else comes in his own name, you will
accept him. John 5:42-43

In the year 2002, the Lord Jesus revealed what true goodness is,
and led me to write about it in the chapter, "The Only Good One"
which appears in the book, "The Promised Blessing to the Nations."
However, the more He revealed and the more I wrote, was the more
I realized that using the word "good" to describe our beloved God
and Lord, was far from being appropriate as it relates to Him. This

is because of the simple fact that in our language and vocabulary, there are so many things that are called good.

It is common to hear people say that they have a good dog, a good cat, etc. This is how common this word is. Therefore, how could we, with this knowledge, use the same word which we have been doing for centuries, that is used for our dog and everything else, without qualifying or distinguishing it, as it is used in relation to our God and Lord? To me, this should not have been and must not continue. This therefore became a concern and a priority for me, which had to be the work of the blessed Holy Spirit in me.

With this concern in my heart, I began to ask my Lord Jesus for a word to set apart the word "good," as it relates to Him. It is now 2007, five years later, when He gave me this word – INESTIMABLE. This word means immeasurable, great, unfathomable, enormous, incalculable, infinite, tremendous, invaluable, not able to be measured, too great to be estimated, and priceless. These meanings were taken from two different dictionaries. This word truly describes so much of who God is, so much so that when I saw its meaning, along with the way it came to me, I believed that this was the answer to my prayer. This is indeed the will of my Father and Lord. "Thank You Lord Jesus."

THE TWO NATURES

You are forgiving and good, O Lord, abounding in
love to all who call to you. Psa. 86: 5

As it is written: "There is no one righteous, not
even one; [11]there is no one who understands, no
one who seeks God. [12]All have turned away, they
have together become worthless; there is no one
who does good, not even one." [13]"Their throats are
open graves; their tongues practice deceit." "The
poison of vipers is on their lips." Rom. 3:10-13

Therefore, this word – "INESTIMABLE" is to be used with the
word "good," whenever it is used to refer to our God, Lord and
His Spirit. Therefore, we are to say, for example, "The inestimable goodness of God," "The Lord is inestimably good," etc. I
do pray that everyone who reads this will gladly adopt this word,
INESTIMABLE to refer to our Lord, God and Father.

"Why do you call me good?" Jesus answered. "No
one is good – except God alone. Luke 18:19

Let us continue with our study. The evidence of satan's nature and
ways are evident and very obvious for all to see, if indeed you want
to see them. However, we do know that by the influence of the very

THE TWO NATURES

devil himself, many are deceived not to accept these truths about the enemy's deceits in their very lives, much less to recognize them to be of him. Is this demonic deception or self-deception? Actually, in many cases, it is both. Why? Because most of the time when the enemy brings his deceits, they are agreed with and embraced to be your own thoughts and feelings, because they are convenient at the time for you. Unless you understand these things you will not be able to discern what is really yours or the enemy's, and for those who do not want truth, in those moments it seems very convenient for them to embrace them, and so they are agreed with and accepted. This is called demonic and self-deception in union, for many have chosen to believe satan's lies without ever questioning them or considering the consequences. Therefore, they remain in agreement with him, many times out of convenience, because they are trapped in their pursuit for carnal satisfaction and for pleasures, etc. They do this rather than believing God's truth and being satisfied in it, and therefore remaining in agreement with Him.

> For this reason, when I could stand it no longer, I sent to find out about your faith. I was afraid that in some way the tempter might have tempted you and our efforts might have been useless. 1 Thess. 3:5

THE TWO NATURES

When we look back to the Garden of Eden, we can see that the moment Adam was deceived by the cunning devices of the enemy, and then decided to join his wife Eve in disobeying God's command to them, they both turned from God. And, unto whom did they turn? They were deceived to turn to satan, and in full agreement and submission to him, they then joined him in his rebellious pursuit to oppose God in every possible way, while covering themselves through pretense, as if none of this was happening. This revealed the deceitful ways of satan in and through them.

> He must not be a recent convert, or he may become conceited and fall under the same judgment as the devil. [7]He must also have a good reputation with outsiders, so that he will not fall into disgrace and into the devil's trap. 1 Tim. 3:6-7

In this type of deceit you could easily find such persons in the church, having a facade of spirituality, while believing it to be the real thing. For, there are deceiving spirits that lead people off to act spiritual. They are able to continue in the church while serving satan, and you will never know. Why? Because on the outside they seem spiritual, and in some cases, even more so than the real Christian, simply because the real Christian does not have to pretend.

THE TWO NATURES

Timothy, my son, I give you this instruction in keeping with the prophecies once made about you, so that by following them you may fight the good fight, [19]holding on to faith and a good conscience. Some have rejected these and so have shipwrecked their faith. 1 Tim. 1:18-19

Adam and Eve's opposition to God became so clear, when shortly after their union with the devil we could see the self-consciousness, the shame to face God with their nakedness, and the fear. These were immediately manifested in and through them by their haste to hide their naked bodies from each other, and by covering themselves with leaves. They further sought to hide themselves from God among the trees of the garden, and people have been doing the same thing ever since – hiding from God, even right there in the church.

All of this came about from the dishonest, deceitful and prideful life that is of the nature of satan, which Adam and Eve were subject to, and which they passed on to us. This resulted in their embarrassment and shame to face the truth before God that they had done wrong, in which case they could have repented. But no! Like so many today in the church, they covered themselves and hid their sins from God, as if that were possible. Yet satan deceives many to believe that yes, it is possible.

The woman said to the serpent, "We may eat fruit from the trees in the garden, ³but God did say, 'You must not eat fruit from the tree that is in the middle of the garden, and you must not touch it, or you will die.'" ⁴"You will not surely die," the serpent said to the woman. ⁵"For God knows that when you eat of it your eyes will be opened, and you will be like God, knowing good and evil." ⁶When the woman saw that the fruit of the tree was good for food and pleasing to the eye, and also desirable for gaining wisdom, she took some and ate it. She also gave some to her husband, who was with her, and he ate it. ⁷Then the eyes of both of them were opened, and they realized they were naked; so they sewed fig leaves together and made coverings for themselves. ⁸Then the man and his wife heard the sound of the LORD God as he was walking in the garden in the cool of the day, and they hid from the LORD God among the trees of the garden. ⁹But the LORD God called to the man, "Where are you?" ¹⁰He answered, "I heard you in the garden, and I was afraid because I was naked; so I hid." ¹¹And he said, "Who told you that you were naked? Have you eaten from the tree that I commanded you not to eat from?" Gen. 3:2-11

Here we must understand that from the day that God created them, Adam and Eve were naked before God and each other, yet they felt no shame. Why? Because there was no sin in them; they knew no evil because God made them good, and therefore they only knew good. This is how God made us in Adam – good, pure, holy and beautiful to behold. However, when sin entered, the result was lies, deceit, pride, hiding, envy and jealousy, the escaping of truth, the justifying themselves, competition, pretense, falsehood, innocence, fear, anxiety, uncertainties, worry, shame, etc., and they immediately became conscious of their nakedness and were ashamed of others seeing it. Shortly thereafter, murder entered.

> Therefore, just as sin entered the world through one man, and death through sin, and in this way death came to all men, because all sinned – Rom. 5:12

> For since death came through a man, the resurrection of the dead comes also through a man. ²²For as in Adam all die, so in Christ all will be made alive. 1 Cor. 15:21-22

THE TWO NATURES

Whereas before, Adam and Eve saw their bodies as pure and beautiful, now they saw them as unclean and no longer pure and holy,
as they had previously seen them. They now saw them through the
eyes of the sinful nature, as something to be ashamed of before
others and before God and in the face of each other, and something
to be lusted after. Therefore, they sought to cover and hide themselves, and we have been doing so ever since. As you can see, not
much has changed in these areas.

> He who does what is sinful is of the devil, because
> the devil has been sinning from the beginning. The
> reason the Son of God appeared was to destroy the
> devil's work. 1 John 3:8

Nothing has changed over all these years. Something very precious has been lost, and what could that be? Could it be the blessed
place we had with God, where we would always know to whom
we belong, and therefore have a sincere love relationship – being
loved by Him and loving our God with our whole heart and being,
where we walk in total obedience to Him, always confident before
Him? Could it also be truth and sincerity of heart and trust in God?
Could it be the surrendering of our lives to the Lord Jesus with all
our heart and being in submission; embracing the ways of the Lord
Jesus, and walking in them in union and conformity with Him;

doing His will from our heart, where we would always be guided by the Holy Spirit in the way of peace with the Lord Jesus, where satisfaction and therefore contentment would be our way? Could it also be that which God had made us to be – godly people, good and pure, holy, faithful, beautiful and more, which were all surrendered to satan by Adam and Eve? satan stole through Adam, all the wonderful and good virtues and things that God gave us, and he corrupted them all.

If it was not for the love of God poured out towards us and for us, we would remain in that place, being slaves to satan and sin forever, without God and without hope in this world. Thanks be to our God and Lord, who sent His only Son to give His precious life to rescue us from such a cruel fate. Thanks be to our great God and Father and our beloved Lord Jesus Christ, who extended mercy and grace to us for which, "We are forever grateful to You for remembering us, and rescuing us from under the wicked and heavy hand of the enemy. Thank You, gracious, beloved Lord Jesus."

> We know that we are children of God, and that the whole world is under the control of the evil one. [20]We know also that the Son of God has come and has given us understanding, so that we may know him who is true. And we are in him who is true

THE TWO NATURES

> – even in his Son Jesus Christ. He is the true God
> and eternal life. [21]Dear children, keep yourselves
> from idols. 1 John 5:19-21

Yes, I believe that something very precious was lost, and this happened all because, through his disobedience, Adam was conquered by satan through deceit. satan then corrupted him by imposing upon him his nature, which we know as the sinful nature. Adam therefore submitted his life along with all that God had placed under his authority and care, to satan. satan took from Adam all that God had given him, and therefore from all his children, and his children's children that would follow, all the way down to us, for all their and our lives. This is why the Lord Jesus said to those who were accusing Him that they belong to their father the devil. This speaks to all who have rejected the Lord Jesus, and continue to reject Him.

> Why is my language not clear to you? Because you
> are unable to hear what I say. [44]You belong to your
> father, the devil, and you want to carry out your
> father's desire. He was a murderer from the begin-
> ning, not holding to the truth, for there is no truth
> in him. When he lies, he speaks his native language,
> for he is a liar and the father of lies. John 8:43-44

THE TWO NATURES

For this reason, today mankind continues to struggle to acknowledge and accept God for who He is. Even those who are called His children, are today struggling with yielding up all areas of their lives to Him, and trusting Him with them. Many refuse to give Him His rightful place in their hearts and lives, even after the Lord Jesus came and died such a cruel death to pay the price for our sins. He did this to destroy the work of satan that was against us, and to forgive us of our sins and save us from a life of sin under the heavy hand of satan. Here God demonstrated His precious love for us through His Sacrificial Atonement to rescue us from the dominion of the devil.

> This is how we know who the children of God are
> and who the children of the devil are: Anyone who
> does not do what is right is not a child of God; nor
> is anyone who does not love his brother. 1 John 3:10

The Lord Jesus freed us from under the heavy hand of the enemy, and so enabled us to oppose and to deny our sinful nature through our flesh, and therefore satan, any further domination over our lives, by fully embracing the life that the Lord Jesus paid for and bought with His precious blood, and gave to us. However, we have yet to embrace it in its fullness, because we have not fully trusted our lives into the hands of the Lord Jesus, and therefore embraced His

divine nature, and at the same time, learn to deny the sinful nature
through the denial of our flesh.

> Then he said to them all: "If anyone would come
> after me, he must deny himself and take up his cross
> daily and follow me. [24]For whoever wants to save
> his life will lose it, but whoever loses his life for me
> will save it. [25]What good is it for a man to gain the
> whole world, and yet lose or forfeit his very self?
> Luke 9:23-25

> ...The reason the Son of God appeared was to destroy
> the devil's work. 1 John 3:8

Even after all that the Lord Jesus did, most of us are still believing
the devil's lies, and therefore continue to hide, like Adam and Eve in
the garden, from our loving God, Lord and Father, to this very day.

In the beginning:

> Then God said, "Let us make man in our image, in
> our likeness, and let them rule over the fish of the
> sea and the birds of the air, over the livestock, over
> all the earth, and over all the creatures that move

along the ground [27]So God created man in his own image, in the image of God he created him; male and female he created them. [28]God blessed them and said to them, "Be fruitful and increase in number; fill the earth and subdue it. Rule over the fish of the sea and the birds of the air and over every living creature that moves on the ground." [29]Then God said, "I give you every seed-bearing plant on the face of the whole earth and every tree that has fruit with seed in it. They will be yours for food. [30]And to all the beasts of the earth and all the birds of the air and all the creatures that move on the ground – everything that has the breath of life in it – I give every green plant for food." And it was so. [31]God saw all that he had made, and it was very good. And there was evening, and there was morning – the sixth day. Gen. 1:26-31

The next thing we see is God coming into the garden looking for Adam and Eve. The Lord called out to Adam, **"Where are you?" He answered, "I heard You in the garden, and I was afraid because I was naked; and so I hid."** God asked him, **"Who told you that you were naked? Have you eaten from the tree that I commanded you not to eat from?"** Adam's response to God was,

THE TWO NATURES

"The woman you put here with me – she gave me some fruit from the tree, and I ate it."

> He answered, "I heard you in the garden, and I was afraid because I was naked; so I hid." [11]And he said, "Who told you that you were naked? Have you eaten from the tree that I commanded you not to eat from?" [12]The man said, "The woman you put here with me – she gave me some fruit from the tree, and I ate it." [13]Then the LORD God said to the woman, "What is this you have done?" The woman said, "The serpent deceived me, and I ate." Gen. 3:10-13

Here we see Adam proclaiming his innocence and accusing God in order to justify himself when he said, **"The woman you put here with me – she gave me some fruit from the tree, and I ate it."** This was an accusation against God, and accusation against God has continued to this very day. The devil loves to use us to accuse God. This is a common practice within and without the church. We also see his wife Eve justifying herself by blaming the serpent – the devil, for her own choice to have listened to satan. To have picked and eaten the fruit in disobedience to God's command to her and her husband, was a deliberate choice on her part.

THE TWO NATURES

These are all ways of the enemy, and therefore ways of the sinful nature we have inherited from our ancestors, Adam and Eve. Therefore, do not be surprised when your choices are similar to theirs, because this nature has not changed over all of these thousands of years, and never will as long as we choose to adhere to it, and so remain satan's possession.

> Be self-controlled and alert. Your enemy the devil prowls around like a roaring lion looking for someone to devour. ⁹Resist him, standing firm in the faith, because you know that your brothers throughout the world are undergoing the same kind of sufferings. 1 Peter 5:8-9

What we are understanding from Genesis Chapter 3, is from a state of being good, pure, innocent and only knowing good, which is how God had made us all in Adam and Eve; when they listened, believed and obeyed the enemy, they were both completely corrupted, and all the evil characteristics of the devil were now present in them. The nature of satan had now become man's nature, and as a result, his beliefs and ways became man's beliefs and ways. This happened because Adam and Eve used their freewill and chose to agree with the devil. In those moments after listening to the devil's lies, and so were deceived, they then chose to take for granted,

THE TWO NATURES

first of all their God, and therefore His Word to them, along with
their place with Him and all that He gave them, and so treated it all
lightly. It therefore became easy for them to listen to another voice,
believe what it said, and turn their backs on their God and Lord.

> Don't you know that when you offer yourselves to
> someone to obey him as slaves, you are slaves to
> the one whom you obey – whether you are slaves
> to sin, which leads to death, or to obedience, which
> leads to righteousness? Rom. 6:16

When Adam and Eve permitted themselves to listen, to reason
with and then to obey satan, they were deceived by him, and were
therefore clothed with his nature. They were then subject to him,
and were carried off to obey him. They were now deceived to
embrace his nature fully with all his evil characteristics, his beliefs
and his ways and walk in them (because at this point they had no
choice), and these we can see revealed through Scripture and in
our very lives.

> Jesus replied, "I tell you the truth, everyone who
> sins is a slave to sin. [35]Now a slave has no perma-
> nent place in the family, but a son belongs to it for-
> ever. John 8:34-35

THE TWO NATURES

Since then, we have been hiding from and escaping God through every possible means, especially through the things we choose to believe from the enemy. From these beliefs come self-goodness and self-righteousness, and accusations such as: God owes me, He has never done anything for me, God does not love me, He has rejected me, He does not want me, etc. Also, there are excuses, justification, dishonesty, lies and deceit, the pride of life, pretense and falsehood, etc. These things come from the nature of satan, for he is the father of deceit and lies, etc.

> You are doing the things your own father does." "We are not illegitimate children," they protested. "The only Father we have is God himself." [42]Jesus said to them, "If God were your Father, you would love me, for I came from God and now am here. I have not come on my own; but he sent me. [43]Why is my language not clear to you? Because you are unable to hear what I say. [44]You belong to your father, the devil, and you want to carry out your father's desire. He was a murderer from the beginning, not holding to the truth, for there is no truth in him. When he lies, he speaks his native language, for he is a liar and the father of lies. [45]Yet because I tell the truth, you do not believe me! John 8:41-45

THE TWO NATURES

Some have also been hiding from and escaping God through the images and defenses they have projected to cover themselves with. This is just as our predecessors Adam and Eve did, as they covered themselves with leaves and hid from the Lord among the trees of the garden. This is really what most of us have been doing all our lives, even those of us who are in the church; although we tend not to want to know or believe that this is what we are doing.

These evil characteristics were imparted to Adam and Eve by the devil through the sinful nature. In their submission to him, these characteristics were also immediately passed on to their children, and we can see the profound effect that this had upon their first-born son, Cain. In Cain, we can see selfishness, pride and self-importance manifested in his choosing not to give God the best from his crop, but rather, to keep it for himself. Yet, when the Lord did not look with favor on his offering, in his pride he became angry, just like many of us do today. I have dealt with Christians who manifested this same characteristic when they did not get their way with God, and so we can see in us, the same sinful nature that was in Cain.

Cain, in his state of self-proclaimed innocence, justified himself to believe that he had done nothing to cause God to look with disfavor on his offering. Therefore, he had a right to be angry, sad, downcast and to feel sorry for himself, and now to believe himself to be a victim of God. Why? Because in his opinion, and according to his fallen nature, he had done nothing that was out of the ordinary to cause God to respond in this way towards him. Does this sound familiar? Here we see the satanic nature that will stop at nothing to vent its evil in God's face through Cain.

> Later she gave birth to his brother Abel. Now Abel kept flocks, and Cain worked the soil. ³In the course of time Cain brought some of the fruits of the soil as an offering to the Lord. ⁴But Abel brought fat portions from some of the firstborn of his flock. The Lord looked with favor on Abel and his offering, ⁵but on Cain and his offering he did not look with favor. So Cain was very angry, and his face was downcast. Gen. 4:2-5

> But if you harbor bitter envy and selfish ambition in your hearts, do not boast about it or deny the truth. ¹⁵Such "wisdom" does not come down from heaven but is earthly, unspiritual, of the devil. ¹⁶For where you have envy and selfish ambition, there you find disorder and every evil practice. James 3:14-16

THE TWO NATURES

This is really the only way that the fallen nature knows to respond. It justifies and proclaims itself to be innocent every step of the way, and in a state of arrogance, it demands to see itself as having rights, before both God and man. So, Cain believed that he had a right to offer God whatever he wanted, and God should have accepted it. And if He did not, Cain, in his demonic, exalted state of demand, believed that he had the right to be angry enough to kill his brother Abel, out of envy and jealousy. Also, in that anger and rage, Cain believed that he had the right to rise up against God and accuse Him. This is the devil's response, which we also see revealed in the sinful nature through the soul and therefore the body, to this very day.

> He who does what is sinful is of the devil, because
> the devil has been sinning from the beginning. The
> reason the Son of God appeared was to destroy the
> devil's work. 1 John 3:8

Indeed, it was God, who Cain in his union with the devil really wanted to kill – if that were possible. But since it was not, satan, through Cain, took out his vengeance against God on Abel, because Abel was the only one at this point who had chosen to be close to God. In the same way the carnal man responds to God to this very day, and it will never change. Why? Because satan will never change, and neither can the sinful nature. The demand of his heart is to be number one, above God – the one who rules. satan has held this position in his heart, and he will not let it go. In his state of arrogance, he even dared to tell the Lord Jesus to worship him.

> The devil led him up to a high place and showed him in an instant all the kingdoms of the world. ⁶And he said to him, "I will give you all their authority and splendor, for it has been given to me, and I can give it to anyone I want to. ⁷So if you worship me, it will all be yours." ⁸Jesus answered, "It is written: `Worship the Lord your God and serve him only.' "
> Luke 4:5-8

This is why the sinful nature and its ways must be put to death. Otherwise, it will reign, taking charge of everything in sight.

When Cain, who was full with rebellion, did not get his way with God, he decided to vent his fury on his brother Abel, whom he was already jealous of. He therefore lured him out into the field, and there Cain murdered him – his own brother, out of jealousy.

Here, the wickedness of sin had now manifested itself to the point where murder is committed. Since then, sin has continued to expand, not only in beliefs, motivations, desires, attitudes and thoughts, but also in all the senses and in all the choices and actions of man.

> At that time many will turn away from the faith and will betray and hate each other, [11]and many false prophets will appear and deceive many people. [12]Because of the increase of wickedness, the love of most will grow cold, [13]but he who stands firm to the end will be saved. Matt. 24:10-13

In less than one generation, we can clearly see that the reality of the satanic nature had so fully and completely vented and revealed itself, through its manifestations in and through the soul and therefore flesh of man, to the point where later, God was sorry that He had made man.

> The LORD saw how great man's wickedness on the earth had become, and that every inclination of the thoughts of his heart was only evil all the time. [6]The LORD was grieved that he had made man on the earth, and his heart was filled with pain. Gen. 6:5-6

The flesh is totally and completely corrupt as we can all see. Its only hope for redemption lies in the Atoning Sacrifice of our beloved and precious Lord Jesus. He came and gave His life on Calvary's Cross to rescue us from the evil state of the sinful nature, which some Scriptures refer to as the body of sin, which is of satan, the devil. Yes, when the Scripture states that the Lord Jesus became sin; this is stating the fact, for He Himself had none. By taking the sins of the world, what He actually did was to take on the full weight of the sinful nature of man in His very body, nailing it to the Cross. There, He put the sinful satanic nature in man to death, so that we would be set free from that demonic, selfish, rebellious, sinful nature and lifestyle, which had totally separated us from God our Father. The Lord Jesus accomplished this, and then declared – "It is finished."

Yet the cleansing of our souls of the ways of the sinful nature goes on through the sanctifying work of the Holy Spirit. This ongoing work of the Holy Spirit, is made possible only because the Lord Jesus broke the power of satan over us through His Sacrificial Atonement on the Cross.

> In him you were also circumcised, in the putting off
> of the sinful nature, not with a circumcision done
> by the hands of men but with the circumcision done
> by Christ, [12]having been buried with him in baptism
> and raised with him through your faith in the power

THE TWO NATURES

of God, who raised him from the dead. [13]When you were dead in your sins and in the uncircumcision of your sinful nature, God made you alive with Christ. He forgave us all our sins, [14]having canceled the written code, with its regulations, that was against us and that stood opposed to us; he took it away, nailing it to the cross. [15]And having disarmed the powers and authorities, he made a public spectacle of them, triumphing over them by the cross. Col. 2:11-15

We have been redeemed by the Blood of the Lamb, and are free to now choose to walk in the newness of life with our God and Lord, remaining in Him and participating in His divine nature. Our Lord has clearly laid this out for us in His Word, and called us to live it out in our everyday life.

satan's nature is filled with hate, a constant state of rebellion, and every other kind of evil. These are all manifested through the evil nature of satan in man, and they are against God. The more I understand this reality, the more I see my need to be grateful to my God and Lord for coming to earth to give His precious life for me to have life – extending mercy and grace to me. At the same time, I also need to be giving Him thanks continually for cleansing me,

and applying death to my sinful nature in areas that He deems
necessary each day. He thereby continues rescuing me from the
prison of that demonic nature, one step at a time and area by area,
through the sanctifying work of His Spirit. "Thank You, beloved
Lord Jesus."

When the Lord asked Cain for his brother, his response to Him was,
"Am I my brother's keeper?" Cain lied, just like his father the
devil. He showed no remorse, and there was no acknowledgement,
and therefore there was no repentance – again – just like his father
the devil. Then, when God judged him for killing his brother, we
see self-pity and accusation towards God in his response. Cain said,
"My punishment is more than I can bear." In other words, God is
unjust. Poor me! He is now a victim and not the victimizer that he
truly is. This is the nature of satan – after it has done its evil work,
it always proclaims itself to be innocent, and a victim of God or
someone else.

> Later she gave birth to his brother Abel. Now Abel
> kept flocks, and Cain worked the soil. ³In the course
> of time Cain brought some of the fruits of the soil
> as an offering to the LORD. ⁴But Abel brought fat
> portions from some of the firstborn of his flock. The
> LORD looked with favor on Abel and his offering,

THE TWO NATURES

⁵but on Cain and his offering he did not look with favor. So Cain was very angry, and his face was downcast. ⁶Then the LORD said to Cain, "Why are you angry? Why is your face downcast? ⁷If you do what is right, will you not be accepted? But if you do not do what is right, sin is crouching at your door; it desires to have you, but you must master it." ⁸Now Cain said to his brother Abel, "Let's go out to the field." And while they were in the field, Cain attacked his brother Abel and killed him. ⁹Then the LORD said to Cain, "Where is your brother Abel?" "I don't know," he replied. "Am I my brother's keeper?" ¹⁰The LORD said, "What have you done? Listen! Your brother's blood cries out to me from the ground. ¹¹Now you are under a curse and driven from the ground, which opened its mouth to receive your brother's blood from your hand. ¹²When you work the ground, it will no longer yield its crops for you. You will be a restless wanderer on the earth." ¹³Cain said to the LORD, "My punishment is more than I can bear." Gen. 4:2-13

We can clearly see that over all these many thousands of years the sinful nature has not changed, and neither has sin since their master, satan, does not change. The sinful nature, through the flesh, continues to oppose God while it pretends spirituality, just as Cain did when he brought offerings to God. Obviously, he did not bring offerings from a sincere heart because he wanted to honor God. No, for based on his heart attitude and choices, he would not. Yet, many in the church are doing the same thing today – bringing their gifts, while their hearts are full of murmuration and accusation against God, and like Cain, they too believe they must compete with their brothers or sisters for God's favor.

In their sinful carnal nature, many keep convincing themselves and others that they are making offerings to God, when in reality what they are doing is seeking to buy God's favor, and at other times appease Him through their efforts. However, because they are deceived to believe that they can indeed bring such offerings to God, they keep right on doing so. But, who are they really making these offerings to? This is the question they need to look into with fear and trembling, because their offerings are usually only to appease God and to buy His favor. This is not possible of course, but that does not stop them.

No, sin has not changed over all these years. Rather, it has only become more sophisticated, in that we now have many more avenues through which to carry it out against God, on a continual basis. This is being done every moment of every day. Today, we do not have to look beyond our own flesh to see the interest, the intent or the will to practice sin, which we should be saying no to, in honor to God.

Because of the sinful nature and its corrupted state through the flesh, the flesh is very susceptible to every kind of sin, and to everything that is convenient to its sinful desires and way of life, for it is governed by the enemy through the sinful nature. It must therefore indulge in selfish satisfaction and carnal pleasures, and it must have its own way, fulfilling its selfish and greedy desires and ambitions, doing its own thing, etc.

The flesh will indulge itself in everything that is pleasing to it, as it is carried along by the devil through the sinful nature. It wants to possess all that its heart desires and demands. It also wants to have everything that it believes will make it feel good and happy, as well as to look good in its own eyes and before men. Yet, it is never truly happy, for the flesh can only sustain its carnal happiness for short periods, and then it disappears. Nevertheless, in its pursuit to make itself happy, it continues seeking after more and more things – the pleasures of life that this carnal world offers, along with its positions and possessions. These the devil, through the sinful nature, pushes on it to convince it that this is the way to happiness. Therefore, he convinces you that if what you are pursuing does not bring happiness, then the next thing or event will. With this deceit in place, the pursuit never ends. Like chasing after a rainbow, happiness keeps eluding you, and God is blamed for it all.

Although it is proven that the soul through the flesh cannot maintain a state of happiness for long periods, yet the devil, through the sinful nature, never ceases in his pursuit to convince the soul and therefore the flesh that it can. And so, the soul just keeps on trying, as if believing that somehow it will succeed one day. But the soul through the flesh will never succeed in sustaining happiness, much less true happiness, because true happiness can only be found in Christ. Nevertheless, the devil keeps on deceiving and convincing you to believe that it can. However, because it cannot find that lasting state of peace, pleasure, happiness and contentment in itself, in its relationships, its status, or in the things it possesses, this becomes yet another reason for accusing and blaming God for its displeasure, dissatisfaction, discontent and misery.

When I mention the flesh in the way that I do, I am actually speaking of the soul being revealed through the flesh/our bodies. For the life that is being lived/revealed through the flesh/body, is really the life of the soul that is being manifested.

THE TWO NATURES

God is therefore always being blamed for the state of unhappiness and misery to which the sinful nature holds the soul, and therefore the flesh. He is also blamed for all the things that the flesh sees as being against it, rather than the true source of its problems, which is its agreement with the devil, living according to the sinful nature which was inherited from our ancestors, Adam and Eve.

The Lord Jesus has put the sinful nature to death in His very body on Calvary's Cross. He therefore freed us to come out of agreement with all that this nature is, enabling us to choose freely against it, by denying ourselves of the ways and things of that nature as He tells us to do, to now live for Him, if we so choose. If we do not choose in this way, then we will continue to live according to the sinful nature – again – as we choose. Many will simply not believe God's Word, which is given us to enable us to come to know our God, Lord and Father, and His will and ways, etc., and therefore believe Him and put our trust in Him. We are then enabled by the Holy Spirit to begin to deny the sinful nature and turn from its evil ways.

> The god of this age has blinded the minds of unbe-
> lievers, so that they cannot see the light of the
> gospel of the glory of Christ, who is the image of
> God. 2 Cor. 4:4

THE TWO NATURES

The sinful nature through the flesh, protects, defends and justifies itself in all things, and at all times. It also honors everything and everyone that honors it and gives it favor. It lies, deceives, and makes excuses to cover its evil practices, while proclaiming itself to be good and innocent. It is selfish, greedy, envious, lustful, covetous and jealous. It demands to have its own way, and we could go on and on.

This is why the Lord Jesus tells us in Luke Chapter 9 verse 23; "**... If anyone would come after me, he must deny himself and take up his cross daily and follow me.**" Here, the Lord Jesus is telling us to deny our sinful nature of the dominant place it holds in our lives, and give that place to Him, because He has freed us to do so. This is a choice that only we can make, and if we do not make it, we will not walk with Him for long. This will be a clear message to the Lord Jesus that our choice is to continue walking according to the sinful nature, which many in the church have chosen to do.

All these evils and more were imposed upon man by the devil through the sinful nature that we have inherited. For these many reasons, the sinful nature through the flesh, hates God. It does all that it can to escape Him, believing that in this way it can achieve that which it believes it deserves. It believes that God is always in its way, hindering it from being happy, and preventing it from its pursuits to be the big, wealthy, powerful, famous, good and great personality it desires and deserves to be, and therefore demands to be. It believes that God is hindering it from doing that which is pleasurous and pleasing to it. So, it does all that it can to shun God and escape Him at every point.

The sinful nature through the flesh demands to have its own way in everything, and when it cannot, it rises up against God. At other times, when it suits its purpose, it will even pretend to love Him. It perfects ways it believes it can use to pacify God, believing that it can indeed deceive Him, "to keep Him off its back" according to it. It believes that if it does not, God will "get it," since He has nothing else to do other than to be always watching to see if it is going to sin, so that He can whack it. This is the lie in which so many in the church are living under. These are the very ways of satan, and in his vengeance against God, he is always pushing us to carry out his will to do evil, and to practice wickedness against God in all of these areas of life and beyond.

and in every sort of evil that deceives those who are perishing. They perish because they refused to love the truth and so be saved. [11]For this reason God sends them a powerful delusion so that they will believe the lie [12]and so that all will be condemned

who have not believed the truth but have delighted
in wickedness. 2 Thess. 2:10-12

Indeed, when we live according to the sinful nature, in reality, we
are nothing more than a tool in the hands of satan to carry out his
will, which primarily is to carry out vengeance against God. In
deceiving us to do this, he is then able to separate us from God. He
accomplishes this through the sins which he uses us to put in the
face of God, to be sure that we end up in hell. These are his two
primary goals: to use us against God, and in the process to keep us
separated from Him, so that in the end we will be destroyed.

> to open their eyes and turn them from darkness to
> light, and from the power of Satan to God, so that
> they may receive forgiveness of sins and a place
> among those who are sanctified by faith in me.'
> Acts 26:18

At the same time, satan is busy convincing us that all our problems
are caused by God, and therefore God is not a good God, but rather
evil, and He definitely does not love us, but rather, He hates us
and is always just waiting to get us. This is the god the devil convinces many to believe in, so that he, the devil, can forever keep
them – God's children – separated from Him. This is so that he can

THE TWO NATURES

continue holding them prisoners through these types of lies, intim-idations, fears, wrong and evil beliefs and concepts about God, etc. What is surprising however, is how many have been deceived to believe these lies of the enemy, and so submit their lives to the fears which they bring.

> Then Peter said, "Ananias, how is it that Satan has so filled your heart that you have lied to the Holy Spirit and have kept for yourself some of the money you received for the land? [4]Didn't it belong to you before it was sold? And after it was sold, wasn't the money at your disposal? What made you think of doing such a thing? You have not lied to men but to God." Acts 5:3-4

By believing the lies of the enemy, many are separated from a life in the only true and living God, who they really do not know. For if they knew God, they would not have believed the lies which the devil told them about Him, and so run from the only true and living God, the only One who truly loves them, who is in reality, their loving God, Lord and Father, and their only Salvation and hope. How do you run from such a One? Yet, many are deceived to do so, as I was.

THE TWO NATURES

The thief comes only to steal and kill and destroy;
I have come that they may have life, and have it
to the full. [11]"I am the good shepherd. The good
shepherd lays down his life for the sheep. [12]The
hired hand is not the shepherd who owns the sheep.
So when he sees the wolf coming, he abandons the
sheep and runs away. Then the wolf attacks the
flock and scatters it. [13]The man runs away because
he is a hired hand and cares nothing for the sheep.
[14]"I am the good shepherd; I know my sheep and
my sheep know me – [15]just as the Father knows me
and I know the Father – and I lay down my life for
the sheep. John 10:10-15

Rather than believe what the devil says about God, they should
have believed what the Scripture says about Him, for if they had,
they would have surely run to Him. The truth is, when anyone
comes to know the God of the Scriptures for who He really is, they
no longer want to run from Him, instead their desire is to run to
Him and to be with Him forever.

My soul faints with longing for your salvation, but
I have put my hope in your word. Psa. 119:81

THE TWO NATURES

How do you run from love, truth, purity and righteousness; from the only One who is truly concerned about you; from the only One who cares about you and has your highest good and interest at heart? How do you run from such an inestimably good God, who always chooses for your highest good, and who alone can rescue you from the dominion of darkness? You cannot, and you will not, unless of course you are totally deceived to believe the lies of the enemy, like I was.

> For he has rescued us from the dominion of dark-
> ness and brought us into the kingdom of the Son he
> loves, [14]in whom we have redemption, the forgive-
> ness of sins. Col. 1:13-14

In reality, we all do yearn, desire and truly want God, because we all desire to be loved, and He, the true and living God truly is the only inestimably Good One. Indeed, we hunger to be loved, yet we run from Him, who is the only One who truly loves us uncondi-tionally. How can this be? Many are kept from truly knowing who their God and Lord is through the lies and deceitful works of the devil, which seem to be always ongoing and coming from all sides. For this reason, many, if not most, do not know of the inestimable goodness, the mercy, the love, the kindness, the forgiveness, the long-suffering, the patience, the faithfulness and the gentleness, of the only inestimably good, true and living God, the great Almighty and the beloved Lord Jesus Christ.

> How great is the love the Father has lavished on us, that we should be called children of God! And that is what we are! The reason the world does not know us is that it did not know him. [2]Dear friends, now we are children of God, and what we will be has not yet been made known. But we know that when he appears, we shall be like him, for we shall see him as he is. [3]Everyone who has this hope in him purifies himself, just as he is pure. 1 John 3:1-3

Some are even led to believe that God only wants to rob them of everything they have, including the rights and liberties which they have held sacred. This causes them to run even further away, not wanting to surrender to this evil god, whom they are deceived to believe that the true and living God is. So yes, the devil has been successful in deceiving many souls to run and hide from their God, using every kind of lie and deceit possible, to convince them that God is not an inestimably good God, but rather a hard, uncaring, unloving and evil God, who only wants to harm them.

THE TWO NATURES

Some have in fact already turned away to follow

Satan. 1 Tim. 5:15

And yes, many believe the devil instead of God's Word, and today they are running and hiding, while no one is chasing them. Indeed, they are full of fear and anxiety, and this is because they believe that one day God will catch up with them. He will then rob them of everything they have, even their very lives. All of this is because they have believed the lies of the devil, and so they are trapped in that circle of deceit, not believing that the Lord Jesus Christ has bought them out from under the control of the devil, and set them free to choose to live in Him and for Him.

The wicked man flees though no one pursues, but

the righteous are as bold as a lion. Prov. 28:1

In many such cases, there is no one to help, because few choose to believe that this state exists. Even the very church, which should be on the front line of this battle, does not believe. Therefore, satan gets away with murder against God's people, and continues to have a free hand in the lives of many souls inside the church, keeping them bound in sin doing his will, and away from God.

Those who oppose him he must gently instruct,
in the hope that God will grant them repentance
leading them to a knowledge of the truth, ²⁶and that
they will come to their senses and escape from the
trap of the devil, who has taken them captive to do
his will. 2 Tim. 2:25-26

Yes, many of us have been deceived to believe that in order to be
happy, we must first of all be good. Then, we must be innocent, we
must have our own way, live according to our own will in order to
pursue our own interests and goals, and have what is called an easy
life. That is why it is so easy for us to be lied to by the enemy. For
these very reasons, Paul had to confront Elymas in the way he did,
for he had chosen to walk hand in hand with the devil, pursuing
his own demonic interest.

Then Saul, who was also called Paul, filled with
the Holy Spirit, looked straight at Elymas and said,
¹⁰"You are a child of the devil and an enemy of
everything that is right! You are full of all kinds of
deceit and trickery. Will you never stop perverting
the right ways of the Lord? ¹¹Now the hand of the
Lord is against you. You are going to be blind, and
for a time you will be unable to see the light of the

THE TWO NATURES

sun." Immediately mist and darkness came over
him, and he groped about, seeking someone to lead
him by the hand. Acts 13:9-11

These lies are so easily and "innocently" believed, agreed with and
received by the carnal mind. This is because it has already been
deceived to believe that if it embraces them, it will have its own
way, along with all the things the enemy convinces it to believe that
it will have, because, according to the carnal mind, it deserves to
have its way in everything. It does not realize that this too is a lie,
for the only ones who will be having their own way are the devil
and his demons, not you, not any of us, although it might seem so
at the time, but we are being deceived.

By these continual lies, the carnal mind continues, by the devil, to
oppose God in everything. Yet, as said before, the flesh in itself is
not inherently wicked or evil, for God did not make it so. However,
the flesh was corrupted by satan – the devil – the evil one, who has
remained the evil force behind all its problems until today.

satan rose up against Israel and incited David to
take a census of Israel. 1 Chr. 21:1

Speaking to us while here on earth, our Lord Jesus said:

THE TWO NATURES

You belong to your father, the devil, and you want
to carry out your father's desire. He was a murderer from the beginning, not holding to the truth,
for there is no truth in him. When he lies, he speaks
his native language, for he is a liar and the father of
lies. John 8:44

Here, the Lord Jesus, who knows all things, is revealing the reality
to us that indeed, the devil is the father of the sinful nature, and
therefore of the natural man – the unredeemed. This means that
everyone, including the redeemed, who live according to the sinful
nature, are under the influence of the devil. Why? Because that
sinful nature is of the devil, and through it he reigns over the lives
of the unredeemed, and all who choose to live according to that
nature, even if they are Christians. If they are, this means that
they are walking according to their sinful nature in obedience to
satan, and walking in disobedience to the Lord Jesus. If it was not
for God's mercy, none of us would survive, for even those of the
redeemed, if they slip back to live according to their sinful nature
they are again, to a great extent, controlled by the devil.

This is why Christians lie, deceive, pretend, live falsely, commit
adultery, sexual immorality, compete with others to be "number
one," envy others, are jealous, resent, hate, disobey God, and do

not humble their hearts and submit to obey their God. This is why they steal, strive to be rich, destroy others, exalt themselves in pride, live in unforgiveness, etc. Much of the church is living this way. It is only because the blessed Holy Spirit continues to pursue us, why anyone is ever rescued from that dark place again.

> For what the law was powerless to do in that it was weakened by the sinful nature, God did by sending his own Son in the likeness of sinful man to be a sin offering. And so he condemned sin in sinful man, [4]in order that the righteous requirements of the law might be fully met in us, who do not live according to the sinful nature but according to the Spirit. [5]Those who live according to the sinful nature have their minds set on what that nature desires; but those who live in accordance with the Spirit have their minds set on what the Spirit desires. Rom. 8:3-5

We also understand from these words of the Lord Jesus in John Chapter 8, verse 44, that He held satan, along with Cain, equally responsible for murdering Abel. He said satan was a murderer from the beginning, for it was satan's nature in Cain by which the first murder was committed. Cain was pushed by the devil himself through his sinful nature when he murdered Abel, and the Lord holds them both equally responsible for that murder, and the consequences will also be for both of them. Murder did not end there. Rather, it began there and it continues up to this day, being pushed by satan and his demons.

The following Scriptures will help us to understand how involved satan is in the struggle of man and nations.

> And I saw an angel coming down out of heaven, having the key to the Abyss and holding in his hand a great chain. ²He seized the dragon, that ancient serpent, who is the devil, or Satan, and bound him for a thousand years. ³He threw him into the Abyss, and locked and sealed it over him, to keep him from deceiving the nations anymore until the thousand years were ended. After that, he must be set free for a short time. Rev. 20:1-3

satan was locked away in the abyss and there was instant peace on the earth. The moment he was released, immediately there were wars across the earth – nations against nations; people against people, all over again.

THE TWO NATURES

When the thousand years are over, Satan will be released from his prison [8]and will go out to deceive the nations in the four corners of the earth – Gog and Magog – to gather them for battle. In number they are like the sand on the seashore. [9]They marched across the breadth of the earth and surrounded the camp of God's people, the city he loves. But fire came down from heaven and devoured them. [10]And the devil, who deceived them, was thrown into the lake of burning sulfur, where the beast and the false prophet had been thrown. They will be tormented day and night for ever and ever. Rev. 20:7-10

This is the evidence that we need, and by God's grace we have it to prove that indeed, our problems are not with flesh and blood, but rather, with satan and his demons.

For our struggle is not against flesh and blood, but against the rulers, against the authorities, against the powers of this dark world and against the spiritual forces of evil in the heavenly realms. Eph. 6:12

THE TWO NATURES

Please read Isaiah Chapter 11, where you will see the peace that the earth will enjoy when satan is taken out of the way, and the Lord Jesus reigns.

> The wolf will live with the lamb, the leopard will lie down with the goat, the calf and the lion and the yearling together; and a little child will lead them. [7]The cow will feed with the bear, their young will lie down together, and the lion will eat straw like the ox. [8]The infant will play near the hole of the cobra, and the young child put his hand into the viper's nest. [9]They will neither harm nor destroy on all my holy mountain, for the earth will be full of the knowledge of the LORD as the waters cover the sea. Isa. 11:6-9

The devil is the god of this age and the lord of the sinful nature. When you live by it, he reigns over you through it, thereby leading you into deeper and deeper sin. Therefore, there will always be problems, uncertainty, fears, doubts, etc. in your life, although you are in the church.

> [16]So I say, live by the Spirit, and you will not gratify the desires of the sinful nature. [17]For the sinful

THE TWO NATURES

nature desires what is contrary to the Spirit, and
the Spirit what is contrary to the sinful nature. They
are in conflict with each other, so that you do not
do what you want. [18]But if you are led by the Spirit,
you are not under law. [24]Those who belong to Christ
Jesus have crucified the sinful nature with its passions and desires. Gal. 5:16-18, 24

Do not be deceived: God cannot be mocked. A man
reaps what he sows. [8]The one who sows to please
his sinful nature, from that nature will reap destruction; the one who sows to please the Spirit, from
the Spirit will reap eternal life. [9]Let us not become
weary in doing good, for at the proper time we will
reap a harvest if we do not give up. Gal. 6:7-9

In the following three passages of Scripture, the Lord Jesus called
satan, **"the prince of this world."** He is the prince of this world,
perpetuating evil and wickedness across the earth. He uses people
against God, and also against each other to wreak havoc and
destroy lives and property. By these deceptive acts, he provokes
more accusation and hostility against God, and turns people and
nations against God and each other. In this, he delights. All this

and more satan is able to do through those who live according to their sinful nature.

> and in regard to judgment, because the prince of this world now stands condemned." John 16:11

> Now is the time for judgment on this world; now the prince of this world will be driven out. [32]But I, when I am lifted up from the earth, will draw all men to myself." John 12:31-32

> I will not speak with you much longer, for the prince of this world is coming. He has no hold on me, John 14:30

satan is also called "god of this age" in 2 Corinthians Chapter 4:

> The god of this age has blinded the minds of unbelievers, so that they cannot see the light of the gospel of the glory of Christ, who is the image of God. 2 Cor. 4:4

he also deceives and blinds the eyes of those in the church who live according to their sinful nature, since they agree with him. In so

THE TWO NATURES

doing, he is able to separate them from their God to carry out his
will against God, because sin separates us from God. That is why
he pushes us with such intensity to sin.

As we can see in the previous Scripture, satan is called, "the god
of this age" who blinds the minds of souls so that they cannot see
the light of the gospel, and so are enabled by it to turn from him to
the Lord Jesus, and be saved. The enemy can and does keep people,
who will not believe the truth, in darkness. The devil blinds them
from seeing and believing the reality of Christ and Calvary through
the Word, turning them to a life of what he calls good works, and
believe me, I know several such souls who are in this state, right
there in the church. The church is loaded down with such souls,
who call themselves good people. The problem with this is that
good people do not need the Lord Jesus.

> Jesus answered them, "It is not the healthy who need
> a doctor, but the sick. [32]I have not come to call the
> righteous, but sinners to repentance." Luke 5:31-32

In the preceding Scriptures on page 52, satan is revealed as the
father of everyone who rejects our Lord Jesus Christ, including
the good, self-righteous souls who are faithful churchgoers. he is
also called the prince of this world, and the god of this age. he is

the head who controls the rulers, the authorities, the powers of this dark world, and the spiritual forces of evil in the heavenly realms.

> This is how we know who the children of God are
> and who the children of the devil are: Anyone who
> does not do what is right is not a child of God; nor
> is anyone who does not love his brother. 1 John 3:10

satan is also the father of those who are deceived to believe that they are really believing in our Lord Jesus, while walking in disobedience to Him and living according to their sinful nature. Yet we know that disobedience is of the nature of satan. So then, if while you think you are believing the Lord Jesus, and at the same time, you are found to be walking in disobedience (sin) to Him, this signifies that you are not believing Him the way you should, and you are walking according to your sinful nature. Those who are sincerely believing in the Lord Jesus in truth and sincerity of heart, cannot deny His Word. Therefore, they do walk in obedience to the Lord Jesus, because believing in Him goes hand in hand with walking in obedience to Him. This is simply the way it is. This does not mean that you will not fail at times, because you will, but the moment that you are conscious of it, you will humble yourself, repent and continue with your Lord.

THE TWO NATURES

No one who lives in him keeps on sinning. No one who continues to sin has either seen him or known him. [7]Dear children, do not let anyone lead you astray. He who does what is right is righteous, just as he is righteous. [8]He who does what is sinful is of the devil, because the devil has been sinning from the beginning. The reason the Son of God appeared was to destroy the devil's work. [9]No one who is born of God will continue to sin, because God's seed remains in him; he cannot go on sinning, because he has been born of God. 1 John 3:6-9

This is how clear-cut our life in Christ should be. The dividing line is – do I believe in the Lord Jesus? Do I believe His Word, and do I agree with His Word, and have I embraced it to be my life? Do I hold to His Word, do I live by His Word, do I trust in His Word, and therefore I am enabled to put all my trust in Him? Do I love the Lord Jesus with all my heart, and thereby choose to obey Him and be faithful to Him? Do I fully embrace truth and sincerity and forgiveness, or do I continue in pride, deceit, lies, dishonesty, unforgiveness and falsehood? Do I know the difference between right and wrong, light and darkness, righteousness and unrighteousness, love and hate, good and bad, truth and lies, etc.?

THE TWO NATURES

This is the life this Scripture is calling us to – a life that can be clearly identified to be that of a child of God, wherever you see it. But it is not that way today because of the darkness that is over the church. For these reasons, the Lord Jesus calls those of us who will choose to follow after Him, to deny ourselves and therefore to no longer live according to our sinful nature, for if we do, we will die. Why? Because that nature is controlled by the devil, and there, sin reigns.

> We know that we are children of God, and that the whole world is under the control of the evil one.
> 1 John 5:19

satan controls much more than any of us want to believe he does, and his influence over this world is much more far reaching than any of us want to believe, and therefore we do not. Yet, he is limited when it comes to serious, sincere and faithful souls, because here, the beloved Lord Jesus is our Lord. He makes the decisions as to what is permitted in the lives of those who are under His Lordship, meaning, those who believe and submit themselves in obedience to His Word, who can be easily led, and who will willingly embrace the sanctifying work of the Holy Spirit. This means that we, who are His obedient children, do not have to waste a moment worrying about what the devil can or cannot do. Of course, this is as long as we love our Lord and are walking in faith – trusting the Lord Jesus, walking in truth and sincerity of heart, in submission, in obedience and being faithful to our Lord and His Word, and doing His will from the heart. These are some of the conditions that are in God's Word, and the testimony of those who remain in Him, and those who continue to be true and faithful to Him.

> Those who obey his commands live in him, and he in them. And this is how we know that he lives in us: We know it by the Spirit he gave us. 1 John 3:24

> During the days of Jesus' life on earth, he offered up prayers and petitions with loud cries and tears to the one who could save him from death, and he was heard because of his reverent submission. [8]Although he was a son, he learned obedience from what he suffered [9]and, once made perfect, he became the source of eternal salvation for all who obey him Heb. 5:7-9

Here I am not saying that we cannot or will not be afflicted by devils, because we all will be in one way or another. Rather, what I am saying is, it is our beloved Lord Jesus who will decide if we need to be tested in that way or not, so whatever happens or is to happen, He will still be in charge of our lives and circumstances. Therefore, we do not have to worry or be afraid, if we put our trust in the Lord Jesus. "Thank You beloved Lord Jesus."

> We know that anyone born of God does not continue to sin; the one who was born of God keeps him safe, and the evil one cannot harm him. 1 John 5:18

However, those souls who say that they belong to the Lord Jesus, yet walk according to how they feel in their flesh and live by it, which means that they are living according to their sinful nature, should worry. You can recognize all the characteristics of satan manifested in the ways of such souls, although they might be in the church proclaiming, "Jesus I love You." Here, you can see manifested in them the lack of trust in the Lord Jesus, and therefore their stubbornness, lies and deceit, arrogance, rebellion, in-submissiveness, disobedience, disrespect and dishonor to the Lord Jesus.

> He answered, "The one who sowed the good seed is the Son of Man. [38]The field is the world, and the good seed stands for the sons of the kingdom. The weeds are the sons of the evil one, [39]and the enemy who sows them is the devil. The harvest is

THE TWO NATURES

the end of the age, and the harvesters are angels.

Matt. 13:37-39

You can also see the fallen nature manifested in their exalting themselves above others, and by their refusal to acknowledge and submit to authority. We can see the devil's hate for truth and his love for lies; his deceit, pride, pretense, falsehood and dishonesty. We can also see his ways manifested in them, in their seeking to please men to gain their favor so that they can go on having their own selfish way – all for self-gratification and to further deny God.

You were running a good race. Who cut in on you
and kept you from obeying the truth? [8]That kind of
persuasion does not come from the one who calls
you. Gal. 5:7-8

Also manifested in the flesh, are the devil's love for darkness and for immorality; his hate for and hiding from truth, from light, and therefore from God, while at the same time claiming to be good and innocent, although his desire to exalt himself continues unabated. You can also see his continual seeking to be acknowledged and honored. You can see too his wanting to be number one, to be the first and the preeminent one, to be acknowledged as the all-important and significant one to be looked up to, and to even be praised.

THE TWO NATURES

The Spirit clearly says that in later times some will abandon the faith and follow deceiving spirits and things taught by demons. ²Such teachings come through hypocritical liars, whose consciences have been seared as with a hot iron. 1 Tim. 4:1-2

All these and more are the ways and works of satan, and therefore the ways of the sinful nature, and those who walk according to it. The Lord Jesus had to put the sinful nature to death in His body to destroy the works of satan that were against us. The Lord Jesus did this as He picked up the sins of the world, nailing them to the Cross. There, He put our sinful nature to death in His very body, so that through it, satan could no longer reign over us at will and thereby hold us captive to sin, for the Lord Jesus tells us that whosoever will may come, and whoever the Son sets free will be free indeed.

That is if spiritual freedom is really what they want. If that is what they want they will have it forever, for that is God's will for us, because:

... if the Son sets you free, you will be free indeed.
John 8:36

THE TWO NATURES

As for you, you were dead in your transgressions and sins, ²in which you used to live when you followed the ways of this world and of the ruler of the kingdom of the air, the spirit who is now at work in those who are disobedient. ³All of us also lived among them at one time, gratifying the cravings of our sinful nature and following its desires and thoughts. Like the rest, we were by nature objects of wrath. ⁴But because of his great love for us, God, who is rich in mercy, ⁵made us alive with Christ even when we were dead in transgressions – it is by grace you have been saved. Eph. 2:1-5

Here, the Lord Jesus freed us to choose without any further fear or intimidation, to say "No" to satan, our flesh, the world and sin, thereby enabling us to come to Him and surrender our lives to His reign. As we are now enabled by the grace of the Lord Jesus, to say "No" to satan, our soul, and therefore our flesh, the world and sin, this is a part of the sanctifying work of the Holy Spirit at work in our lives, as He continues to cleanse us and begins to apply death to the satanic, sinful nature in our souls and therefore our bodies, area by area. This continues to free us up to sincerely submit ourselves in obedience to the Lord Jesus from then on.

THE TWO NATURES

Those who oppose him he must gently instruct,
in the hope that God will grant them repentance
leading them to a knowledge of the truth, [26]and that
they will come to their senses and escape from the
trap of the devil, who has taken them captive to do
his will. 2 Tim. 2:25-26

This frees up our soul, and therefore our body, to bow its knees to
the reign of our Lord Jesus; and yes, it will, but only as it is being
cleansed and death is being applied to it by the Holy Spirit. It is
a process, and it takes time, but it is happening and will continue
to happen if we persist and steadfastly continue in the Lord Jesus.

As we choose by God's grace, to humble our hearts before the Lord
Jesus and walk in submission and obedience to Him, choosing
along with Him to deny our flesh, the Holy Spirit continues the long
process of sanctifying us. At the same time, He applies death area
by area to the sinful nature, through which the devil functions. As
stated before, this will then free up the soul and therefore the body,
to now bow its knees and surrender its ways to the King of kings
and Lord of lords, our dear and beloved Lord Jesus Christ, for His
will to be done in and through the soul and body.

THE TWO NATURES

Once a person surrenders his life to the reign of our beloved Lord Jesus, and comes into agreement with Him in His Word, the sanctifying work of the Holy Spirit begins. He is then enabled by God's grace, to deny his flesh in those areas where it rises up to have its own way to sin against God. The blessed Holy Spirit is then able to apply death to those areas, bringing them into subjection to the reign of the Lord Jesus.

But if Christ is in you, your body is dead because of sin, yet your spirit is alive because of righteousness. [11]And if the Spirit of him who raised Jesus from the dead is living in you, he who raised Christ from the dead will also give life to your mortal bodies through his Spirit, who lives in you. [12]Therefore, brothers, we have an obligation – but it is not to the sinful nature, to live according to it. [13]For if you live according to the sinful nature, you will die; but if by the Spirit you put to death the misdeeds of the body, you will live, Rom. 8:10-13

We always carry around in our body the death of Jesus, so that the life of Jesus may also be revealed in our body. [11]For we who are alive are always being

THE TWO NATURES

given over to death for Jesus' sake, so that his life may be revealed in our mortal body. 2 Cor. 4:10-11

Am I saying that the sinful nature, through the flesh, will eventually surrender its opposition to God voluntarily? No, that is not what I am saying, for it will never give up of its own accord, because it is controlled by the enemy. What I am saying is the Holy Spirit will sanctify us over time, allowing us to come into agreement with Him more and more as time goes by, according to His Word and will, and so remain in Him. As we do, He will put to death the misdeeds of the body, which are of the soul, by applying to our soul the finished work of the Lord Jesus on Calvary's Cross. This thereby brings both soul and body into compliance and subjection to the Lordship of the Lord Jesus, since it is the sinful nature in the soul that functions through the body, and imposes its sin upon the body.

However, this will only happen as we take our place of death with the Lord Jesus, and remain in Him, whereby we are enabled by the blessed Holy Spirit to deny our flesh, and therefore the sinful nature. We choose along with Him to do so, by taking it to Him in prayer when He makes us conscious of its manifestation, asking Him to cleanse us of it.

THE TWO NATURES

He then puts to death the sinful nature and its ways, area by area, as it is manifested in and through the soul and therefore the flesh/body, by its usual sinning. This diminishes its power step by step, thereby subjecting the soul and therefore the body/flesh to the reign of our beloved Lord Jesus. This is applying the finished work of the beloved Lord Jesus on Calvary's Cross to our very soul, and therefore our body. In this way, He brings the reality of the finished work in His body on Calvary's Cross, which is already the reality in our spirit, and makes it the reality in our very soul and therefore in our body, and in our daily lives.

> He told them still another parable: "The kingdom of heaven is like yeast that a woman took and mixed into a large amount of flour until it worked all through the dough." Matt. 13:33

Accordingly, the life of the Lord Jesus will begin to expand and to be revealed in and through the whole man. Someone might ask, do you mean the flesh/body also? Yes, I mean in and through the whole man, who is spirit, soul and body. Then, there will no longer be a struggle between the flesh and the spirit, because here the Lord Jesus reigns Lord over all, for they are now in full agreement and therefore subjection and submission to the Lord Jesus, obeying Him and doing His will from the heart.

We must understand that the body cannot submit apart from the soul. For the body to submit, submission must first take place in the heart, and therefore the soul, since the functioning of the body is from the soul; while the soul and the body are empowered with life from the spirit.

> But he took her by the hand and said, "My child, get up!" [55]Her spirit returned, and at once she stood up. Then Jesus told them to give her something to eat. [56]Her parents were astonished, but he ordered them not to tell anyone what had happened. Luke 8:54-56

> But if Christ is in you, your body is dead because of sin, yet your spirit is alive because of righteousness. Rom. 8:10

> Since we have now been justified by his blood, how much more shall we be saved from God's wrath through him! [10]For if, when we were God's enemies, we were reconciled to him through the death of his Son, how much more, having been reconciled, shall we be saved through his life! Rom. 5:9-10

THE TWO NATURES

For every living soul belongs to me, the father as well as the son – both alike belong to me. The soul who sins is the one who will die. Ezek. 18:4

He redeemed my soul from going down to the pit, and I will live to enjoy the light.' [29]"God does all these things to a man – twice, even three times – [30]to turn back his soul from the pit, that the light of life may shine on him. Job 33:28-30

Obviously, when we first came to the Lord Jesus, He had to immediately cleanse and bring death to many areas of our sinful nature, without which we would never be able to even begin a walk with Him. However, there are many areas remaining that have yet to be cleansed and to be put to death. Those are the areas that need this ongoing cleansing work of the Holy Spirit to put those areas to death; freeing us from continual sinning in those areas, as we continue to participate in the divine nature. This work is called the sanctifying work of the Holy Spirit, so that the finished work of the Lord Jesus on Calvary's Cross will become the reality not only as it has in our spirit, but also in our souls and bodies.

But we ought always to thank God for you, brothers loved by the Lord, because from the beginning God

THE TWO NATURES

chose you to be saved through the sanctifying work of the Spirit and through belief in the truth. [14]He called you to this through our gospel, that you might share in the glory of our Lord Jesus Christ. [15]So then, brothers, stand firm and hold to the teachings we passed on to you, whether by word of mouth or by letter. 2 Thess. 2:13-15

and in every sort of evil that deceives those who are perishing. They perish because they refused to love the truth and so be saved. 2 Thess. 2:10

Therefore, get rid of all moral filth and the evil that is so prevalent and humbly accept the word planted in you, which can save you. James 1:21

The putting to death of the ways of the sinful nature is absolutely necessary for the life of Christ to continue expanding in us, and therefore be manifested in and through the body, and this does not happen instantly as we would like it to. It happens over time, area by area, as we continue by God's grace to persevere and to submit ourselves, through faith, to the leading of the blessed Holy Spirit, in obedience to His Word, and as we continue to remain faithful to the Lord Jesus.

THE TWO NATURES

This means that we have come into agreement with our Lord Jesus
through His Word, and by His Word, our minds are now being
renewed from the old ways of believing, desiring, thinking and
choosing. We are therefore being turned from the old self, the world
and the ways of the devil, as manifested in and through the sinful
nature, to God, becoming like our Lord Jesus in nature. This happens as we choose to participate in the divine nature, by the guidance of the Holy Spirit – being made holy as He is holy. This of
course is according to the light that we have.

We are also becoming more and more like Christ every day, as we
choose to take on His very nature as revealed in His Word, experiencing it through our participation in it. His purity will then begin
to be desired and embraced by us, and we will no longer want or
seek after recognition or honor for ourselves. Our purpose now is
to become more and more like Christ, in true righteousness and
holiness.

> But he who unites himself with the Lord is one with
> him in spirit. 1 Cor. 6:17

All this has to do with the blessed Holy Spirit putting to death the
old satanic or sinful nature, as He extends the reign and lordship
of the Lord Jesus over the whole man, area by area. However, this

will only happen as we continue to hold to His Word, and by it participate in His divine nature, which is laid out in His Word. We participate in His divine nature, by believing the Scripture, coming into agreement with it, embracing it to be our life, obeying it and surrendering our life in submission to it. In this way, we can be led by the Holy Spirit, according to His Word, so that we will experience His blessed, ongoing work in our daily life.

> Since, then, you have been raised with Christ, set your hearts on things above, where Christ is seated at the right hand of God. [2]Set your minds on things above, not on earthly things. [3]For you died, and your life is now hidden with Christ in God. [4]When Christ, who is your life, appears, then you also will appear with him in glory. Col. 3:1-4

> You were taught, with regard to your former way of life, to put off your old self, which is being corrupted by its deceitful desires; [23]to be made new in the attitude of your minds; [24]and to put on the new self, created to be like God in true righteousness and holiness. Eph. 4:22-24

THE TWO NATURES

Do not lie to each other, since you have taken off your old self with its practices [10]and have put on the new self, which is being renewed in knowledge in the image of its Creator. Col. 3:9-10

Therefore, I urge you, brothers, in view of God's mercy, to offer your bodies as living sacrifices, holy and pleasing to God – this is your spiritual act of worship. [2]Do not conform any longer to the pattern of this world, but be transformed by the renewing of your mind. Then you will be able to test and approve what God's will is – his good, pleasing and perfect will. Rom. 12:1-2

Here we are choosing to go forward in conformity with our Lord, to be like Him in nature as we are in spirit. At the same time, the opposition from the sinful nature continues to diminish day by day, week by week, month after month and year after year, as the blessed Holy Spirit continues to cleanse it and apply death to it. This must be our goal and pursuit, and therefore our heart's desire and attitude before God, not some of the time, but on an ongoing basis, continually and forever. This tells us that indeed, we are growing closer and closer to our blessed Lord as each day goes by.

Here, the blessed Holy Spirit is able, in His very gentle way, to continue applying death to the sinful nature and its carnal ways, diminishing its power step by step. He diminishes its power to continue going its own way, sinning against God, as He cleanses us and applies the death of our Lord Jesus on the Cross to it, thereby putting it to death bit by bit; freeing the soul and therefore the body, and bringing them into subjection to the Holy Spirit, through the same death. In this way, the Holy Spirit is putting an end to the evil ways of the sinful nature – its corruption, its opposition, and its disagreement with the ways of the Lord Jesus and His Word, by putting it to death step by step, day by day, as we continue in agreement with Him.

As a result of this, the life of the Lord Jesus now will be able to flow more and more freely to the soul, and from the soul through the body to carry out God's will, as death is being applied to the sinful nature. In this way the soul and therefore the body, are being freed from their slavery to the selfish desires and their greed and envy for this world and the evil thereof, from the dominion of the devil, from his influence and reasoning to cause us to sin, and from his desires and his will. I am being sanctified to live for my God and Lord. "Thank You dearest beloved Lord Jesus."

> We know that we are children of God, and that the
> whole world is under the control of the evil one.
> 1 John 5:19

This will result in our spirit no longer being hindered by the carnal
nature through our soul and therefore our body, struggling against
and opposing it, which it has been experiencing all along. The soul
(and therefore the body) will now be able to rest and enjoy its God,
Lord and Father. All its heart desires now, is to love, honor, cherish
and obey its Father and Lord and to be with Him, united in Spirit,
nature and purpose; not only some of the time, but every moment
of every second, of every minute, of every hour, of every day and
night, for ever and ever, now and for eternity.

> I have been crucified with Christ and I no longer
> live, but Christ lives in me. The life I live in the
> body, I live by faith in the Son of God, who loved
> me and gave himself for me. Gal. 2:20

> Those who belong to Christ Jesus have crucified the
> sinful nature with its passions and desires. Gal. 5:24

Here, the whole man's desire is to be always gazing upon the
Person of his beloved Lord, God and Father; loving Him, desiring

Him and admiring Him, while desiring this to be his eternal occu-
pation. This is liberty – not carnal, external or worldly, but rather,
internal and eternal liberty for the spirit and soul. The Holy Spirit
can now pour out in us and through us, more grace to move us on
into more and more light in our Lord Jesus.

As you can see, when your purpose is the satisfying of your soul
with that which is spiritual, and this is your priority, this will further
empower your soul, for you are in full agreement with what the
Holy Spirit wants, and therefore with what the Lord Jesus wants,
according to His will and ways for your life. On the other hand, as
long as your desires and choices are toward your sinful nature, this
means that you are not being sanctified. In such a case, the soul
will only intensify its struggle against the things of the Spirit, to go
its own way and to do its own thing to satisfy its own selfish lust
and greed, for these are the ways of the sinful nature with which it
has now come into agreement. In that state there can be no peace;
there is only misery.

These are all barriers in the flesh which will obstruct you in your
pursuit of your Lord. This is so, because by pursuing those desires
to satisfy the cravings of the soul and flesh for carnal and worldly
passions, pleasures and things, you should know that you have
again joined your sinful nature. This happens simply because the

THE TWO NATURES

soul wants to go its own way according to the sinful nature, and that way is always the way of the world and the enemy, which is contrary to the ways of God. When this occurs, the work of the Holy Spirit cannot proceed, and we suffer the loss.

> Do not love the world or anything in the world. If anyone loves the world, the love of the Father is not in him. [16]For everything in the world – the cravings of sinful man, the lust of his eyes and the boasting of what he has and does – comes not from the Father but from the world. [17]The world and its desires pass away, but the man who does the will of God lives forever. 1 John 2:15-17

The work of the Spirit is limited by the carnal choices of the soul when its choices are towards the sinful nature, because in such lives there is no longer any sincere prayer by the soul, and God's Word is not heeded. Therefore, the love and the desire for the Lord, the choices that are usually made towards Him, the trust in God, the submission, the obedience and the faithfulness to Him, the agreement with Him in His Word, along with the other types of choices, communication, etc., that should be taking place in such souls with the Lord Jesus, are simply not happening. The whole man therefore suffers the loss of all this and more, as a result of the lack of such

THE TWO NATURES

pursuits by the soul. Only as the soul surrenders itself to embrace the sanctifying work of the Holy Spirit, can these divisions and opposition be resolved.

> for you are receiving the goal of your faith, the sal-
> vation of your souls. 1 Peter 1:9

Therefore, a continual and sincere response to the beloved Lord Jesus, will only be possible as we continue to deny ourselves of the ways of the sinful nature (and more so if we really want to do this), trusting the blessed Holy Spirit to cleanse us and bring death to the old nature, and thereby freeing our soul and body through His ongoing sanctifying work in us.

It is because of the sinful nature why there is no obedience to our Lord Jesus on the part of many souls, and why they say "No" to Him. It is because of the sinful nature and its domination over our soul and therefore our body, caused by our agreement with its ways, why many deny the Lord Jesus. The flesh therefore is the barometer of our spiritual life. The Lord Jesus said:

> ..."If anyone would come after me, he must deny
> himself and take up his cross daily and follow me.
> Luke 9:23

THE TWO NATURES

In the same way, any of you who does not give up
everything he has cannot be my disciple. Luke 14:33

To the Jews who had believed him, Jesus said, "If
you hold to my teaching, you are really my disciples. [32]Then you will know the truth, and the truth
will set you free." John 8:31-32

Because we have chosen to die with Christ Jesus, which in itself
makes the statement that we are finished with a life that is according
to the ways of the sinful nature and the world, this enables us to
deny our soul and therefore our flesh. This in itself is a sign that
tells us that we are really walking with the beloved Lord Jesus. It
is the actual denial of the soul and therefore the flesh that tells the
Holy Spirit that we are truly finished with the ways of our sinful
nature. It is our denial of its selfish desires, rights, demands, selfish
ambitions, greed for wealth, fame, power, exalted life to show off,
positions, possessions, worldly pleasures and things, its demand
to have its own way, etc., that tells us that we are indeed finished
with that old sin life.

Therefore, by the denial of the ways of that old selfish sinful lifestyle, which is of the sinful nature, and therefore the soul/body, on
a daily, moment-by-moment basis, we are declaring our separation

from it; to be further united with the Lord Jesus more each day, and so to be able to live with and for Him.

> For Christ's love compels us, because we are con-
> vinced that one died for all, and therefore all died.
> [15]And he died for all, that those who live should no
> longer live for themselves but for him who died for
> them and was raised again. [16]So from now on we
> regard no one from a worldly point of view. Though
> we once regarded Christ in this way, we do so no
> longer. [17]Therefore, if anyone is in Christ, he is a
> new creation; the old has gone, the new has come!
> 2 Cor. 5:14-17

Have I chosen to die to the selfish, prideful desires, the images I project before men to show myself to be other than I really am, along with the carnal feelings, thoughts, worldly plans and plea-sures, selfish ambitions, etc. that are of the sinful nature, and that are contrary to the ways of our Lord Jesus? Do I therefore choose to deny them on a day-to-day, moment-by-moment basis as they appear? If I am doing this, then this is the sign that I am walking with the beloved Lord Jesus, with a sincere faith that pro-duces action.

THE TWO NATURES

If on the other hand, I am not denying the flesh, this is the sign that tells me that I am not walking with the Lord Jesus in truth and sincerity, because to walk with Him, I must deny my flesh its selfish, self-indulgent, carnal way of life that is contrary to God's will for my life. In other words, I should stop wanting my own way, going my own way, or having my own way. I should not only stop doing these things, but I should also be opposing those desires and pursuits that are contrary to the ways of the Lord Jesus, to now embrace the things and ways of Christ, for in my surrender to Him, I abandoned my ways and will, and I accepted His will and ways to be mine.

I must also face the fact that if I am not denying myself to follow the Lord Jesus as He has ordered, but instead I am following my own beliefs, ideas, inclinations and thoughts, this tells me that I am back walking in my sinful nature, where I can have my own way without having to deny myself of anything.

Although these signs should be obvious to all of us, yet many choose to ignore them, and are deceived to believe that they are walking with the Lord Jesus. This deceit is convenient to such persons, for their pursuit is to satisfy their flesh. Once that is so, these souls will continue to be led off by the enemy through their choices to willfully continue in their rebellion, sinning against God. This says clearly that they are not yet willing to turn from the ways of the sinful nature, or from the ways of the world.

> You adulterous people, don't you know that friend-
> ship with the world is hatred toward God? Anyone
> who chooses to be a friend of the world becomes an
> enemy of God. James 4:4

The understanding the beloved Lord Jesus gives us in Luke Chapter 5, verses 37-39 is simply that He cannot put the Holy Spirit into a heart that has chosen the sinful nature to be their way of life. For Him to give you the Holy Spirit, you must first repent of your old ways – sin – believe in the Lord Jesus, and trust your life to Him so that He can give you a new spirit. Then with that new spirit, He can now give you the Holy Spirit. The Lord Jesus is also saying to us that He knows that most souls want Him to give them the Holy Spirit while they are still in their corrupted, evil state. They are deceived to believe the lie that they are good in their own eyes, and because they are in the church, they are believing that they are therefore worthy to receive the Holy Spirit. This, He cannot do.

However, these persons do not care about the state they are in, or if they have sincerely received the Lord Jesus. They just want Him to give them the Holy Spirit, along with all the other promises/

blessings that are in His Word. They want all this as an add-on to
their sinful ways, to continue living out their selfish way of life, and
they will have it no other way. They want it all, so that they can go
on living in the way that they have chosen and are accustomed to.
At the same time, some even believe that they have the approval
of God and man to go on living this way, while others could not
care less what God or man thinks. In spite of this, they all want the
assurance of going to heaven when they leave this earth.

> And no one pours new wine into old wineskins.
> If he does, the new wine will burst the skins, the
> wine will run out and the wineskins will be ruined.
> [38]No, new wine must be poured into new wineskins.
> [39]And no one after drinking old wine wants the new,
> for he says, `The old is better.' " Luke 5:37-39

The beloved Lord Jesus continues to reveal in this Scripture that
no one who is enjoying the old life – old wine, which in fact is the
ways of their sinful nature, really wants the new. This is because
they believe that the old life "tastes" better to them than the new,
for in the old life they are free to have their own way and to possess
their hearts' desires, and to have all the pleasure they desire. They
can therefore lust and fantasize without limit, living the "good old
carnal life," according to them.

THE TWO NATURES

This too is a lie and a deceit of the devil, and you therefore must not believe it. For if you do, you will be carried off by the enemy to continue doing his will, while you are being deceived to believe that by living the way you want, it is completely your will that you are carrying out. This is a lie, for it is not all your will, although it seems so to you, but rather, it is the devil's will you are carrying out in agreement with him.

> But I am afraid that just as Eve was deceived by the serpent's cunning, your minds may somehow be led astray from your sincere and pure devotion to Christ. 2 Cor. 11:3

In every case that we have denied the Lord Jesus and said "No" to Him, we have done so because of the desires of the heart to satisfy the flesh, driven by the sinful nature, with the devil behind it all. Many souls believe that if they obey the Lord Jesus, they will not have the liberty that they feel they need to be able to live the way they want, or to have the pleasures and things that they desire and want to pursue and have. Because of the fear they feel to give up these things, they refuse to surrender their life to the Lord Jesus and trust Him with it, believing that to obey the Lord Jesus, is to lose out on all those carnal things that they would like to hold on to or to obtain.

THE TWO NATURES

Looking at this from another perspective – they believe that if they deny the Lord Jesus, they will have these liberties, pleasures and things that they desire. This too is a lie of the enemy, because no one can ever have all that their heart desires in any area of that old life. The enemy however, deceives many to believe this lie, and those who believe him are carried away captive by him to pursue the rainbow – the impossible. In the process, they are trapped by him and suffer great loss, and they then end up blaming God for all the problems that follow.

> A man's own folly ruins his life, yet his heart rages
> against the Lord. Prov. 19:3

The Lord Jesus speaks of the "narrow gate" in Matthew Chapter 7 verses 13-14. To the carnal Christian, He is saying that the narrow gate is too uncomfortable for him, for it is the way of righteousness. He therefore cannot enter it, and even if he could, he would not. Why? Because he is aware that if he were to, he would not be able to have his own way, neither would he be able to satisfy his carnal desires there. For there, the Lord Jesus reigns as Lord over the truly righteous, and they are satisfied with His ways and with His provisions. As a result, they no longer want that which they once called their own ways and things, which are of the sinful nature.

Now they only want that which is of the Lord Jesus, for His ways are satisfying and pleasing to them.

> "Enter through the narrow gate. For wide is the gate
> and broad is the road that leads to destruction, and
> many enter through it. [14]But small is the gate and
> narrow the road that leads to life, and only a few
> find it. Matt. 7:13-14

Our beliefs, desires, thoughts, choices and responses towards the Lord Jesus, tell us whether we indeed have a spiritual life or not. For instance: are we laying down our life and trusting it to the Lord Jesus completely on an ongoing basis, whereby we are choosing to deny our carnal beliefs, desires, thoughts, feelings, pleasures, greed, selfish ambitions, etc., that are all of the sinful nature? If we are not, then are we really walking with the beloved Lord Jesus, or are we just pretending that we are, or are we deceived by the enemy to believe that we are? Or, maybe we are even deceiving ourselves to believe that we are, when in reality, we are not. If this is you, then you are a genuine, one hundred percent, false Christian.

After we have examined ourselves, we may conclude that indeed we are only pretending and simply acting out a Christian life, maybe to pacify our guilt, appease our conscience, to please others, or to be

THE TWO NATURES

accepted by them. If this is what we are doing, isn't that the carnal nature – the old man, the satanic nature, carrying out his old tricks by pretending before men that he is walking with the Lord Jesus, while in the heart he continues to be in rage against Him? It could be that you are just deceived, but whatever it is or is not, shouldn't you examine yourselves to be sure of where you are in the faith – if indeed you are?

> Examine yourselves to see whether you are in the faith; test yourselves. Do you not realize that Christ Jesus is in you – unless, of course, you fail the test? 2 Cor. 13:5

> For such men are false apostles, deceitful workmen, masquerading as apostles of Christ. [14]And no wonder, for Satan himself masquerades as an angel of light. [15]It is not surprising, then, if his servants masquerade as servants of righteousness. Their end will be what their actions deserve. 2 Cor. 11:13-15

Indeed, being the liar and deceiver that he is, the "best" that the carnal man can do, is to pretend he is walking with the Lord Jesus so that he will be accepted in the church as a Christian, which many have been doing. This is all that he can do and nothing else. He does this to accomplish his own purpose, he thinks, not realizing that he is only carrying out the will of his father the devil. Sadly, he doesn't believe that this is what he is doing.

The Lord Jesus asks for obedience that is of faith, and not for works, self-efforts or sacrifice. Therefore, nothing we do in that carnal state has any spiritual value or importance, as in that state we cannot obey the Lord Jesus, and so we cannot walk with Him.

We obey the Lord Jesus, not by sacrificing, self-efforts or works of any kind which are part of the Law and that old deceitful life of pretense and falsehood. Rather, we obey the Lord Jesus out of a heart of love and faith – the Lord Jesus speaks, and so by faith, we believe and obey Him. We therefore do not take the flesh into account in choosing to obey the Lord Jesus. Rather, we obey Him, whether it is convenient or pleasing to the flesh or not.

If at any time we are faced with resistance of any kind to the Word of God – any displeasure, hesitation or fear to yield to and obey the Lord Jesus, we must quickly acknowledge it for what it is – sin. We must then surrender it and oppose it, taking it to the Lord Jesus in repentance.

THE TWO NATURES

> We demolish arguments and every pretension that
> sets itself up against the knowledge of God, and we
> take captive every thought to make it obedient to
> Christ. 2 Cor. 10:5

We need to understand that the devil, using our sinful nature through the soul and therefore the flesh, will oppose us as we choose to deny it and its sinful ways. This opposition will only diminish as we continue to submit to be sanctified by the Holy Spirit and reject its evil ways, having our trust in the Lord Jesus, thereby walking in obedience to Him. As we do this, the Holy Spirit is then able to continue putting to death the sinful nature and its ways as He cleanses us. This liberates us to choose more freely to obey the Lord Jesus, without the continual resistance and opposition of the sinful nature through the soul, to the flesh.

> Since the children have flesh and blood, he too
> shared in their humanity so that by his death he
> might destroy him who holds the power of death
> – that is, the devil – [15]and free those who all their
> lives were held in slavery by their fear of death.
> Heb. 2:14-15

THE TWO NATURES

The obedience that the Lord Jesus calls us to is an obedience that comes by faith, which enables us to make sincere choices and the actions that follow, toward Him. Therefore, if we do not obey the Lord Jesus by denying ourselves, we just will not obey Him in anything else. This is because the devil, through the sinful nature, is always impulsing and pushing us to go his way and obey him instead of the Lord Jesus, through the temptations that he brings to us. he does this by enticing us to satisfy the selfish lust for pleasures, greed, rights and demands of the sinful nature through the flesh, along with its greed for more, its demand to have carnal happiness to feel good carnally about itself, to lift itself up in pride over others, etc. All this and more, is pushed on us by satan through the sinful nature, to keep us sinning against the Lord Jesus.

We need to understand that living according to the sinful nature is disobedience, and therefore sin against the Lord Jesus. However, most do not see this as sin.

> The Spirit gives life; the flesh counts for nothing.
> The words I have spoken to you are spirit and they
> are life. John 6:63

Therefore, in order to obey the Lord Jesus, we must deny our soul through our flesh, and therefore the sinful nature; otherwise, we

THE TWO NATURES

just will not obey the Lord Jesus. Why? Because the ways of the
Spirit and the ways of the soul and therefore the flesh are contrary
one to the other, and our tendency is to honor our soul, through
our flesh, over the things of the Spirit. In this way, we find that the
needs and ways of the soul and therefore the flesh are always being
met, while the ways of the Lord Jesus are ignored.

> Because you are sons, God sent the Spirit of his
> Son into our hearts, the Spirit who calls out, "Abba,
> Father." Gal. 4:6

> because through Christ Jesus the law of the
> Spirit of life set me free from the law of sin and
> death. Rom. 8:2

The demands of the flesh through the thoughts and feelings can be
so strong and overpowering at times that many believe them, give
in to them and embrace them, even though it means sinning against
the Lord Jesus. In those times many do not consider their Lord, and
so cry out to Him for help. Rather, they just submit to their feelings
and give in to them, and are therefore carried off by them.

Many will not deny any of their feelings in order to honor their
Lord. Therefore, if they feel bad, and disobeying the Lord Jesus,

that is, to commit sin against Him, will make them feel good, that is precisely what they will do then, and on a continual basis. This is the state of many in the church.

> So I say, live by the Spirit, and you will not gratify the desires of the sinful nature. [17]For the sinful nature desires what is contrary to the Spirit, and the Spirit what is contrary to the sinful nature. They are in conflict with each other, so that you do not do what you want. Gal. 5:16-17

What is important here is not whether we feel good or bad, or how much we have to deny ourselves to be able to obey our Lord Jesus. What is important is: will we honor our Lord, and walk with Him in the submission and obedience that is of faith? Here we do not have to be contemplating on how, or how much we have to deny ourselves to obey the Lord Jesus. What we see is simply a need to humble ourselves to be able to honor our Lord by obeying Him.

We are therefore not calculating or reasoning about what we did to obey, or what we have to do to obey, or what we had to deny ourselves of to be able to obey Him, or how we have suffered in order to obey Him, or what we had to go through to obey Him. Such an attitude is of the old life – the old sinful nature. This is the old self keeping account of its own good works and sacrifices. This gives credit to the old nature and only feeds pride, which leads to more sacrificing, and further separates one from God.

> As for you, you were dead in your transgressions and sins, [2]in which you used to live when you followed the ways of this world and of the ruler of the kingdom of the air, the spirit who is now at work in those who are disobedient. Eph. 2:1-2

We must understand that whatever we believe we are doing towards our Lord Jesus, has no significance at all outside of faith. Without faith, all that we can do and will be able to do, is to offer self-righteous acts and sacrifices by our own understanding and efforts, which will only be to our own glory. This is sin against God. Nevertheless, this is all that the carnal Christian can do, and which he does, to then take pride in it. Why? Because it is his works, as it was not done through God. Therefore, he has a right to glory and take pride in his own works.

> Those along the path are the ones who hear, and then the devil comes and takes away the word from their hearts, so that they may not believe and be saved. Luke 8:12

THE TWO NATURES

Some will also do the very things that the Lord Jesus requires of them. However, they do them in a carnal way for men to see (this is what is called to show-off), and to bring them acknowledgement, praise, carnal satisfaction and gratification. In the process, they add these to their self-importance, self-goodness and self-glory, all of which really come out of a life of selfishness, dishonesty and pride – the self-life. Here, self-righteousness and pride reign as the driving forces and power behind that self-life, because they do not trust the Lord Jesus for His help, and indeed in their state they cannot, much less to do the things that God requires in faith and humility, to honor Him. No, they cannot, so they do their own works to honor themselves. Pride therefore multiplies in such lives because of falsehood/dishonesty, and so nothing they do can ever be done unto the Lord Jesus.

The mouth makes great boasts of a life with the Lord Jesus, while in the heart, the devil, through the sinful nature, is governing the life. he does this through the beliefs, desires and thoughts, along with the feelings and impressions which he inflicts upon the soul and therefore the flesh, through the sinful nature.

You cannot continue to justify the ways of the sinful nature through your flesh, following its dictates, while at the same time you are proclaiming that you are walking with the Lord Jesus. Therefore, by the denial of the sinful nature through the soul and therefore the flesh, or the lack thereof, you are able to determine whether or not you are walking with the Lord Jesus.

> "'These people honor me with their lips, but their hearts are far from me. 'They worship me in vain; their teachings are but rules taught by men.' " Matt. 15:8-9

> But then they would flatter him with their mouths, lying to him with their tongues; ³⁷their hearts were not loyal to him, they were not faithful to his covenant. Psa. 78:36-37

If you are yielding to the desires and ways of the flesh and the world, you are not walking with the Lord Jesus. Rather, you are living according to your sinful nature. On the other hand, if in faith, you have faced these desires and ways of the sinful nature through the flesh head-on as they rise up, and you choose to deny yourself of them, repent of them, say no to them, and surrender them to your Lord Jesus, this is denying your flesh. Then, you are sincerely walking with the Lord Jesus.

THE TWO NATURES

Although the soul through the body/flesh is yearning to go its own carnal way to enjoy its pleasures, yet, if you acknowledge that these are sins against the Lord Jesus, and reject them for what they are – sin – repent of them, and surrender that area to the Lord Jesus, then you will continue with your Lord Jesus. You will then be able to draw from Him the strength you need to stand against these desires, and continue to say no to them, and yes to your Lord Jesus. This you are able to do, because in your heart you have sincerely died to these carnal desires, and have truly surrendered your life to your Lord Jesus.

Even if I caused you sorrow by my letter, I do not regret it. Though I did regret it – I see that my letter hurt you, but only for a little while – [9]yet now I am happy, not because you were made sorry, but because your sorrow led you to repentance. For you became sorrowful as God intended and so were not harmed in any way by us. [10]Godly sorrow brings repentance that leads to salvation and leaves no regret, but worldly sorrow brings death. [11]See what this godly sorrow has produced in you: what earnestness, what eagerness to clear yourselves, what indignation, what alarm, what longing, what concern, what readiness to see justice done. At every

THE TWO NATURES

point you have proved yourselves to be innocent in

this matter. 2 Cor. 7:8-11

If you respond in these ways, then you can say with all sincerity of heart that you are walking with the Lord Jesus; for this is remaining in Him. Your motivation for doing so however, must be that you really desire to live in and for your God, Lord and Father to honor Him, and you are no longer willing to deliberately sin against your Lord. If all of this is your disposition and reality, then you are the Lord's, and you are living in Him and with Him. Yes, you are then walking with the beloved Lord Jesus.

Over time, the Holy Spirit has been putting to death the sinful nature in those of us who are being sanctified, freeing us of its power and influence, so that we can be free to live for the Lord Jesus, without the usual carnal desires, resistance and pull from that evil nature. This is as a result of the sanctifying work of the Holy Spirit, as He cleanses us and applies the finished work of the Lord Jesus on Calvary's Cross to our very souls, and therefore our bodies. In so doing, He brings to bear the death of the sinful nature, even as it took place on Calvary's Cross in the body of the Lord Jesus, making it real in our very souls and bodies, through the sanctifying/ cleansing work of the Holy Spirit.

So it is written: "The first man Adam became a living being"; the last Adam, a life-giving spirit. [46]The spiritual did not come first, but the natural, and after that the spiritual. [47]The first man was of the dust of the earth, the second man from heaven. [48]As was the earthly man, so are those who are of the earth; and as is the man from heaven, so also are those who are of heaven. [49]And just as we have borne the likeness of the earthly man, so shall we bear the likeness of the man from heaven. 1 Cor. 15:45-49

The beloved Lord Jesus took back from satan, all that satan took from Adam. Therefore, as satan was victorious over Adam, even more so, the Lord Jesus was victorious over satan through His death on the Cross, followed by His Resurrection. In his push to put the Lord Jesus to death, satan was deceived, not knowing it would work against him – his defeat. Had he known this, he would not have led them to put the Lord Jesus to death. Rather, he would have worked to avoid putting the Lord Jesus to death.

For as in Adam all die, so in Christ all will be made alive. 1 Cor. 15:22

THE TWO NATURES

This continues to reveal the fact that the flesh is not inherently evil, for it was not made evil nor with evil intent or purposes – rather, God made it good.

> Let us examine our ways and test them, and let us return to the Lord. Lam. 3:40

CHAPTER 2

TWO NATURES

Have you ever wondered how some who are called Christians, could have done some of the outrageous things that they have done? "How are such things possible?" Some have also asked: "Those who have done these terrible things, are they really Christians?" The answer is yes – at least some of them are. These things happen because ever since they came to the Lord Jesus, they have never sought to sincerely lay down their lives to Him, and so to be sanctified/cleansed from the ways of the sinful nature. They would then have begun to be united to their Lord, thereby becoming one in agreement and purpose with the Word and ways of the Lord Jesus, by taking on His divine nature. Instead, they continued to live according to their sinful nature, the result of which is this horrible disobedience to their Lord, and so they continue to do what they have been doing – committing outrageous acts/sinning.

> Do not be deceived: God cannot be mocked. A man reaps what he sows. [8]The one who sows to please his sinful nature, from that nature will reap destruction; the one who sows to please the Spirit, from the Spirit will reap eternal life. [9]Let us not become weary in doing good, for at the proper time we will reap a harvest if we do not give up. Gal. 6:7-9

Let us look at it from another angle. To carry out any such acts, as some have done, which are so outrageous and contrary to the ways of the Lord Jesus and His Word, they must first have turned from their Lord, back to their carnal sinful nature. There, they again feel free from the constraints of God's Word, and are therefore able to do such outrageous things. Only in this way can those who are called Christians, if indeed they really are, do those outrageous things which so many have done, and for that matter, carry out any act that is so contrary to their Lord, His Word and His will for their lives. It is only when they have turned from their Lord, back to their old carnal nature that such things are possible. In fact, when you live according to that nature, it is very easy to understand why such things happen. This I will try to explain, as the blessed Holy

Spirit gives me the understanding, and continues to lead and guide me through these writings.

> Those who live according to the sinful nature have their minds set on what that nature desires; but those who live in accordance with the Spirit have their minds set on what the Spirit desires. [6]The mind of sinful man is death, but the mind controlled by the Spirit is life and peace; Rom. 8:5-6

Let me now explain this more thoroughly with the guidance and the understanding that the Lord Jesus is giving me. There are two natures: one is called the divine nature, and the other the sinful or carnal nature. The divine nature is of God, and is clearly laid out in His Word, and in which He has called us to participate. (See 2 Peter, Chapter 1). The other is the sinful nature, which is of the devil, under which we have lived from the day we were born and came into this world, until the day we came to Christ and were saved. When we were saved, we all should then have taken the next step, which is to learn from and of the Lord Jesus in His Word, and as a result submit ourselves in obedience to the Holy Spirit for Him to begin His sanctifying/cleansing work in our souls, to cleanse us from the ways of the sinful nature. This is also clearly laid out in God's Word.

THE TWO NATURES

To come to Christ, a decision had to be made in our hearts, or should
have been made, to turn from the ways of the sinful or carnal nature
by God's grace, through the faith given us to believe in the Lord
Jesus Christ, and surrender our lives to Him by acknowledging our
sins and repenting of them. These are the sins we had practiced all
our lives and lived out against our God and Lord, when we lived
according to the sinful nature in full agreement and obedience to
the ways of that nature.

> As for you, you were dead in your transgressions
> and sins, [2]in which you used to live when you fol-
> lowed the ways of this world and of the ruler of the
> kingdom of the air, the spirit who is now at work
> in those who are disobedient. [3]All of us also lived
> among them at one time, gratifying the cravings
> of our sinful nature and following its desires and
> thoughts. Like the rest, we were by nature objects
> of wrath. [4]But because of his great love for us, God,
> who is rich in mercy, [5]made us alive with Christ
> even when we were dead in transgressions – it is
> by grace you have been saved. [6]And God raised
> us up with Christ and seated us with him in the
> heavenly realms in Christ Jesus, [7]in order that in
> the coming ages he might show the incomparable

THE TWO NATURES

riches of his grace, expressed in his kindness to us in Christ Jesus. [8]For it is by grace you have been saved, through faith – and this not from yourselves, it is the gift of God – [9]not by works, so that no one can boast. [10]For we are God's workmanship, created in Christ Jesus to do good works, which God prepared in advance for us to do. Eph. 2:1-10

To be able to repent, a decision had to be made in our heart to turn from those sins – that old way of life which we had lived – to the Lord Jesus, believing in Him and therefore putting our trust in Him, and we were forgiven of our sins. We were then born-again of His Spirit, that is, we were given a new spirit, while our souls were redeemed. This now allows us to begin to walk with the Lord Jesus, and to come to knowledge of Him so that we can begin to participate in His divine nature, as we hold to His teaching/Word and continue in it. At the same time, our souls are being sanctified by the Holy Spirit.

By this gospel you are saved, if you hold firmly to the word I preached to you. Otherwise, you have believed in vain. 1 Cor. 15:2

THE TWO NATURES

Once you were alienated from God and were enemies in your minds because of your evil behavior.
²²But now he has reconciled you by Christ's physical body through death to present you holy in his
sight, without blemish and free from accusation –
²³if you continue in your faith, established and firm,
not moved from the hope held out in the gospel.
This is the gospel that you heard and that has been
proclaimed to every creature under heaven, and of
which I, Paul, have become a servant. Col. 1:21-23

Therefore, get rid of all moral filth and the evil that
is so prevalent and humbly accept the word planted
in you, which can save you. James 1:21

To the Jews who had believed him, Jesus said, "If
you hold to my teaching, you are really my disciples. ³²Then you will know the truth, and the truth
will set you free." John 8:31-32

You, however, did not come to know Christ that way.
²¹Surely you heard of him and were taught in him
in accordance with the truth that is in Jesus. ²²You
were taught, with regard to your former way of life,

to put off your old self, which is being corrupted by its deceitful desires; [23]to be made new in the attitude of your minds; [24]and to put on the new self, created to be like God in true righteousness and holiness. Eph. 4:20-24

Do not lie to each other, since you have taken off your old self with its practices [10]and have put on the new self, which is being renewed in knowledge in the image of its Creator. Col. 3:9-10

Therefore, I urge you, brothers, in view of God's mercy, to offer your bodies as living sacrifices, holy and pleasing to God – this is your spiritual act of worship. [2]Do not conform any longer to the pattern of this world, but be transformed by the renewing of your mind. Then you will be able to test and approve what God's will is – his good, pleasing and perfect will. Rom. 12:1-2

In reply Jesus declared, "I tell you the truth, no one can see the kingdom of God unless he is born again." John 3:3

THE TWO NATURES

Therefore, if anyone is in Christ, he is a new creation;
the old has gone, the new has come! 2 Cor. 5:17

One of the answers as to why so many, after being saved, can carry
out outrageous acts, or for that matter go on deliberately sinning,
is found in 2 Peter, Chapter 1:2-11.

> Grace and peace be yours in abundance through the
> knowledge of God and of Jesus our Lord. [3]His divine
> power has given us everything we need for life and
> godliness through our knowledge of him who called
> us by his own glory and goodness. [4]Through these
> he has given us his very great and precious prom-
> ises, so that through them you may participate in the
> divine nature and escape the corruption in the world
> caused by evil desires. 2 Peter 1:2-4

This Scripture calls us to participate in the divine nature through the
sanctifying work of the Holy Spirit, and in so doing we are enabled
by God's grace to escape the corruption in the world. However, we
are the only ones who can choose in agreement with the Holy Spirit
to be sanctified; no one else can choose for us. We are the only ones
who can choose which direction our lives will take – the way of the
divine nature or the way of the carnal sinful nature.

THE TWO NATURES

This decision is solidly placed in our hands and in our hands alone. This is called freewill, because we are free to exercise it in any direction we choose, for God has made us free moral agents. So, if we choose to go in the direction of the divine nature, which we are invited to do, we are certainly free to do so. On the other hand, if we choose to continue in the way of the carnal sinful nature, we are also free to do so, even after we have received the Lord Jesus.

What I have come to realize is; our beloved Lord Jesus gently pursues us, but He never forces Himself on anyone. He will not force anyone to receive Salvation; neither will He force anyone to remain in Him, or to be sanctified after they have come to Him and are saved. It is up to each one of us to face our need to be cleansed/sanctified of the ways of the sinful nature, and continue to surrender our souls/lives in prayer to the Holy Spirit to be cleansed.

> Sanctify them by the truth; your word is truth.
> John 17:17

The Lord Jesus has invited us to come to Him. In the process, He will woo us with His inestimable goodness, love, gentleness and purity, while He pours out grace on us every step of the way, to open our eyes and to soften our hardened hearts. He woos us until

He wins us over, and brings us to that place where we voluntarily choose to say yes to Him.

"Yes Lord Jesus; we have chosen to live in You and with You and for You, beloved Lord Jesus. We have chosen to turn our backs on the world, the carnal nature, sin and the devil, to now embrace You, beloved Lord Jesus, submit our lives to You, and to walk in submission and obedience to You, and to be faithful to You, Your Word and Your ways, to honor You. This is not for a time, or until something happens that displeases us, or comes with the intent for us to retreat from You again. No, but rather, this is for eternity, for we have surrendered our all to You, and we have chosen death with You, so as to be able to live with You forever."

> Consider therefore the kindness and sternness of God: sternness to those who fell, but kindness to you, provided that you continue in his kindness. Otherwise, you also will be cut off. Rom. 11:22

> Now if we died with Christ, we believe that we will also live with him. Rom. 6:8

I must again emphasize here, that the Lord Jesus does not force us to do anything. Rather, He has freed us, and invites us to participate in the divine nature, because we do have the liberty to choose to live according to either nature. We are given these choices, and we must choose. The Lord Jesus has given us this liberty. He warns us in His Word however, that we are not to live according to the sinful nature, for if we do, we will die. In the same way He had warned Adam and Eve, but they disobeyed Him and died spiritually that day, and would also now die physically. This and several similar warnings are stated throughout God's Word. Therefore, everyone who chooses to live according to the sinful nature will suffer the consequence that is established in God's Word, which is spiritual death, as Adam did.

> Be imitators of God, therefore, as dearly loved children ²and live a life of love, just as Christ loved us and gave himself up for us as a fragrant offering and sacrifice to God. ³But among you there must not be even a hint of sexual immorality, or of any kind of impurity, or of greed, because these are improper for God's holy people. ⁴Nor should there be obscenity, foolish talk or coarse joking, which are out of place, but rather thanksgiving. ⁵For of this you can be sure: No immoral, impure or greedy person – such a man is an idolater – has any inheritance in the kingdom of Christ and of God. ⁶Let

THE TWO NATURES

no one deceive you with empty words, for because
of such things God's wrath comes on those who
are disobedient. [7]Therefore do not be partners with
them. [8]For you were once darkness, but now you
are light in the Lord. Live as children of light [9](for
the fruit of the light consists in all goodness, righteousness and truth) [10]and find out what pleases the
Lord. [11]Have nothing to do with the fruitless deeds
of darkness, but rather expose them. Eph. 5:1-11

I believe the word "participate," is the key to unlock the door for us
to understand and to answer the earlier questions asked, regarding
the outrageous things that some of those who are called Christians
choose to do or practice, and therefore – are they really Christians?
Here we must understand, that yes, our beloved Lord Jesus has
died, and with His precious blood He has bought us out from under
the heavy hand of the devil and sin, forgiven us our sins, given us
a new spirit, redeemed our souls, and placed us on the road for our
souls to be sanctified by the blessed Holy Spirit, preparing us for
eternity in heaven with our Father and Lord.

Since we have these promises, dear friends, let us
purify ourselves from everything that contaminates

THE TWO NATURES

body and spirit, perfecting holiness out of reverence
for God. 2 Cor. 7:1

For the love of money is a root of all kinds of evil.
Some people, eager for money, have wandered from
the faith and pierced themselves with many griefs.
[11]But you, man of God, flee from all this, and pursue
righteousness, godliness, faith, love, endurance and
gentleness. [12]Fight the good fight of the faith. Take
hold of the eternal life to which you were called
when you made your good confession in the presence of many witnesses. 1 Tim. 6:10-12

However, along with these blessings, we have the liberty to further
choose at any time, whether we want to continue in the Lord Jesus
or not. Will we choose to humble ourselves, deny ourselves and
surrender the life in submission and obedience to the Lord Jesus,
according to His dictates, and therefore be faithful to Him? This
choice is still ours, even after He has saved us and forgiven us our
sins, to now cleanse us from the ways of the sinful nature through
the sanctifying work of His Spirit. I will now lay out a series of
Scriptures to confirm what has been said so far.

THE TWO NATURES

But we ought always to thank God for you, brothers loved by the Lord, because from the beginning God chose you to be saved through the sanctifying work of the Spirit and through belief in the truth. [14]He called you to this through our gospel, that you might share in the glory of our Lord Jesus Christ. 2 Thess. 2:13-14

It is God's will that you should be sanctified: that you should avoid sexual immorality; [4]that each of you should learn to control his own body in a way that is holy and honorable, [5]not in passionate lust like the heathen, who do not know God; [6]and that in this matter no one should wrong his brother or take advantage of him. The Lord will punish men for all such sins, as we have already told you and warned you. [7]For God did not call us to be impure, but to live a holy life. [8]Therefore, he who rejects this instruction does not reject man but God, who gives you his Holy Spirit. 1 Thess. 4:3-8

May God himself, the God of peace, sanctify you through and through. May your whole spirit, soul and body be kept blameless at the coming of our

Lord Jesus Christ. [24]The one who calls you is faithful and he will do it. 1 Thess. 5:23-24

"Now I commit you to God and to the word of his grace, which can build you up and give you an inheritance among all those who are sanctified. Acts 20:32

Peter, an apostle of Jesus Christ, To God's elect, strangers in the world, scattered throughout Pontus, Galatia, Cappadocia, Asia and Bithynia, [2]who have been chosen according to the foreknowledge of God the Father, through the sanctifying work of the Spirit, for obedience to Jesus Christ and sprinkling by his blood: Grace and peace be yours in abundance. 1 Peter 1:1-2

For the grace of God that brings salvation has appeared to all men. [12]It teaches us to say "No" to ungodliness and worldly passions, and to live self-controlled, upright and godly lives in this present age, [13]while we wait for the blessed hope – the glorious appearing of our great God and Savior, Jesus Christ, [14]who gave himself for us to redeem

THE TWO NATURES

us from all wickedness and to purify for himself a people that are his very own, eager to do what is good. [15]These, then, are the things you should teach. Encourage and rebuke with all authority. Do not let anyone despise you. Titus 2:11-15

But God demonstrates his own love for us in this: While we were still sinners, Christ died for us. [9]Since we have now been justified by his blood, how much more shall we be saved from God's wrath through him! [10]For if, when we were God's enemies, we were reconciled to him through the death of his Son, how much more, having been reconciled, shall we be saved through his life! Rom. 5:8-10

because by one sacrifice he has made perfect forever those who are being made holy. Heb. 10:14

and, once made perfect, he became the source of eternal salvation for all who obey him. Heb. 5:9

We are therefore Christ's ambassadors, as though God were making his appeal through us. We implore you on Christ's behalf: Be reconciled to God. [21]God made him who had no sin to be sin for us, so that in him we might become the righteousness of God. 2 Cor. 5:20-21

How great is the love the Father has lavished on us, that we should be called children of God! And that is what we are! The reason the world does not know us is that it did not know him. [2]Dear friends, now we are children of God, and what we will be has not yet been made known. But we know that when he appears, we shall be like him, for we shall see him as he is. [3]Everyone who has this hope in him purifies himself, just as he is pure. 1 John 3:1-3

[2]To the church of God in Corinth, to those sanctified in Christ Jesus and called to be holy, together with all those everywhere who call on the name of our Lord Jesus Christ—their Lord and ours: [18]For the message of the cross is foolishness to those who are perishing, but to us who are being saved it is the power of God. 1 Cor. 1:2, 18

Do not lie to each other, since you have taken off your old self with its practices [10]and have put on the

THE TWO NATURES

new self, which is being renewed in knowledge in the image of its Creator. Col. 3:9-10

You were taught, with regard to your former way of life, to put off your old self, which is being corrupted by its deceitful desires; [23]to be made new in the attitude of your minds; [24]and to put on the new self, created to be like God in true righteousness and holiness. [25]Therefore each of you must put off falsehood and speak truthfully to his neighbor, for we are all members of one body. Eph. 4:22-25

This is the message we have heard from him and declare to you: God is light; in him there is no darkness at all. [6]If we claim to have fellowship with him yet walk in the darkness, we lie and do not live by the truth. [7]But if we walk in the light, as he is in the light, we have fellowship with one another, and the blood of Jesus, his Son, purifies us from all sin. [8]If we claim to be without sin, we deceive ourselves and the truth is not in us. [9]If we confess our sins, he is faithful and just and will forgive us our sins and purify us from all unrighteousness. [10]If we claim we have not sinned, we make him out to be a liar and his word has no place in our lives. 1 John 1:5-10

Since we have these promises, dear friends, let us purify ourselves from everything that contaminates body and spirit, perfecting holiness out of reverence for God. 2 Cor. 7:1

Sanctify them by the truth; your word is truth. [18]As you sent me into the world, I have sent them into the world. [19]For them I sanctify myself, that they too may be truly sanctified. John 17:17-19

Now, brothers, I want to remind you of the gospel I preached to you, which you received and on which you have taken your stand. [2]By this gospel you are saved, if you hold firmly to the word I preached to you. Otherwise, you have believed in vain. 1 Cor. 15:1-2

...just as Christ loved the church and gave himself up for her [26]to make her holy, cleansing her by the washing with water through the word, [27]and to present her to himself as a radiant church, without

stain or wrinkle or any other blemish, but holy and
blameless. Eph. 5:25-27

Therefore, I urge you, brothers, in view of God's
mercy, to offer your bodies as living sacrifices, holy
and pleasing to God – this is your spiritual act of
worship. [2]Do not conform any longer to the pattern
of this world, but be transformed by the renewing
of your mind. Then you will be able to test and
approve what God's will is – his good, pleasing and
perfect will. Rom. 12:1-2

[19]Nevertheless, God's solid foundation stands firm,
sealed with this inscription: "The Lord knows those
who are his," and, "Everyone who confesses the
name of the Lord must turn away from wickedness."
[22]Flee the evil desires of youth, and pursue righteousness, faith, love and peace, along with those
who call on the Lord out of a pure heart. [23]Don't
have anything to do with foolish and stupid arguments, because you know they produce quarrels.
2 Tim. 2:19, 22-23

But whenever anyone turns to the Lord, the veil is taken away. [17]Now the Lord is the Spirit, and where the Spirit of the Lord is, there is freedom. [18]And we, who with unveiled faces all reflect the Lord's glory, are being transformed into his likeness with ever-increasing glory, which comes from the Lord, who is the Spirit. 2 Cor. 3:16-18

Therefore we do not lose heart. Though outwardly we are wasting away, yet inwardly we are being renewed day by day. [17]For our light and momentary troubles are achieving for us an eternal glory that far outweighs them all. [18]So we fix our eyes not on what is seen, but on what is unseen. For what is seen is temporary, but what is unseen is eternal. 2 Cor. 4:16-18

Then Jesus said to his disciples, "If anyone would come after me, he must deny himself and take up his cross and follow me. [25]For whoever wants to save his life will lose it, but whoever loses his life for me will find it. [26]What good will it be for a man if he gains the whole world, yet forfeits his soul? Or what can a man give in exchange for his soul? [27]For the

THE TWO NATURES

Son of Man is going to come in his Father's glory
with his angels, and then he will reward each person
according to what he has done." Matt. 16:24-27

Jesus replied, "The hour has come for the Son of
Man to be glorified. ²⁴I tell you the truth, unless
a kernel of wheat falls to the ground and dies, it
remains only a single seed. But if it dies, it produces
many seeds. ²⁵The man who loves his life will lose
it, while the man who hates his life in this world
will keep it for eternal life. ²⁶Whoever serves me
must follow me; and where I am, my servant also
will be. My Father will honor the one who serves
me. John 12:23-26

"Enter through the narrow gate. For wide is the gate
and broad is the road that leads to destruction, and
many enter through it. ¹⁴But small is the gate and
narrow the road that leads to life, and only a few
find it. Matt. 7:13-14

So I say, live by the Spirit, and you will not gratify
the desires of the sinful nature. ¹⁷For the sinful
nature desires what is contrary to the Spirit, and

the Spirit what is contrary to the sinful nature. They are in conflict with each other, so that you do not do what you want. [18]But if you are led by the Spirit, you are not under law. [19]The acts of the sinful nature are obvious: sexual immorality, impurity and debauchery; [20]idolatry and witchcraft; hatred, discord, jealousy, fits of rage, selfish ambition, dissensions, factions [21]and envy; drunkenness, orgies, and the like. I warn you, as I did before, that those who live like this will not inherit the kingdom of God. [22]But the fruit of the Spirit is love, joy, peace, patience, kindness, goodness, faithfulness, [23]gentleness and self-control. Against such things there is no law. [24]Those who belong to Christ Jesus have crucified the sinful nature with its passions and desires. [25]Since we live by the Spirit, let us keep in step with the Spirit. [26]Let us not become conceited, provoking and envying each other. Gal. 5:16-26

In the same way, any of you who does not give up everything he has cannot be my disciple. Luke 14:33

But you, man of God, flee from all this, and pursue righteousness, godliness, faith, love, endurance and gentleness. [12]Fight the good fight of the faith. Take hold of the eternal life to which you were called when you made your good confession in the presence of many witnesses. 1 Tim. 6:11-12

Therefore, rid yourselves of all malice and all deceit, hypocrisy, envy, and slander of every kind. [2]Like newborn babies, crave pure spiritual milk, so that by it you may grow up in your salvation, [3]now that you have tasted that the Lord is good. 1 Peter 2:1-3

And we also thank God continually because, when you received the word of God, which you heard from us, you accepted it not as the word of men, but as it actually is, the word of God, which is at work in you who believe. 1 Thess. 2:13

Your boasting is not good. Don't you know that a little yeast works through the whole batch of dough? [7]Get rid of the old yeast that you may be a new batch without yeast – as you really are. For Christ, our Passover lamb, has been sacrificed. [8]Therefore let us keep the Festival, not with the old yeast, the yeast

THE TWO NATURES

of malice and wickedness, but with bread without yeast, the bread of sincerity and truth. 1 Cor. 5:6-8

"If, while we seek to be justified in Christ, it becomes evident that we ourselves are sinners, does that mean that Christ promotes sin? Absolutely not! [18]If I rebuild what I destroyed, I prove that I am a lawbreaker. [19]For through the law I died to the law so that I might live for God. [20]I have been crucified with Christ and I no longer live, but Christ lives in me. The life I live in the body, I live by faith in the Son of God, who loved me and gave himself for me. Gal. 2:17-20

"I am the true vine, and my Father is the gardener. [2]He cuts off every branch in me that bears no fruit, while every branch that does bear fruit he prunes so that it will be even more fruitful. [3]You are already clean because of the word I have spoken to you. [4]Remain in me, and I will remain in you. No branch can bear fruit by itself; it must remain in the vine. Neither can you bear fruit unless you remain in me. [5]"I am the vine; you are the branches. If a man remains in me and I in him, he will bear much fruit;

THE TWO NATURES

apart from me you can do nothing. ⁶If anyone does not remain in me, he is like a branch that is thrown away and withers; such branches are picked up, thrown into the fire and burned. John 15:1-6

'Now get up and stand on your feet. I have appeared to you to appoint you as a servant and as a witness of what you have seen of me and what I will show you. ¹⁷I will rescue you from your own people and from the Gentiles. I am sending you to them ¹⁸to open their eyes and turn them from darkness to light, and from the power of Satan to God, so that they may receive forgiveness of sins and a place among those who are sanctified by faith in me.' Acts, 26:16-18

We always carry around in our body the death of Jesus, so that the life of Jesus may also be revealed in our body. ¹¹For we who are alive are always being given over to death for Jesus' sake, so that his life may be revealed in our mortal body. 2 Cor. 4:10-11

Put to death, therefore, whatever belongs to your earthly nature: sexual immorality, impurity, lust, evil desires and greed, which is idolatry. ⁶Because

THE TWO NATURES

of these, the wrath of God is coming. [7]You used to walk in these ways, in the life you once lived. [8]But now you must rid yourselves of all such things as these: anger, rage, malice, slander, and filthy language from your lips. [9]Do not lie to each other, since you have taken off your old self with its practices [10]and have put on the new self, which is being renewed in knowledge in the image of its Creator. Col. 3:5-10

A man is not a Jew if he is only one outwardly, nor is circumcision merely outward and physical. [29]No, a man is a Jew if he is one inwardly; and circumcision is circumcision of the heart, by the Spirit, not by the written code. Such a man's praise is not from men, but from God. Rom. 2:28-29

For we are to God the aroma of Christ among those who are being saved and those who are perishing. [16]To the one we are the smell of death; to the other, the fragrance of life. And who is equal to such a task? 2 Cor. 2:15-16

THE TWO NATURES

But since we belong to the day, let us be self-controlled, putting on faith and love as a breastplate,
and the hope of salvation as a helmet. [9]For God did
not appoint us to suffer wrath but to receive salvation through our Lord Jesus Christ. [10]He died for us
so that, whether we are awake or asleep, we may
live together with him. 1 Thess. 5:8-10

As God's fellow workers we urge you not to receive
God's grace in vain. [2]For he says, "In the time of
my favor I heard you, and in the day of salvation
I helped you." I tell you, now is the time of God's
favor, now is the day of salvation. 2 Cor. 6:1-2

We want each of you to show this same diligence
to the very end, in order to make your hope sure.
[12]We do not want you to become lazy, but to imitate
those who through faith and patience inherit what
has been promised. Heb. 6:11-12

In a large house there are articles not only of gold
and silver, but also of wood and clay; some are for
noble purposes and some for ignoble. [21]If a man
cleanses himself from the latter, he will be an

THE TWO NATURES

instrument for noble purposes, made holy, useful to the Master and prepared to do any good work. [22]Flee the evil desires of youth, and pursue righteousness, faith, love and peace, along with those who call on the Lord out of a pure heart. 2 Tim. 2:20-22

And do this, understanding the present time. The hour has come for you to wake up from your slumber, because our salvation is nearer now than when we first believed. [12]The night is nearly over; the day is almost here. So let us put aside the deeds of darkness and put on the armor of light. [13]Let us behave decently, as in the daytime, not in orgies and drunkenness, not in sexual immorality and debauchery, not in dissension and jealousy. [14]Rather, clothe yourselves with the Lord Jesus Christ, and do not think about how to gratify the desires of the sinful nature. Rom. 13:11-14

Timothy, my son, I give you this instruction in keeping with the prophecies once made about you, so that by following them you may fight the good fight, [19]holding on to faith and a good conscience.

THE TWO NATURES

Some have rejected these and so have shipwrecked
their faith. 1 Tim. 1:18-19

Then he said to them all: "If anyone would come
after me, he must deny himself and take up his cross
daily and follow me. [24]For whoever wants to save
his life will lose it, but whoever loses his life for me
will save it. [25]What good is it for a man to gain the
whole world, and yet lose or forfeit his very self?
Luke 9:23-25

May I never boast except in the cross of our Lord
Jesus Christ, through which the world has been crucified to me, and I to the world. Gal. 6:14

But if Christ is in you, your body is dead because of
sin, yet your spirit is alive because of righteousness.
[11]And if the Spirit of him who raised Jesus from the
dead is living in you, he who raised Christ from
the dead will also give life to your mortal bodies
through his Spirit, who lives in you. [12]Therefore,
brothers, we have an obligation – but it is not to the
sinful nature, to live according to it. [13]For if you live
according to the sinful nature, you will die; but if

THE TWO NATURES

by the Spirit you put to death the misdeeds of the body, you will live, Rom. 8:10-13

who through faith are shielded by God's power until the coming of the salvation that is ready to be revealed in the last time. [6]In this you greatly rejoice, though now for a little while you may have had to suffer grief in all kinds of trials. [7]These have come so that your faith – of greater worth than gold, which perishes even though refined by fire –may be proved genuine and may result in praise, glory and honor when Jesus Christ is revealed. [8]Though you have not seen him, you love him; and even though you do not see him now, you believe in him and are filled with an inexpressible and glorious joy, [9]for you are receiving the goal of your faith, the salvation of your souls. 1 Peter 1:5-9

Over the past two thousand years, many have chosen to believe in the Lord Jesus, and so have embraced His Atoning Sacrifice for themselves. Some have chosen to continue in Him for eternity. However, there are those who have chosen not to continue after starting with Him. Still many others have simply chosen to reject the Lord Jesus after reading His Word, saying that it is

contradictory, confusing, too confining and hard for them to understand. Some have even said that He has asked too much of them,
along with many other similar excuses.

> Anyone who runs ahead and does not continue in
> the teaching of Christ does not have God; whoever
> continues in the teaching has both the Father and
> the Son. 2 John 1:9

> The Spirit clearly says that in later times some will
> abandon the faith and follow deceiving spirits and
> things taught by demons. ²Such teachings come
> through hypocritical liars, whose consciences have
> been seared as with a hot iron. 1 Tim. 4:1-2

The reason for all these excuses however, is simply that they do not
want to give up their old life style. Sanctification then becomes an
obstacle to going on with our Lord Jesus. For many, being cleansed
from their old way of life is, to them, giving up too much, and to be
sanctified is not a blessing, but rather a curse. According to them,
they will lose too much of their possessions, their position/status,
time, and even their liberty to go their own way and to do their own
thing. To give this up is simply asking too much of them.

THE TWO NATURES

Therefore, since we are surrounded by such a great
cloud of witnesses, let us throw off everything that
hinders and the sin that so easily entangles, and let
us run with perseverance the race marked out for
us. [2]Let us fix our eyes on Jesus, the author and per-
fecter of our faith, who for the joy set before him
endured the cross, scorning its shame, and sat down
at the right hand of the throne of God. [3]Consider
him who endured such opposition from sinful men,
so that you will not grow weary and lose heart.
Heb. 12:1-3

The intent of the Lord Jesus has always been to give us all the
opportunity and liberty to exercise our freewill, and we have all
done so. At the same time, His desire has always been for us to
choose to come home to Him. Those of us who have believed in
the Lord Jesus, and have received His Atoning Sacrifice for ourselves, and have truly surrendered our lives to Him, and have continued in Him, being sanctified/cleansed from our old way of life
by the Holy Spirit, will receive eternal life. Our soul will therefore
live eternally with our God, Lord and Father in heaven where our
spirit is. On the other hand, those who have rejected the sanctifying
work of His Spirit for themselves will receive the consequence
for such choices, although they had received the Lord Jesus. The

point that is being made here is, you cannot live according to your sinful nature and expect your soul to go to heaven. The Scriptures are very clear about this subject. It states that if you live according to your sinful nature you will die.

> Therefore, brothers, we have an obligation – but it is not to the sinful nature, to live according to it. [13]For if you live according to the sinful nature, you will die; but if by the Spirit you put to death the misdeeds of the body, you will live, Rom. 8:12-13

> Do not be deceived: God cannot be mocked. A man reaps what he sows. [8]The one who sows to please his sinful nature, from that nature will reap destruction; the one who sows to please the Spirit, from the Spirit will reap eternal life. [9]Let us not become weary in doing good, for at the proper time we will reap a harvest if we do not give up. Gal. 6:7-9

Again, to further confirm what I have just said, I invite you to read 1 Corinthians 15:2, Colossians 1:21-23, Galatians 5:1-26, John 8:31-32, etc.

THE TWO NATURES

The reason for this is heaven is a home of righteousness. Therefore, there will be no deceitful, puffed-up, prideful, arrogant, lying, deceiving and exalted souls in heaven. Neither will there be any wickedness, sexual immorality, evil, rebellion, having your own way, doing your own thing, perversion, selfishness, envy, jealousy, greed, hate, stealing, rape, murder, etc. All this wickedness is lived out by those who live according to the sinful nature, and it will come to its end here on this earth. As we acknowledge them, and in sincerity of heart renounce them and repent of them, we will then be cleansed of those old ways and patterns of living/sin that belong to the old nature. They will either come to their end here through the sanctifying work of God's Spirit, or they will come to their end in hell – one way or another, they will end. For these reasons, God has given us this precious blessing of repentance and sanctification to cleanse us of all these old ways of life/sin, preparing us to come home to be with Him as His holy children, living in true submission and obedience to Him – our God, Lord and Father.

> For the grace of God that brings salvation has appeared to all men. [12]It teaches us to say "No" to ungodliness and worldly passions, and to live self-controlled, upright and godly lives in this present age, [13]while we wait for the blessed hope – the glorious appearing of our great God and Savior,

THE TWO NATURES

Jesus Christ, [14]who gave himself for us to redeem us from all wickedness and to purify for himself a people that are his very own, eager to do what is good. [15]These, then, are the things you should teach. Encourage and rebuke with all authority. Do not let anyone despise you. Titus 2:11-15

Be imitators of God, therefore, as dearly loved children [2]and live a life of love, just as Christ loved us and gave himself up for us as a fragrant offering and sacrifice to God. Eph. 5:1-2

For you not to embrace the sanctification/cleansing work of the blessed Holy Spirit, is to turn away from the ways of your holy Lord, and reject them. As I write, I can already hear the voices of the rebellious saying, "I do not believe you, and I do not believe what you are saying." That too is freewill in action, for we are free to believe or to reject God's truth, along with those lying voices and deceiving impressions that come to us from the enemy.

Those who refuse to be cleansed will therefore face the consequence of their choices, although according to them, they had received the Lord Jesus.

THE TWO NATURES

"Not everyone who says to me, `Lord, Lord,' will enter the kingdom of heaven, but only he who does the will of my Father who is in heaven. Matt. 7:21

This calls for patient endurance on the part of the saints who obey God's commandments and remain faithful to Jesus. [13]Then I heard a voice from heaven say, "Write: Blessed are the dead who die in the Lord from now on." "Yes," says the Spirit, "they will rest from their labor, for their deeds will follow them." Rev. 14:12-13

However, if you suffer as a Christian, do not be ashamed, but praise God that you bear that name. [17]For it is time for judgment to begin with the family of God; and if it begins with us, what will the outcome be for those who do not obey the gospel of God? [18]And, "If it is hard for the righteous to be saved, what will become of the ungodly and the sinner?" [19]So then, those who suffer according to God's will should commit themselves to their faithful Creator and continue to do good. 1 Peter 4:16-19

THE TWO NATURES

When the Scripture says, if it is hard for the righteous to be saved, it is speaking to this very point of sanctification. Those who choose to go through this cleansing process of the Holy Spirit, will in time be set free from most of the ways of the sinful nature, to be firmly united with their God and Lord, doing His will from their hearts without having to struggle against the constant pull on them to fulfill the desires of the sinful nature through their soul, and therefore their flesh. This is one of the many benefits of being sanctified by the Holy Spirit. For those who refuse to submit themselves to go through this cleansing work of the Holy Spirit, it will be impossible for them to be saved from that filthy ungodly way of life that is of the sinful nature, for it is only the Holy Spirit who can cleanse you from the ways of the sinful nature – the old way of life – and no one else.

As we can see, our beloved Lord Jesus did not shed His precious blood to compel any of us to come to Him, or to be sanctified/ cleansed. Rather, He did this so that every one of us would be free to be able to choose freely and willingly to either come to Him, or not to come at all. Even those who have come to Him still have the liberty and the option to remain in Him, to continue being sanctified or not. Neither does He compel those who have come to Him to remain in Him, and to partake of the divine nature. Rather, He invites them to do so, while at the same time revealing the consequences for those who refuse to. Therefore, it will be by our own choosing that we will either go to be with our Father in heaven, or end up in hell.

> Watch out that you do not lose what you have worked for, but that you may be rewarded fully. [9]Anyone who runs ahead and does not continue in the teaching of Christ does not have God; whoever continues in the teaching has both the Father and the Son. [10]If anyone comes to you and does not bring this teaching, do not take him into your house or welcome him. [11]Anyone who welcomes him shares in his wicked work. 2 John 1:8-11

Those who refuse to live according to the divine nature, and therefore live according to their sinful nature, do carry out outrageous acts, even though they are Christians. They have never chosen to continue according to the requirements of the Lord Jesus in His Word, and therefore grow up in their Salvation. This means that they have never chosen to submit themselves to the sanctifying process of the Holy Spirit, for Him to cleanse them of the ways of the sinful nature, and therefore of their sins. However, nothing or no one can compel them to do so in order for them to continue in the Lord Jesus, participating in the divine nature, although such persons could be in the church, and many of them are.

> The Spirit clearly says that in later times some will abandon the faith and follow deceiving spirits and things taught by demons. ²Such teachings come through hypocritical liars, whose consciences have been seared as with a hot iron. 1 Tim. 4:1-2.

There are many such cases in the church, because there are so many diverse personalities who call themselves Christians; and whether they are or not, no one really knows. This is because the devil is always there working to deceive us, to entice us back into the old way of life for us to once again be trapped under the heavy burden and weight of sin.

> No, but the sacrifices of pagans are offered to demons, not to God, and I do not want you to be participants with demons. ²¹You cannot drink the cup of the Lord and the cup of demons too; you cannot have a part in both the Lord's table and the table of demons. ²²Are we trying to arouse the Lord's jealousy? Are we stronger than he? 1 Cor. 10:20-22

THE TWO NATURES

Whenever that old way of life is embraced, the result will be the same old selfish choices and way of life. At times, many, according to the feelings and impressions received in their flesh, are deceived to believe that this is what they want when in reality they do not. But, because they follow their feelings instead of coming to the knowledge of God's Word to enable them to choose what they truly want, they end up being further deceived to embrace and live out that which they feel, while being miserable doing so.

This always results in them falling into a state of disappointment with self. Discouragement then follows, which leads to frustration, accusation, condemnation, doubt and then to withdrawal. At this point, if there is no acknowledgement and repentance, then giving up is usually the option that they choose, rather than turning to the Lord Jesus in repentance and asking for His help.

> See to it, brothers, that none of you has a sinful,
> unbelieving heart that turns away from the living
> God. [13]But encourage one another daily, as long
> as it is called Today, so that none of you may be
> hardened by sin's deceitfulness. [14]We have come
> to share in Christ if we hold firmly till the end the
> confidence we had at first. [15]As has just been said:
> "Today, if you hear his voice, do not harden your

hearts as you did in the rebellion." [16]Who were they
who heard and rebelled? Were they not all those
Moses led out of Egypt? [17]And with whom was he
angry for forty years? Was it not with those who
sinned, whose bodies fell in the desert? [18]And to
whom did God swear that they would never enter
his rest if not to those who disobeyed? [19]So we see
that they were not able to enter, because of their
unbelief. Heb. 3:12-19

For many, having their own way to satisfy the greed and lust of the
flesh, along with all kinds of other selfish and carnal desires and
ambitious acts, etc., are the choices that they would rather make
than to surrender their lives to the Lord Jesus. The devil can plant
all such desires and feelings on us, but it is only when we agree
with them and embrace them, that he is able to use them to trap us
and tie us up in them. Once he has done this, then he is able to use
them to seduce us back into the ways of the carnal sinful nature,
so as to imprison us there once again. Many fall for these tricks of
the enemy and are again trapped in them by him.

It is for freedom that Christ has set us free. Stand
firm, then, and do not let yourselves be burdened
again by a yoke of slavery. Gal. 5:1

THE TWO NATURES

Therefore, since we are surrounded by such a great cloud of witnesses, let us throw off everything that hinders and the sin that so easily entangles, and let us run with perseverance the race marked out for us. Heb. 12:1

The sad thing is, many have been trapped in such pursuits and are carried off to do the devil's will, without ever taking seriously the fact that they are being deceived by him. And in reality, many do not care. There are still others who want to be deceived, and therefore choose to be deceived to escape what they call, "this confining life in Christ." Through these choices, they have turned their backs on their Lord Jesus, and have ended up being trapped by the enemy in their carnal sinful nature, to their own shame and loss. In this state, they can and will commit outrageous acts. The problem with this is the consequences of such acts affect all of us Christians one way or another.

People who want to get rich fall into temptation and a trap and into many foolish and harmful desires that plunge men into ruin and destruction. [10]For the love of money is a root of all kinds of evil. Some people, eager for money, have wandered from the faith and pierced themselves with many griefs.

THE TWO NATURES

> [11]But you, man of God, flee from all this, and pursue
> righteousness, godliness, faith, love, endurance and
> gentleness. [12]Fight the good fight of the faith. Take
> hold of the eternal life to which you were called
> when you made your good confession in the pres-
> ence of many witnesses. 1 Tim. 6:9-12

For some, because of the outrageous acts they have committed,
those very acts have driven them back to the Lord Jesus in a serious
way, while others are driven further in the other direction to continue living according to their sinful nature, committing even more
outrageous acts. This kind of, in the Lord and out of the Lord, is
really a serious matter in the church, but this is so because of our
desire to satisfy the flesh, and of course, we do have the freewill to do so.

> I am astonished that you are so quickly deserting the
> one who called you by the grace of Christ and are
> turning to a different gospel – [7]which is really no
> gospel at all. Evidently some people are throwing
> you into confusion and are trying to pervert the
> gospel of Christ. Gal. 1:6-7

THE TWO NATURES

I know that most Christians do not believe that they can actually desert the One who called them, but these things do happen. In fact, they are common everyday occurrences in the lives of many who call themselves Christians, yet refuse to submit themselves to be sanctified so that their souls may be cleansed. Thanks to the blessed Holy Spirit, who makes us conscious of these choices that so many make. Those who heed the prompting of the Holy Spirit, and repent of these choices and actions that led them away from their Lord, will again enjoy sweet fellowship with the Lord Jesus. On the other hand, those who do not will continue having their own way in their carnal success or failure, whichever it may be. As a result, they will experience separation from their Lord, along with the dryness, emptiness and loneliness of soul, and the torment of once again being under the heavy hand of the devil, which such choices bring.

> My brothers, if one of you should wander from the truth and someone should bring him back, [20]remember this: Whoever turns a sinner from the error of his way will save him from death and cover over a multitude of sins. James 5:19-20

The ways of the beloved Lord Jesus are so different. He does not push Himself on us. Rather, He pursues us with His inestimable

THE TWO NATURES

goodness, love and gentleness, giving us His precious grace to enlighten and convince us of His inestimable goodness and love for us. As time goes by, the Lord Jesus further convinces us of our great need for Him. In the process, He brings us to that place by His grace, where we are now able to make the decision to either go with Him or away from Him. Some decide to go with the Lord Jesus, while sadly, many others turn their backs on His grace and choose to go the way of their flesh and the world, which is really the way of the sinful nature and therefore the devil. One thing is clear however, the choice will always be ours as to whom we will serve – whether the beloved Lord Jesus or the devil.

> Some have in fact already turned away to follow
> Satan. 1 Tim. 5:15

There are those who, on a daily basis, continue to go back and forth between the divine nature and the sinful nature. When the blessed Holy Spirit makes them aware of their state, rather than quickly repent and turn back to their Lord, some will linger and resist Him for a time. Then, they will repent and return to the Lord Jesus, to again participate in the divine nature. For some, this process is repeated several times per week, all according to their feelings, circumstances, needs, and their relationships, etc. Still, there are those who will struggle for weeks resisting God's grace to them, before choosing to return to their Lord Jesus. There are still others who will never return to Him.

However, this habitual going back and forth will not be permitted to continue forever. At a point, it will have to either come to an end, or be put to an end, and only our beloved Lord Jesus knows when that time will come.

> Remain in me, and I will remain in you. No branch can bear fruit by itself; it must remain in the vine. Neither can you bear fruit unless you remain in me. [5]"I am the vine; you are the branches. If a man remains in me and I in him, he will bear much fruit; apart from me you can do nothing. [6]If anyone does not remain in me, he is like a branch that is thrown away and withers; such branches are picked up, thrown into the fire and burned. John 15:4-6

Nevertheless, there are those who do repent immediately when the blessed Holy Spirit makes them conscious that they have sinned, and so they continued with their Lord and did not turn from Him. In these cases, it is as if nothing had happened – as if they had not sinned. In such cases, sin was not counted against them. When we

respond in this way, our sins are washed away and forgotten by
our Lord Jesus.

> Simply let your 'Yes' be 'Yes,' and your 'No,' 'No';
> anything beyond this comes from the evil one.
> Matt. 5:37

There are still others who, when they have sinned, waver and hesi-
tate for a long period of time, to then continue on in their rebellious
ways. This explains why Christians at times doubt God and their
Salvation, and why they are so unfaithful to their Lord and God.

> At that time many will turn away from the faith and
> will betray and hate each other, [11]and many false
> prophets will appear and deceive many people.
> [12]Because of the increase of wickedness, the love
> of most will grow cold, [13]but he who stands firm to
> the end will be saved. Matt. 24:10-13

Please understand that every time you doubt the Lord Jesus and your
Salvation, or every time you feel bored or tired with a life in Christ,
or dissatisfied with your Christian life, these are signs that you are
back in your old carnal nature. Or, when you are frustrated with
your spiritual progress, or impatient with waiting upon the Lord

Jesus for whatever reason, these too are signs that you are back in your sinful nature, wanting things to happen in your life according to your own understanding, agenda, timing, will and ways.

Also, when you want to do works of sacrifices before the Lord Jesus to speed up the spiritual process in your life, making what you call, "spiritual choices" to impress the Lord Jesus, or to pacify Him, or to prove your worth with the motivation to get your way with Him in return, these too are signs that you are back in your old carnal nature, and are carrying out its usual tricks, to in the end have you accuse the Lord and demand of Him. Yes, you could even drift back into your old nature without knowing it, for the signs that tell you that you are back there are usually taken for granted.

I have found that no one wants to believe that they are back in their sinful nature, or that they have strayed and have turned from their Lord. Most of us are too "spiritual" to acknowledge such failings. This is nothing less than spiritual pride and falsehood operating through that dishonest sinful nature.

When you are tired of life in general, wanting to give up, or when you are worried and preoccupied with yourself – being self-centered, or are yielding to negative thoughts, feelings and impressions, and you are agreeing with them, these are signs that you are in your sinful nature, receiving demonic thoughts and impressions. Here, you are being led by the devil to once again embrace boredom, negativism and preoccupation; burdened with life's weight and worries, living according to your sinful nature, while believing this to be a life in Christ. You are then used by the devil through the sinful nature to accuse God, deceived to believe that the Christian life is hard and therefore God is unjust, for look at the burden you are under.

But no, that is not a life in Christ. These problems are a result of your refusal to submit yourself and come into agreement with your Lord, and therefore obey Him in His Word, thereby submitting yourself to be sanctified/cleansed of the ways of your sinful nature so that you can come to know what a life in Christ is all about. In this way, the life of being preoccupied with yourself, worrying, accusing, judging for evil purposes, being dissatisfied, reasoning with the Word of God, unfaithfulness, demanding justice, and being a victim who is always crying "poor me," feeling sorry for yourself etc., will begin to come to an end. All these are sins in your life that the devil uses to bog you down. These are some of the very sins that the Holy Spirit wants to cleanse you of to liberate you, so that you will be free to begin to live for and with your Lord. In other words, you need to sincerely acknowledge your sinful ways to be able to submit yourself to the Holy Spirit through repentance and prayer, surrendering your all to Him, along with those areas where sin has you bound, to be cleansed of it.

> We are therefore Christ's ambassadors, as though God were making his appeal through us. We implore you on Christ's behalf: Be reconciled to God. [21]God made him who had no sin to be sin for us, so that in him we might become the righteousness of God. 2 Cor. 5:20-21

The things that we worry about or are preoccupied with, are things that we possess in our hearts. In turn they possess us, and so keep us preoccupied with them. For these reasons, our Lord tells us that unless we give up everything, we cannot be His disciples. Many of us are possessed. Our hearts are filled to overflowing with this world, its things and its ways, and so we are self-centered to the point where most of our thoughts are on self. As a result, self becomes the center of our focus rather than the Lord Jesus, and we are held prisoners there, and for many that is their reality.

> In the same way, any of you who does not give up everything he has cannot be my disciple. Luke 14:33

THE TWO NATURES

If they have escaped the corruption of the world by
knowing our Lord and Savior Jesus Christ and are
again entangled in it and overcome, they are worse
off at the end than they were at the beginning. [21]It
would have been better for them not to have known
the way of righteousness, than to have known it and
then to turn their backs on the sacred command that
was passed on to them. [22]Of them the proverbs are
true: "A dog returns to its vomit," and, "A sow that
is washed goes back to her wallowing in the mud."
2 Peter 2:20-22

Therefore, if you have accepted a life of boredom, negativism and
worry to be a life in Christ, then this simply proves that you do not
know what a life in Christ really is. And, because you do not know,
the enemy is then able to deceive you to believe that the miserable
state in which you are walking, is a life in Christ. You however
chose to be so deceived, because this is convenient to your flesh,
as it gives you a time of carnal pleasure, feelings of liberty, etc.,
away from Christ and the constraint of His Word.

When there is a lack of interest in, and opposition to hearing God's
Word or going to church, and at the same time you feel attracted
to the world and the things and pleasures thereof and you do not

oppose them, but rather you agree with them, all these and more are signs that indeed, you are back in agreement with your old carnal sinful nature. There, the devil feeds you with all kinds of lies through negative thoughts and feelings, to discourage you. There, he will reason with you, and if you are the type who will reason back with him, then you will be carried off by him, for no one will ever win an argument with the devil.

> Avoid godless chatter, because those who indulge in it will become more and more ungodly. [17]Their teaching will spread like gangrene. Among them are Hymenaeus and Philetus, [18]who have wandered away from the truth. They say that the resurrection has already taken place, and they destroy the faith of some. [19]Nevertheless, God's solid foundation stands firm, sealed with this inscription: "The Lord knows those who are his," and, "Everyone who confesses the name of the Lord must turn away from wickedness." 2 Tim. 2:16-19

The problem with all this is no one can out-reason the devil. You will lose at every point, while believing that you are winning and having your own way, when it is really the devil who is having his way, in and through your life. Consequently, you will be tied up in knots even more by him. In the process, he will drain and wear you down, and you will end up being even more confused and frustrated. At this point, many choose to yield to their feelings and give up, rather than to resist them by standing firm in faith, holding to the Word of truth and trusting their Lord and remaining in Him. Many do not do this, because they are deceived to believe that to choose the way of faith is difficult and hard. This is a lie of the enemy.

> Timothy, guard what has been entrusted to your care. Turn away from godless chatter and the opposing ideas of what is falsely called knowledge, [21]which some have professed and in so doing have wandered from the faith. Grace be with you. 1 Tim. 6:20-21

> … If you do not stand firm in your faith, you will not stand at all.' " Isa. 7:9b

The thing to do when you have these types of problems and you agree with them, is to recognize that you are back in your old nature. You should therefore quickly choose the way of faith, and humble your heart and ask your Lord to help you. Then, with His help, you are to immediately repent and return to your Lord Jesus, again by putting your trust in Him; resisting the pride that the devil will hit you with for the purpose of hindering you from wanting to do so.

It is important for you to know that these types of problems are not part of the divine nature. Why? Because that nature is of God. When you were saved, God placed His nature before you through His Word. You were then invited by Him to participate in His divine nature by coming to His Word, where He lays it out for us all to see and to know Him and His ways. When you embrace this and come into agreement with it there in His Word, and bring it home to your heart, this will then lead to a transformed mind, which results in a transformed life.

> Grace and peace be yours in abundance through the knowledge of God and of Jesus our Lord. ³His divine power has given us everything we need for life and godliness through our knowledge of him who called us by his own glory and goodness. ⁴Through these he has given us his very great and precious promises, so that through them you may participate in the divine nature and escape the corruption in the world caused by evil desires. ⁵For this very reason, make every effort to add to your faith goodness; and to goodness, knowledge; ⁶and to knowledge,

THE TWO NATURES

self-control; and to self-control, perseverance; and to perseverance, godliness; [7]and to godliness, brotherly kindness; and to brotherly kindness, love. [8]For if you possess these qualities in increasing measure, they will keep you from being ineffective and unproductive in your knowledge of our Lord Jesus Christ. [9]But if anyone does not have them, he is nearsighted and blind, and has forgotten that he has been cleansed from his past sins. 2 Peter 1:2-9

This renewed mind now leads to a whole new way of believing, desiring, thinking, choosing and acting. The Word has now become our life, and by it we now live. It now determines all that we believe, desire, think, choose and do, and how we do them, and this is the way we want it to be. This is participating in the divine nature.

Therefore, I urge you, brothers, in view of God's mercy, to offer your bodies as living sacrifices, holy and pleasing to God – this is your spiritual act of worship. [2]Do not conform any longer to the pattern of this world, but be transformed by the renewing of your mind. Then you will be able to test and approve what God's will is – his good, pleasing and perfect will. Rom. 12:1-2

THE TWO NATURES

So I tell you this, and insist on it in the Lord, that you must no longer live as the Gentiles do, in the futility of their thinking. [18]They are darkened in their understanding and separated from the life of God because of the ignorance that is in them due to the hardening of their hearts. [19]Having lost all sensitivity, they have given themselves over to sensuality so as to indulge in every kind of impurity, with a continual lust for more. [20]You, however, did not come to know Christ that way. [21]Surely you heard of him and were taught in him in accordance with the truth that is in Jesus. [22]You were taught, with regard to your former way of life, to put off your old self, which is being corrupted by its deceitful desires; [23]to be made new in the attitude of your minds; [24]and to put on the new self, created to be like God in true righteousness and holiness. [25]Therefore each of you must put off falsehood and speak truthfully to his neighbor, for we are all members of one body. [26]"In your anger do not sin": Do not let the sun go down while you are still angry, [27]and do not give the devil a foothold. [28]He who has been stealing must steal no longer, but must work, doing something useful

THE TWO NATURES

with his own hands, that he may have something to
share with those in need. Eph. 4:17-28

When we choose to surrender our lives to the Lord Jesus, we are
choosing in obedience to our God and Lord to remain in dependency upon Him to keep us, so that we will not do those outrageous things that so many do, because we have embraced an active
faith in our Lord Jesus. We therefore walk in a state of trust, truth,
submission, obedience, faithfulness, etc., to our Lord. This will
be our state, for we have chosen to remain in our Lord, believing
and trusting, with our hope fixed in our God and Lord. Therefore,
we are being built up daily in Him in all these areas of faith, truth,
love, humility, submission, obedience, faithfulness, peace, contentment, satisfaction, etc., as we choose to remain participating in the
divine nature. This is all part of being sanctified, and a sign that
we are really surrendering the life more and more each day to our
Lord, to be cleansed.

There is no rejection of God when our intention is consistently
towards Him, and our interest is in His Word and the new nature;
neither will there be any discontent, rebellion, hostility, accusation
or frustration towards our Lord. None of these negative attitudes
and responses that are natural to, and reside in the old carnal sinful
nature, are a part of you when you have seriously embraced God's

Word, and therefore His divine nature to be your life, and growing in it daily as you are being sanctified. Your focus and pursuit will then be the things of God's nature, and as long as you remain participating in it, these other things will only appear as temptations to move you. However, they cannot, because your life is in the Lord Jesus, and that is where you desire and want to be, and this has become your purpose and pursuit, for this is what you want. Therefore, you will not be moved, because you would have had the truth of your Lord to hold to, as He holds you, His faithful one, in Him.

> For the time will come when men will not put up with sound doctrine. Instead, to suit their own desires, they will gather around them a great number of teachers to say what their itching ears want to hear. ⁴They will turn their ears away from the truth and turn aside to myths. ⁵But you, keep your head in all situations, endure hardship, do the work of an evangelist, discharge all the duties of your ministry.
> 2 Tim. 4:3-5

The Lord Jesus calls us to come to Him in His Word and learn from Him. As we do, we find that as we learn from Him, we are learning to believe, submit, obey, trust and love Him more and more each day, etc. We are also coming into agreement with Him there in His Word, where now our beliefs, thoughts, choices and actions are conforming to His Word. As a result, we are now being conformed to His ways more and more each day, becoming one with Him in nature. This happens as we participate in His divine nature, as it is revealed in His Word, and is embraced to be our life.

> Put to death, therefore, whatever belongs to your earthly nature: sexual immorality, impurity, lust, evil desires and greed, which is idolatry. [6]Because of these, the wrath of God is coming. [7]You used to walk in these ways, in the life you once lived. [8]But now you must rid yourselves of all such things as these: anger, rage, malice, slander, and filthy language from your lips. [9]Do not lie to each other, since you have taken off your old self with its practices [10]and have put on the new self, which is being renewed in knowledge in the image of its Creator. Col. 3:5-10

The question is: can we be tempted while we are in our Lord Jesus? Yes, we are tempted while we are in our Lord Jesus, participating in the divine nature. Through the temptation that comes our way, we are given the responsibility and opportunity to choose on a continual basis, who we will serve; whether the Lord Jesus, or the devil through the old carnal sinful nature, for we are tempted with the things and ways of the world through the sinful nature. These have come to test our hearts, for us to choose over and over again the way we want to go. If, for instance, the ways of the Lord Jesus are what we want, then that is the way we will always choose to go. On the other hand, if the ways of the sinful nature and the world is the way we want to go, then our choices will be to that nature and the world. The testing of our hearts will reveal the truth as to where our allegiance lies, whether to the Lord Jesus or elsewhere.

> "Now fear the LORD and serve him with all faith-
> fulness. Throw away the gods your forefathers wor-
> shiped beyond the River and in Egypt, and serve
> the LORD. [15]But if serving the LORD seems unde-
> sirable to you, then choose for yourselves this day
> whom you will serve, whether the gods your fore-
> fathers served beyond the River, or the gods of the
> Amorites, in whose land you are living. But as for
> me and my household, we will serve the LORD."
> Josh. 24:14-15

However, when you are tempted, if you acknowledge those temptations to be of the enemy, being pushed on you by him through

your old sinful nature, and then quickly call on your Lord for help to resist them, you will find that His help is there with you. At times His help is not always immediate, for He sometimes gives us time to exercise the faith He has given us to trust Him, and to resist and oppose the tempter and those temptations against our soul, mind and body, which at times can be heavy.

Our Lord Jesus permits this to teach and prepare us today, to enable us to take our stand tomorrow against further onslaught of the enemy through the sinful nature, in and against our flesh/body. He allows this to happen to help us to learn and to grow and take our stand in faith in our Lord Jesus, and deny our flesh of those things that are of the sinful nature. In other words, saying no to sin. If you do this, trusting in your Lord, you will be victorious, for it is our Lord Jesus who tells us to deny ourselves in order to follow Him.

Please be sure however, that you do not come into agreement with those temptations, regardless of how forcefully they are being pushed on you, because they come to slay you and tie you up in sin. If you agree with them, they will become yours, and you will then carry them out, only to fall under the condemnation that will follow. If you do not resist and oppose these temptations by faith, trusting in your Lord Jesus, always calling on Him for help, you will succumb to them. You will join your old nature once more, and from there, oppose your Lord and resist Him all over again.

This is how simple it is to fall back into living according to your sinful nature, for by your agreeing with the temptations that come, you are sinning against your Lord. And you will automatically continue in them unless you choose to acknowledge that you have sinned, and repent of them. As you can see, falling back into the sinful nature is only a decision away, but that decision could also have been towards the Lord Jesus to remain in Him.

> Formerly, when you did not know God, you were slaves to those who by nature are not gods. ⁹But now that you know God – or rather are known by God – how is it that you are turning back to those weak and miserable principles? Do you wish to be enslaved by them all over again? ¹⁰You are observing special days and months and seasons and years! ¹¹I fear for you, that somehow I have wasted my efforts on you Gal. 4:8-11.

This is how rebellion begins at times – by your first accepting the temptations that come to you, and agreeing with them. They will then become your beliefs. The consequences of believing those lies

THE TWO NATURES

and temptations will be murmuration and accusation against God and man for your misery that will automatically follow – then a state of rebellion ensues.

This will happen because by believing and agreeing with these temptations, what you have done is to accept them to become your own beliefs and desires, upon which you are now going to act.

> "Are you so dull?" he asked. "Don't you see that nothing that enters a man from the outside can make him `unclean'? [19]For it doesn't go into his heart but into his stomach, and then out of his body." (In saying this, Jesus declared all foods "clean.") [20]He went on: "What comes out of a man is what makes him `unclean.' [21]For from within, out of men's hearts, come evil thoughts, sexual immorality, theft, murder, adultery, [22]greed, malice, deceit, lewdness, envy, slander, arrogance and folly. [23]All these evils come from inside and make a man `unclean.' "
> Mark 7:18-23

We must choose that which we want at all times and in all situations. For if you do not know who you are in Christ and what you are about or what you want, the devil will know for you and he

THE TWO NATURES

will tell you what you want, where you are to go, what you are to do and how you are to do it. He will push you to take his lies to be your truth, and when you do, you will walk in them and carry them out while believing that it is your will, or even God's will you are carrying out.

> "Son of man, say to the house of Israel, `This is what you are saying: "Our offenses and sins weigh us down, and we are wasting away because of them. How then can we live?"' [11]Say to them, `As surely as I live, declares the Sovereign LORD, I take no pleasure in the death of the wicked, but rather that they turn from their ways and live. Turn! Turn from your evil ways! Why will you die, O house of Israel?'
> [12]"Therefore, son of man, say to your countrymen, `The righteousness of the righteous man will not save him when he disobeys, and the wickedness of the wicked man will not cause him to fall when he turns from it. The righteous man, if he sins, will not be allowed to live because of his former righteous-ness.' [13]If I tell the righteous man that he will surely live, but then he trusts in his righteousness and does evil, none of the righteous things he has done will be remembered; he will die for the evil he has done.

THE TWO NATURES

¹⁴And if I say to the wicked man, `You will surely die,' but he then turns away from his sin and does what is just and right – ¹⁵if he gives back what he took in pledge for a loan, returns what he has stolen, follows the decrees that give life, and does no evil, he will surely live; he will not die. ¹⁶None of the sins he has committed will be remembered against him. He has done what is just and right; he will surely live. ¹⁷"Yet your countrymen say, `The way of the Lord is not just.' But it is their way that is not just. ¹⁸If a righteous man turns from his righteousness and does evil, he will die for it. ¹⁹And if a wicked man turns away from his wickedness and does what is just and right, he will live by doing so. ²⁰Yet, O house of Israel, you say, `The way of the Lord is not just.' But I will judge each of you according to his own ways." Ezekiel 33:10-20

So I say, live by the Spirit, and you will not gratify the desires of the sinful nature. ¹⁷For the sinful nature desires what is contrary to the Spirit, and the Spirit what is contrary to the sinful nature. They are in conflict with each other, so that you do not do what you want. Gal. 5:16-17

THE TWO NATURES

We must also be aware that out of His great love for us, our beloved Lord Jesus will, from time to time, allow us to be tempted. This is to reveal to us the true condition of our hearts, so that wherever evil is found, whether we are aware or unaware of its presence, or whether we are holding on to it deliberately, or have fallen into it unawares, we will face it in truth and sincerity, and in repentance before our beloved Lord Jesus, turn from it so that He can cleanse us of wickedness and evil. By doing so, He can then move us forward on to further growth, maturity and purity, which will automatically bring us closer to Him, as the Lord Jesus teaches us to resist sin and handle difficulties in a more mature way. This is sanctification. All that the beloved Lord Jesus permits in our lives will always be for our highest good. This we can count on. In this case, all that He wants to do is to cleanse and purify us.

The question will then be asked, "How will I know when I am participating in the divine nature?" You will know that you are when you are sincerely believing God's Word, agreeing with it, and are therefore putting your trust in the Lord Jesus with your whole heart. Also, when you are holding to His Word and acting upon it by wanting and embracing His ways, where His Word now becomes your point of reference and therefore your direction in life. It is in His Word that His divine nature is laid out, and if you do not believe it enough to act upon it, you will not sincerely participate in the divine nature.

The divine nature is God's nature. As you read His Word, you will see His nature revealed, beginning with God is good (inestimably). He is: love, truth, sincere, honest, faithful, trustworthy, righteous, just, patient, forgiveness, merciful, always giving, generous, He suffers long, etc. His divine nature calls us to: love your neighbor as yourself, love your enemies, pray for those who hate you and despitefully use you, those who persecute you, etc. When you have come into agreement with these and begin to pray for them, while putting them into practice in your own life as you learn to submit in obedience to your Lord Jesus, then you will know that you have begun to participate in the divine nature.

Indeed, I think that you could sum it all up in few words – stop sinning against God by turning whole-heartedly to Him, and obey His Word. As you do, you will see His nature revealed right there in His Word. You are to embrace it prayerfully to be your life, and as you do, you are being transformed. But do not forget to pray and ask the Lord Jesus for it, and trust Him to help you to bring it home and put it in practice in your life, for it to become your ways. Then you will see it begin to be revealed in your very life.

THE TWO NATURES

Every good and perfect gift is from above, coming
down from the Father of the heavenly lights, who
does not change like shifting shadows. James 1:17

The goal of this command is love, which comes
from a pure heart and a good conscience and a sincere faith. ⁶Some have wandered away from these
and turned to meaningless talk. 1 Tim. 1:5-6

Another sign that can help you to know whether or not you are participating in the divine nature, is whether your desires are towards
the Lord Jesus or towards the world to satisfy your flesh, with its
selfish ambition and greed, its lust for self-gratification, etc. If you
find that they are towards the flesh and the world, and you have
accepted that to be what you want, then that will be a sign to you
that you are not believing the Word or trusting in the Lord Jesus.
Therefore, you are not, and will not be participating in the divine
nature. You will simply continue to have your own way as usual,
living according to your sinful nature, pleasing yourself.

"Therefore say to the house of Israel, `This is what
the Sovereign LORD says: Repent! Turn from your
idols and renounce all your detestable practices!
⁷" `When any Israelite or any alien living in Israel

THE TWO NATURES

separates himself from me and sets up idols in his
heart and puts a wicked stumbling block before his
face and then goes to a prophet to inquire of me, I
the LORD will answer him myself. [8]I will set my
face against that man and make him an example and
a byword. I will cut him off from my people. Then
you will know that I am the LORD. Ezek. 14:6-8

The difference between the divine nature and the sinful nature is
as radical as day is from night. Yes, the difference is that radical.
When you are in your carnal sinful nature, your interest is yourself; your pursuit is to satisfy your flesh in every way you can. Your
desires and personal interests are to have everything go your way.
They are also to have as much pleasure as you can in order to make
yourself happy. Your interests and pursuits are always to fulfill your
selfish ambitions in every possible way, along with possessing your
heart's desires across the board. In this way, you can then gloat over
these pursuits and take pride in them, exalting yourself in your own
eyes and before others with one purpose, and that is to show-off.

There is no room there in such hearts for the Lord Jesus, for He is
a bother to that old nature. He is in your way, and you want Him
out so that you can go on with what you call, "your life" – having
your own way in whatever you might choose to pursue. According

to those old beliefs and habits, having the Lord Jesus around will rob you of your liberty to pursue your carnal goals.

> Blessed is the man who does not fall away on
> account of me." Luke 7:23

In this belief, you believe that you cannot have any fun at all, and according to you, who wants to live like that – no one! However, these things are never thought about or spoken of so blatantly, because most souls are ashamed to face the reality of their motives for believing what they believe, desiring what they desire, thinking what they think, planning what they plan, and doing what they do. They therefore carry out these selfish desires and acts by hiding from their true motives, or by simply giving themselves other reasons for doing what they do, by following that which the enemy tells them through their feelings and thoughts.

> Who is wise? He will realize these things. Who is
> discerning? He will understand them. The ways of
> the LORD are right; the righteous walk in them, but
> the rebellious stumble in them. Hosea 14:9

Generally, people think of themselves as too "good" to be caught thinking or speaking in this way, and so they cover it. Yet, they

THE TWO NATURES

might even call on the Name of the Lord Jesus, and even ask for His help. But this is all in vain, because their asking for help is not sincere and is therefore not from faith, and without faith no one can please the Lord, for although they are believing that nothing will ever happen, yet they are praying. This attitude helps to keep them in that place of deceit, believing that they are still in the Lord Jesus, although they should have knowledge, or at least suspect or sense that something is wrong.

In reality, what so many are believing in are the words that they have spoken, and a choice that they may have made here and there, like going to church or "praying" or doing what they call a good deed. By those acts, words and choices, they have now convinced themselves that they are trusting the Lord Jesus, even though they know that they might not be doing so. This will now lead them to further accusation against the Lord Jesus when things do not go the way they expect them to. In such cases, you can be assured that things will never go the way they desire, because the devil is leading such lives, and he will only lead them into further and further deceit to keep them accusing God.

> Therefore, dear friends, since you already know this,
> be on your guard so that you may not be carried
> away by the error of lawless men and fall from your

secure position. [18]But grow in the grace and knowledge of our Lord and Savior Jesus Christ. To him be
glory both now and forever! Amen. 2 Peter 3:17-18

All these desires are pushed by the devil through your old sinful
nature, possibly because you have come into agreement with him.
And if you continue to listen to his lies, he will convince you never
to return to your Lord Jesus. This he does by appealing to your flesh
through the sinful nature, showing you ways to satisfy its greed and
lust, and at the same time, how to justify yourself for indulging it.

Here he deceives you to believe that by remaining in the Lord Jesus,
you are missing out on all the fun things in life, the pleasures and
the liberty to do as you please, etc. Many believe his lies and are
carried off by him, to once again live according to the old sinful
nature. Some remain in this state permanently, while others do so
for a time. There are still others who are sincere, and as they were
enabled by the grace of our Lord Jesus to escape the enemy's grasp,
did so, to forever remain in their Lord.

Watch out that you do not lose what you have
worked for, but that you may be rewarded fully.
[9]Anyone who runs ahead and does not continue in
the teaching of Christ does not have God; whoever

THE TWO NATURES

continues in the teaching has both the Father and the
Son. [10]If anyone comes to you and does not bring
this teaching, do not take him into your house or
welcome him. [11]Anyone who welcomes him shares
in his wicked work. 2 John 1:8-11

When you are in your carnal nature, you can do outrageous things
against God and man. However, when you are participating in the
divine nature, you will notice that there is love for God and tenderness towards Him, because that is where your heart is. Therefore,
your choice is to honor Him because you believe His Word and are
enjoying it, and so that is where you choose to focus your attention.
There are also deeper levels of believing God's Word, putting your
faith in Him, and a wanting and desiring more of Him. Here, your
priority and principal desire and pursuit are no longer to satisfy
the flesh with the pleasures and things of this life, and although
the enemy brings back all kinds of things from that life to entice
you away from your Lord Jesus, you will reject them, for you are
finished with sin and therefore the world and that way of life.

Many have succumbed to such temptations, while others have
remained true to their Lord, because their desires for and trust
in their God are steadfast. Therefore, they choose accordingly,
feeding their spirit man with the things of the Spirit. At the same

time, they also choose to trust their natural life according to the flesh, along with all its needs, to the Lord Jesus, because He satisfies its needs according to His will when we truly and sincerely trust Him with it all.

> So do not worry, saying, 'What shall we eat?' or 'What shall we drink?' or 'What shall we wear?' [32]For the pagans run after all these things, and your heavenly Father knows that you need them. [33]But seek first his kingdom and his righteousness, and all these things will be given to you as well. Matt. 6:31-33

> As God's fellow workers we urge you not to receive God's grace in vain. [2]For he says, "In the time of my favor I heard you, and in the day of salvation I helped you." I tell you, now is the time of God's favor, now is the day of salvation. 2 Cor. 6:1-2

As I have said before, here I am not talking about a carnal "feel good" or happiness. I am talking about a living hope within your spirit and soul, which keeps you in tune with your God and Lord, for you have trusted your all to your Lord Jesus with your whole heart. In this way, you are fully participating in the divine nature,

THE TWO NATURES

which keeps you occupied with your God and Lord, becoming like Him in nature, because you have chosen it to be yours.

This is exciting! Here, there is no room for boredom or self-centeredness, which would disallow us from looking beyond ourselves to our Lord Jesus, and therefore rob us of our place in our God. This would then result in us giving ourselves over to the frustration of the enemy, to be further distressed.

The Scripture says that we are to test ourselves to see whether or not we are in the faith (2 Cor. 13:5). This is the best test that one could ever give themselves. Indeed, this is a sure test, because when you are in the new life there is faith, which allows you to trust your life and everything else into the hands of the Lord Jesus, and rest from the struggles of life.

> Find rest, O my soul, in God alone; my hope comes
> from him. Psa. 62:5

> "To the angel of the church in Pergamum write:
> These are the words of him who has the sharp, dou-
> ble-edged sword. [13]I know where you live – where
> Satan has his throne. Yet you remain true to my
> name. You did not renounce your faith in me, even

in the days of Antipas, my faithful witness, who

was put to death in your city – where Satan lives.

Rev. 2:12-13

On the other hand, when you are in the old nature, there is only

worry, fear, uncertainty, anxiety, etc., although at other times there

can be a carnal, demonic peace that deceives you to believe that

you are in the Lord Jesus, or at least convinces you that all is

well. This is why at times, souls are confused as to whether or not

they are Christians. It also clarifies for us, the reason why most

Christians doubt their God at times – they simply have left their

Lord and are back in their sinful nature. Therefore, if you cannot

trust and rest in your Lord, you should test yourself to see whether

or not you are in the Lord Jesus, simply by: Am I believing the

Lord Jesus, am I holding to His Word, and therefore am I trusting

Him in all areas of my life?

Timothy, my son, I give you this instruction in

keeping with the prophecies once made about you,

so that by following them you may fight the good

fight, [19]holding on to faith and a good conscience.

Some have rejected these and so have shipwrecked

their faith. 1 Tim. 1:18-19

THE TWO NATURES

There are those who have left their Lord and are quite at home in their misery, living according to the old sinful nature, having no desire to be away from it at all, while believing that they are sincerely walking with the Lord Jesus. For many, this is what a Christian life is all about – pleasing their flesh and having their own way. This is the example that they see before them every day, and therefore this is all that they know. Moreover, teachings are lacking in these areas where they are desperately needed now.

Another reason for this state is when there is no serious commitment to a spiritual life in the Lord Jesus to begin with, and consequently they see nothing there that they desire to pursue, because their focus is on the natural – the physical. Such souls, nevertheless, go on as if this is not their reality, while at the same time they will tell you that they want to go to heaven. However, how can anyone want to go to heaven to be with a God and Lord who they do not want to be with while here on the earth? This does not make any sense.

The question was: why have some who are called Christians, done some of the outrageous things that they have done? I believe the question has been answered for those who need an answer. Nevertheless, here it is again. Those who are called Christians, do outrageous things simply because they have turned from their Lord,

and have again returned to follow the ways of their sinful nature –
their old place of abode.

> Blessed is the man who does not fall away on
> account of me." Luke 7:23

For some, it seems to be more beneficial and more convenient to
remain in the carnal sinful nature, and to continue living there the
kind of life they prefer, rather than to remain in the Lord Jesus,
participating in the divine nature, where they have to be denying
their flesh and opposing sin. According to their beliefs, why do
this, when a spiritual life can be had without any of this, when it
can even be faked? The false life is always an option for such folks.

> For when I brought your forefathers out of Egypt
> and spoke to them, I did not just give them com-
> mands about burnt offerings and sacrifices, 23but
> I gave them this command: Obey me, and I will
> be your God and you will be my people. Walk in
> all the ways I command you, that it may go well
> with you. 24But they did not listen or pay attention;
> instead, they followed the stubborn inclinations of
> their evil hearts. They went backward and not for-
> ward. 25From the time your forefathers left Egypt

THE TWO NATURES

until now, day after day, again and again I sent you
my servants the prophets. ²⁶But they did not listen
to me or pay attention. They were stiff-necked and
did more evil than their forefathers.' Jer. 7:22-26

But my righteous one will live by faith. And if
he shrinks back, I will not be pleased with him."
³⁹But we are not of those who shrink back and are
destroyed, but of those who believe and are saved.
Heb. 10:38-39

You could also simply believe that since you have received the Lord
Jesus, and are going to heaven, all is well that ends well. So, why
deny yourself of anything and suffer any inconvenience or discomfort – you are going to heaven anyway. There are also those who
reason that spiritual maturity takes too long to come about. Many
are therefore not willing to wait, and so they are deceived to leave
the Lord Jesus, believing that they can go and achieve their spiritual
goals carnally. In the same way that you might have heard of the
"one hundred percent, genuine, simulated leather," likewise, there
are the one hundred percent, genuine, false Christians.

Now, brothers, I want to remind you of the gospel I
preached to you, which you received and on which

THE TWO NATURES

you have taken your stand. ²By this gospel you are
saved, if you hold firmly to the word I preached
to you. Otherwise, you have believed in vain.
1 Cor. 15:1-2

Of course, some of those who have turned away will again repent
and turn back to their Lord, while others will not. Still, there are
those who will be back and forth, over and over again. For some,
this is the state in which they have walked, and still there are those
who are not even aware that they have left their Lord and are back
in their sinful nature. Some have never spent enough time in God's
Word to learn of it, and how to apply it to their lives so that they
could learn to walk in His ways, much less to appreciate the difference between the two natures. Therefore, the devil deceives them to
believe, among other things, that being in their carnal sinful nature
is one and the same as walking according to the divine nature. Or,
he simply deceives them to believe that there are no benefits to
their self-image or their flesh to be gained by obeying God's Word
and participating in the divine nature, and so why waste their valu-
able time with something that is of no carnal value to them. They
therefore believe and agree with the devil, and so do not continue
in their Lord.

THE TWO NATURES

See to it, brothers, that none of you has a sinful,
unbelieving heart that turns away from the living
God. Heb. 3:12

"No one sews a patch of unshrunk cloth on an old
garment, for the patch will pull away from the garment, making the tear worse. [17]Neither do men pour
new wine into old wineskins. If they do, the skins
will burst, the wine will run out and the wineskins
will be ruined. No, they pour new wine into new
wineskins, and both are preserved." Matt. 9:16-17

Even though there are all of these problems, our beloved Lord
Jesus, instead of programming us to do His will, still invites us to
participate in the divine nature. He will not force us to do so. He
will not intimidate us, or coerce us to get us to participate in the
divine nature. He uses the word participate, which means voluntary
choice and action (which He has given us the grace to do). And
this is what He wants from us: a willingness to want His ways, and
then choose to embrace them and walk in them. When we do, this
gives us more grace to walk in them.

Our beloved Lord Jesus only uses love to woo us, and to invite us to
participate in the divine nature. Of course, once you are committed

to be His child, He will then discipline you when it is needed, as a good father must. If you should go off into sin, He will bring it to your attention. If you respond and repent willingly, you will continue with Him, as if nothing had happened. If you do not, He will again repeat His warning. If you still do not respond, He might rebuke you and discipline you. This He does in several ways to bring you to repentance, such as: through His Word, through others, through sicknesses, afflictions, circumstances and withholding from you, etc., in order to bring you back on the straight and narrow path, and to keep you on it as a pure child of God, if you will so choose to remain in Him.

And you have forgotten that word of encouragement that addresses you as sons: "My son, do not make light of the Lord's discipline, and do not lose heart when he rebukes you, [6]because the Lord disciplines those he loves, and he punishes everyone he accepts as a son." [7]Endure hardship as discipline; God is treating you as sons. For what son is not disciplined by his father? [8]If you are not disciplined (and everyone undergoes discipline), then you are illegitimate children and not true sons. [9]Moreover, we have all had human fathers who disciplined us and we respected them for it. How much more

THE TWO NATURES

should we submit to the Father of our spirits and live! [10]Our fathers disciplined us for a little while as they thought best; but God disciplines us for our good, that we may share in his holiness. [11]No discipline seems pleasant at the time, but painful. Later on, however, it produces a harvest of righteousness and peace for those who have been trained by it. Heb. 12:5-11

Once you were alienated from God and were enemies in your minds because of your evil behavior. [22]But now he has reconciled you by Christ's physical body through death to present you holy in his sight, without blemish and free from accusation – [23]if you continue in your faith, established and firm, not moved from the hope held out in the gospel. This is the gospel that you heard and that has been proclaimed to every creature under heaven, and of which I, Paul, have become a servant. Col. 1:21-23

Precisely what causes one to be separated from their Lord? How is this possible? The beloved Lord Jesus tells us in John Chapter 15 verses 4-5, to remain in Him and He will remain in us, for without Him we can do nothing. This Scripture is the key to be able to

THE TWO NATURES

understand this problem. For example, as long as my dependency and trust remain in the Lord Jesus to do the things I do, with the full knowledge that I can do nothing without Him, and therefore I need to look to Him to lead and guide me in everything that I need to do, I will have His help.

However, the moment I believe that I, in myself, am capable of doing anything without the Lord Jesus, I will of course go and do it. The moment I choose to believe this, and set out to do it in my own strength, if after being prompted by the blessed Holy Spirit that I am straying into self-dependency/sin, and I ignore Him and continue on that path, then I will be separated from my Lord. By my own choice, with such action, I have made a clear statement that I can do without the help of the Holy Spirit. This is self-dependency and not Christ dependency. Therefore, in such a case, the Lord Jesus cannot help me.

To continue under the guidance of the Holy Spirit, I must first acknowledge that I am insufficient in myself and I need His help. I must then submit myself and pray to receive His help and guidance on a continual ongoing basis. In this, I have made a clear statement that I have turned from the sin of self-dependency, and the sin of ignoring the blessed Holy Spirit's guidance, repented of them, and acknowledged my need for His help. If I am sincere in my acknowledgement and repentance, I will receive His help; if I am not, I won't.

Self-dependency is one of the many reasons for being separated from the Lord Jesus. It signifies that I am back in my old carnal nature, and all that I will do from then on will only be carnal, and no longer spiritual. For in that nature, I do not have the help of the Lord Jesus to do anything from a spiritual perspective. I will however, have all the help of demons to carry out all the evil that one wants to do, such as believing all kinds of evil, harboring all kinds of ill feelings, wrong and even evil desires and thoughts, making wrong choices, and carrying out wrong actions, which are all of the old nature, pushed by the enemy.

> but I see another law at work in the members of my body, waging war against the law of my mind and making me a prisoner of the law of sin at work within my members. Rom. 7:23

> The acts of the sinful nature are obvious: sexual immorality, impurity and debauchery; [20]idolatry and witchcraft; hatred, discord, jealousy, fits of rage, selfish ambition, dissensions, factions [21]and envy; drunkenness, orgies, and the like. I warn you, as

THE TWO NATURES

I did before, that those who live like this will not
inherit the kingdom of God. Gal. 5:19-21

Therefore, my brothers, be all the more eager to
make your calling and election sure. For if you
do these things, you will never fall, [11]and you will
receive a rich welcome into the eternal kingdom of
our Lord and Savior Jesus Christ. [12]So I will always
remind you of these things, even though you know
them and are firmly established in the truth you now
have. 2 Peter 1:10-12

For example, I have gotten angry several times with my brethren
for straying back into the old life, and I have rebuked them for
doing so. However, this type of anger is for their highest good, and
so it is unselfish. Therefore, it would not be sin. I find that the grace
of God is always there to help me take this stand, trusting Him for
the understanding as to how I should handle those situations. In
such cases, I am doing these things in Him, and therefore there is
no separation from Him.

"In your anger do not sin": Do not let the sun go
down while you are still angry, Eph. 4:26

THE TWO NATURES

On the other hand, if I were to get angry with my brethren and rebuke them for some selfish, carnal and personal reason, and in so doing, choose for my highest good rather than theirs, that would be sin. And when the blessed Holy Spirit brings this sin to my attention, if I humble myself, acknowledge my sin in sincerity before Him, repenting of it, I would then continue with my Lord in the light of His presence, as if nothing had happened.

> But if we walk in the light, as he is in the light, we have fellowship with one another, and the blood of Jesus, his Son, purifies us from all sin. [8]If we claim to be without sin, we deceive ourselves and the truth is not in us. [9]If we confess our sins, he is faithful and just and will forgive us our sins and purify us from all unrighteousness. 1 John 1:7-9

However, if I do not heed the prompting of the Holy Spirit to acknowledge and repent of my sin or sins, and if, after He has prompted me a few times I continue in that state, refusing to acknowledge and repent of them, I will be separated from my Lord. This happens because, by not yielding to the prompting of the blessed Holy Spirit in obedience to the Lord Jesus, I have therefore chosen to reject or ignore His counsel, in disobedience to Him.

THE TWO NATURES

This would be as if telling Him that I do not need, nor do I want His help or guidance.

This attitude is one that says I'll do it myself. This brings further separation between my Lord and me, for by my choices and actions, I have made a clear statement that I have chosen not to remain in the Lord Jesus. The next thought will then be accusatory towards Him, because I would now be back in the old sinful nature, being instructed by the enemy to see God as an unreasonable, hard, unloving and unjust God, etc. This then will begin a series of accusations against the Lord Jesus. These are some of the ways the enemy uses to continue his attacks of deception against us.

When the blessed Holy Spirit makes you conscious of your act or state of sin, do not reason it away. Rather, quickly obey Him by humbling your heart, receive what He is showing you, repent of your rebellious ways, and return to the bosom of your Lord. If you do this, you will be forgiven and embraced by your Father and Lord, to once again have sweet fellowship with Him. You must however, again choose to participate in the divine nature. All this will be your choice of course, for it is placed there in His Word for all who so choose to participate in it.

What does it mean to participate in the divine nature? Simply, it means to adopt that which is God's nature as revealed in and through His Word to be yours, given to you by God, and begin to walk according to it by putting it into practice in your daily, moment-by-moment walk. As the Scriptures say: **"Rather, clothe yourselves with the Lord Jesus Christ, and do not think about how to gratify the desires of the sinful nature."** (Rom. 13:14) Then, by the grace given you, you need to remain in your Lord by trusting Him, and holding firmly to faith, truth and sincerity of heart, while at the same time choosing to do those things that He requires of you in His Word, in submission and obedience to Him.

Be imitators of God, therefore, as dearly loved children ²and live a life of love, just as Christ loved us and gave himself up for us as a fragrant offering and sacrifice to God. ³But among you there must not be even a hint of sexual immorality, or of any kind of impurity, or of greed, because these are improper for God's holy people. ⁴Nor should there be obscenity, foolish talk or coarse joking, which are out of place, but rather thanksgiving. ⁵For of this you can be sure: No immoral, impure or greedy person – such a man is an idolater – has any inheritance in the kingdom of Christ and of God. ⁶Let

no one deceive you with empty words, for because
of such things God's wrath comes on those who
are disobedient. ⁷Therefore do not be partners with
them. Eph. 5:1-7

These are things that are good and right, and are in agreement with
the requirements of the Lord Jesus and His ways which are laid out
in His Word, according to the understanding and guidance He gives
us by His blessed Holy Spirit, and through the precious promises
He has given us through His Word. There, we will come to know
the things that are pleasing to Him and learn to do them, rather
than the things that are pleasing to our flesh, because when we
live only according to the things that please our flesh, we are living
according to our sinful nature. We are then carried off by those
feelings that are of the carnal nature, to again make our choices by
them, which only leads to further degrading of ourselves and more
sinning against our Lord.

Those who belong to Christ Jesus have crucified the
sinful nature with its passions and desires. ²⁵Since
we live by the Spirit, let us keep in step with the
Spirit. Gal. 5:24-25

THE TWO NATURES

When the Holy Spirit makes you conscious of sin, if you do not choose to humble yourself and repent, but rather choose to puff yourself up in the pride of the old carnal sinful nature, your heart will only become harder and harder. At the same time, you will be distancing yourself from the Lord Jesus even further, accusing Him every step of the way for your own wrong choices and actions, to the point where you will become resentful of Him. You could even become bitter against your Lord for no reason. If you continue on this path, you will eventually reject your Lord, again going back to hating Him, which is the way of the old sinful nature.

> See to it, brothers, that none of you has a sinful, unbelieving heart that turns away from the living God. ¹³But encourage one another daily, as long as it is called Today, so that none of you may be hardened by sin's deceitfulness. ¹⁴We have come to share in Christ if we hold firmly till the end the confidence we had at first. ¹⁵As has just been said: "Today, if you hear his voice, do not harden your hearts as you did in the rebellion." Heb. 3:12-15

> Blessed is the man who always fears the LORD, but he who hardens his heart falls into trouble. Prov. 28:14

THE TWO NATURES

The quickest way to leave your Lord Jesus, to again be in agreement with the old carnal nature, is to stop trusting Him. Once you have done this, you are automatically back in your old nature. Then lies, deceit and dishonesty would again be your life, and this would be the sign that you are now living according to your sinful nature. Self-defense, justification, escaping truth, disobedience and rejection of authority would be further signs. Then, there would be accusation to the Lord. Pretense and falsehood would then follow, because you are now living a false life. Exalting and puffing yourself up in pride, and even looking and talking down to others could also follow. Believing yourself to be deserving, and seeing yourself as innocent, worthy, number one, better than others and above them, independent in yourself, and demanding to have your own way, are all signs that you have left the Lord Jesus and joined the carnal nature. Envy and jealousy are also signs. Going your own way, doing your own thing, not looking to the Lord Jesus for the answer for the small things – these are also signs.

Another way to know that you have left your Lord would be through worrying. Why? Because worrying is a sign that you have picked up the weight of your life, and are again in control of it where you are no longer trusting it to your Lord Jesus for Him to carry it and manage it. This says that you are out of faith, and you are therefore no longer in your Lord, but rather you are back with your sinful nature.

> Praise be to the Lord, to God our Savior, who daily
> bears our burdens. Selah [20]Our God is a God who
> saves; from the Sovereign Lord comes escape from
> death. Psa. 68:19-20

When the Holy Spirit makes you conscious of your state in any of these areas, please humble your heart, acknowledge that you have strayed from the Lord Jesus, repent, and return to Him. The Lord Jesus tells us that if we remain in Him, He will remain in us. He also tells us to come to Him with all of our burdens, and lay them down to Him.

> "Come to me, all you who are weary and burdened,
> and I will give you rest. [29]Take my yoke upon you
> and learn from me, for I am gentle and humble in
> heart, and you will find rest for your souls. [30]For my
> yoke is easy and my burden is light." Matt. 11:28-30

It is also easy to take control of your life from the Lord Jesus when you are afraid. You would think that at such times, God's children would run to Him where they are safe and secure. But no; many take control of their lives instead, choosing to trust themselves rather than the beloved Lord Jesus. As they do, they are again in their old carnal nature, where there is no trust in the Lord Jesus. This leads to them taking more control, which in turn leads them even further away from their Lord, then doubt takes over. I have worked with many such persons.

Whatever the reason that causes these souls to take control of their lives, when they do, it is as if they have no spiritual life in them at all. They are as cold and turned off to the Lord Jesus as a degenerate soul is, only more rebellious. This the Lord Jesus has placed before me seven days per week, through those He has placed with me, without exception. They all manifest the same rejection and even profound hostility towards the Lord Jesus when they have turned from Him. But when the Holy Spirit allows me to pray for them, and they again repent and turn back to the Lord Jesus, the difference is as day and night. The tenderness for the Lord Jesus is present; the submission and obedience are there. Everything that is of the divine nature is there. It is as if I am dealing with two different persons. The change from the carnal to the divine and vice versa is that radical.

These are dangerous games that people play with their lives, and there are many who are trapped outside the Lord Jesus in their

THE TWO NATURES

rebellion and are never able to return, and so their rebellion continues to increase until bitterness takes over and their hostility to the Lord increases.

The Lord Jesus permitted me to witness two such cases recently, one after the other, where Christians were taken over by the enemy to the point where even their features were changed. They proclaimed that they are innocent and have no need to repent. Their state of resentment, hate, hostility and rejection of God was so real, that it defied everything that has to do with God's Word. This is what can happen when you turn away from the Lord Jesus back to your sinful nature. We are to take heed.

It is only now in the year 2010 as I continue these writings, that the Holy Spirit made me conscious that He has kept this reality before me for thirty-three years now, through the very souls He has placed with me. This is to confirm the reality of the need to be sanctified/cleansed from the ways of the sinful nature – the work of satan in the lives of Christians, as has been laid out through these writings and those that will follow. The Lord Jesus has been convincing me of this and confirming it seven days per week before my very eyes, and I did not know that this was what He was doing, until He made it so clear that I could not deny it.

THE TWO NATURES

In fact, when we were with you, we kept telling you that we would be persecuted. And it turned out that way, as you well know. ⁵For this reason, when I could stand it no longer, I sent to find out about your faith. I was afraid that in some way the tempter might have tempted you and our efforts might have been useless. 1 Thess. 3:4-5

I know of souls who leave the Lord Jesus for the simplest reasons, such as: feeling tired, or not having the things at hand that they desire to eat or wear, or for not being able to go where they want to go, at the time they want to go. Others leave Him for the slightest discomfort or sickness they feel, or for not having the relationships they desire. There are also those who leave the Lord Jesus for not being able to live in the neighborhood they desire, or for not being satisfied with the wife or husband that they have, or because of problems in their families. They also leave Him because they are tempted with the possessions and even the families of others, along with the things of the world – selfish ambition, money, position, possessions, power, fame, carnal liberty, pleasures, etc.

This, in the Lord Jesus and away from Him, is a continual battle for most Christians, only they do not see these choices and actions as turning from the Lord Jesus. Rather, they see this as normal because this is what they practice all throughout their Christian lives. Therefore, being in the Lord Jesus and out of the Lord Jesus means nothing to them – it is a normal way of life, and so many souls do not even know that this is what they are doing.

As simple and even foolish as these things might sound to some, nevertheless they are real and should be taken seriously, so that when we fall in any of these areas, rather than seeing it as normal, begin to see it as sin to be repented of. For all these are signs of deep dissatisfaction in the heart with a life in the Lord Jesus, pushed by the devil.

There are many who believe that they should suffer no wants, no discomforts, no sicknesses, no pains, no displeasures, no difficulties at all, no dissatisfactions, no problems with others, etc. Therefore, when these things happen, because of their beliefs, they cannot handle them. So they give up, believing that the Lord Jesus did nothing for them; He only brought them more problems than they already have.

Some are distracted when they go to the grocery store or the clothing store, the car showroom, etc., for they are envious of the things they see there. They are also envious of the things that they see on television. They therefore become obsessed with these things,

and through them, they are carried off by the enemy to pursue possessing such things, filling their hearts with them, leaving no room
there for the things of the Lord Jesus. Therefore, at the slightest
problem, they give up. They are also envious of the world and the
things of others, and so become discontented with their lives, what
they have, their circumstances and even with themselves. They then
become tied up in the desires for such things, forgetting who they
are in the Lord Jesus, and are soon carried off by the enemy, who
again controls their lives so that they will once again be under the
weight and worries of life, fears and anxiety, and accusations etc.
against the Lord Jesus, which are of the old nature, while blaming
the Lord Jesus for it all. These are all reasons to ask your Lord to
show you the root of your problems, because they all go much
deeper than they appear. Let us look at Simon in Acts.

> [13]Simon himself believed and was baptized. And
> he followed Philip everywhere, astonished by the
> great signs and miracles he saw. [17]Then Peter and
> John placed their hands on them, and they received
> the Holy Spirit. [18]When Simon saw that the Spirit
> was given at the laying on of the apostles' hands, he
> offered them money [19]and said, "Give me also this
> ability so that everyone on whom I lay my hands
> may receive the Holy Spirit." [20]Peter answered:

THE TWO NATURES

"May your money perish with you, because you
thought you could buy the gift of God with money!
[21]You have no part or share in this ministry, because
your heart is not right before God. [22]Repent of this
wickedness and pray to the Lord. Perhaps he will
forgive you for having such a thought in your heart.
[23]For I see that you are full of bitterness and captive
to sin." Acts 8:13, 17-23

Some will even turn from their Lord for something as simple as
not feeling good in their flesh. Such persons believe that because
they have given their lives to the Lord Jesus, He should keep them
feeling good, and according to them, if He does not, He is not
worthy of them. Believe it or not, this is the mentality of many who
call themselves Christians and are faithful churchgoers.

Some even leave the Lord Jesus because they are not satisfied with
their faces or their bodies. So, in that state of discontent, they leave
Him to have their own way to go and fix themselves through plastic
surgery, or whatever other means available to achieve this end. This
is dissatisfaction with the way they were made. Therefore, a state
of rebellion against God exists deep within their hearts, and they
might not even be aware of it, or want to be aware of such beliefs
in their hearts. For many believe that they are too good to have such

beliefs, and so they hide from facing them, covering them with a false spiritual fervor. Such hearts are full of accusation against God, according to them, for making them the way they are, and they are not willing to face such accusations in their hearts.

However, these things are usually buried deep within the heart, and most souls are not conscious that this is their true state, and still others do not want to know, since these are not easy to face. In this way, they continue in them, never understanding why they cannot get close to the Lord Jesus.

But how does one get close to the Lord Jesus, when you believe that God made you to look and feel the way you do – bad about yourself – which is totally unacceptable to you? No, you will not; for according to you, now you are going to have to fix that which you believe God has messed up, which you cannot, yet you are determined.

We need to understand with clarity that the way each of us as individuals appear or look, depends solely on who our individual parents chose to marry or partner with and have children, and not on God. Because, when God made Adam and Eve, He declared all He had made to be good. So, by that declaration, we know that God made us good, perfect, beautiful, whole and sane. Therefore, everyone who has come out of the womb different from this is a result of the fall, and therefore sin, the devil, and our parents' and their ancestors, and the choices they and we make, for sin warped everything. Yet, God is blamed, accused and judged as evil for making people ugly, deformed, disease-stricken, some without limbs, others joined together, etc. All these are caused by the fall, sin and therefore satan – yet God is blamed for it all.

> Therefore, get rid of all moral filth and the evil that
> is so prevalent and humbly accept the word planted
> in you, which can save you. James 1:21

The enemy uses all the tragic illnesses, deformities and more, to deceive and tempt the children of God, and in many cases carry them off to murmur against their Lord and God and to accuse Him. When, by the Holy Spirit, they have come to their senses and realize what they have been doing, at this point many are ashamed of the way they have been living before the Lord Jesus, and are condemned by the devil. At such times, some will even say, "But the Scripture says that there is no condemnation to those who are in Christ Jesus our Lord." That is a fact, but for this Scripture to be applied in your life, you must remain in your Lord Jesus, and I emphasize "in," and sincerely believe the Scriptures, and not use them for your convenience. In so doing, you will be able to trust the Lord Jesus, and Him alone, for it refers specifically to those who are in Christ. However, if you leave Him to go back into your carnal nature to fulfill the desires of that nature, you will be condemned, and there is no doubt about that, because condemnation is of the devil, and is therefore a part of the sinful nature.

> Therefore, there is now no condemnation for those who are in Christ Jesus, ²because through Christ Jesus the law of the Spirit of life set me free from the law of sin and death. Rom. 8:1-2

> Anyone who runs ahead and does not continue in the teaching of Christ does not have God; whoever continues in the teaching has both the Father and the Son. 2 John 1:9

> Therefore, brothers, we have an obligation – but it is not to the sinful nature, to live according to it. ¹³For if you live according to the sinful nature, you will die; but if by the Spirit you put to death the misdeeds of the body, you will live, Rom. 8:12-13

> Consider therefore the kindness and sternness of God: sternness to those who fell, but kindness to

you, provided that you continue in his kindness.
Otherwise, you also will be cut off. Rom. 11:22

Remain in me, and I will remain in you. No branch
can bear fruit by itself; it must remain in the vine.
Neither can you bear fruit unless you remain in
me. 5"I am the vine; you are the branches. If a man
remains in me and I in him, he will bear much fruit;
apart from me you can do nothing. 6If anyone does
not remain in me, he is like a branch that is thrown
away and withers; such branches are picked up,
thrown into the fire and burned. John 15:4-6

Most Christians do not take these Scriptures to be the reality for
their lives. If they did, this going back and forth from the divine
nature to the carnal nature would not be happening at all, much
less with such frequency. We know that some go back and forth at
will, simply because they are not finished with the old ways of the
sinful nature, and therefore sin, and so to them it is not a problem.

Most of those who are back and forth from the divine nature to
the carnal nature, are souls who have never sincerely embraced
the divine nature, nor chose to walk according to it. Again, they
might not have been taught these things, and so they do not know

of them, and therefore, no importance is given to them. If this is so, then they were short-changed in the teaching they have received. Yet they have God's Word, and therefore they are without excuse.

I remember someone saying to me that if he gave up everything to the Lord Jesus, what then would he have left, meaning, that he would lose all control over everything in his life. In his case, lies, deceit, pride, falsehood, demanding to be number one and pretense, were a great part of his life. In other words, without the dishonest life he would not be able to hide, justify or escape his wrong and evil desires, choices and actions. So if he cannot hide, how then will he manage, control or defend himself against God and man?

Therefore, if he gives up everything to the Lord Jesus, he would not see himself giving up sin, but rather, he would see himself giving up his control to justify, defend and protect himself, especially against God. He, like so many others, is simply not willing to trust the Lord Jesus with his life. To such persons, maintaining control over their own lives and circumstances means everything to them, even if it leads them to hell. This is how strongly some have held to the old way of life – the sinful nature. They refuse to come to the light of the Gospel and sincerely believe.

THE TWO NATURES

"Go up and down the streets of Jerusalem, look around and consider, search through her squares. If you can find but one person who deals honestly and seeks the truth, I will forgive this city. ²Although they say, `As surely as the LORD lives,' still they are swearing falsely." ³O LORD, do not your eyes look for truth? You struck them, but they felt no pain; you crushed them, but they refused correction. They made their faces harder than stone and refused to repent. ⁴I thought, "These are only the poor; they are foolish, for they do not know the way of the LORD, the requirements of their God. ⁵So I will go to the leaders and speak to them; surely they know the way of the LORD, the requirements of their God." But with one accord they too had broken off the yoke and torn off the bonds. Jer. 5:1-5

Those who obey his commands live in him, and he in them. And this is how we know that he lives in us: We know it by the Spirit he gave us. 1 John 3:24

For too many, surrendering all to the lordship of the Lord Jesus Christ is a little too much to ask, and so they continue to go back and forth, as it is convenient. In so doing, they are deceived to believe that they are in control of their lives and destiny. Only the beloved Lord Jesus knows for sure what will be the conclusion of such lives. Will He permit such souls to continue like this forever? Or, will He at a point say, enough is enough, and cut them off as He did with the children of Israel in the desert because they rebelled over and over again, and refused to trust and obey their God through Moses? The Lord Jesus said, **"If you want to enter life, obey the commandments."** (Matt. 19:17)

One thing we know, and that is, our blessed God is patient with all of us, not wanting anyone to perish, but rather that all would come to repentance. Therefore, He gives all of us lots of time to come to a place where we will choose to let go the life completely to Him. Many have done so, while many others have not, and still others will not, to their own sorrow and shame.

> We must pay more careful attention, therefore, to what we have heard, so that we do not drift away. ²For if the message spoken by angels was binding, and every violation and disobedience received its just punishment, ³how shall we escape if we ignore such a great salvation? This salvation, which was first announced by the Lord, was confirmed to us by those who heard him. Heb. 2:1-3

THE TWO NATURES

Many souls do not stay believing the Lord Jesus, and therefore they cannot remain in Him. To remain in the Lord Jesus, we must stay believing Him in His Word, and therefore place our trust in Him. It is only when we believe His Word and stay believing it, that we will be able to stay trusting Him. If we do not stay believing the Word of the Lord Jesus, we will not be able to stay trusting Him. Indeed, we cannot, for it is only when we stay believing Him that we are enabled by faith, and the blessed Holy Spirit, to stay trusting the Lord Jesus. When we stop believing the Lord Jesus in His Word, we will automatically stop trusting Him, and therefore stop participating in the divine nature.

> To the Jews who had believed him, Jesus said, "If you hold to my teaching, you are really my disciples. [32]Then you will know the truth, and the truth will set you free." John 8:31-32

There are some however, who in their old nature, are deceived to believe that they are trusting in the Lord Jesus. But this trust is only mental and emotional, and so it is false, for it is of the sinful nature. It therefore comes and goes according to how they feel. They are also deceived to believe they are trusting the Lord Jesus, through the many words that they speak. By saying it enough times, they actually believe their own words of how much they love and trust the Lord Jesus. They are therefore deceived by their own words. As said before, by saying this often enough, they literally believe the words of their own mouth, which then becomes their reality, rather than the truth of God's Word that should have been in their hearts, which clearly tells them that what their feelings, emotions and thoughts are telling them through their body and mouths, is a lie.

There are those souls who believe that they are good. So they set out to confirm their goodness and their spirituality through what they see as their service to the church – through Bible reading, much prayer and what they call repentance, and even through using the name of the Lord Jesus, and talking with others about Him.

In their minds, good people are supposed to be spiritual, and so they feel obligated to put forth a spiritual image. Therefore, they use all that they do and say to give themselves a sense of spirituality, especially before others, but this is all carnal and of the sinful nature. They are deceived to believe that through the service they offer to the Body, or because of it, that they are trusting the Lord Jesus, even though there is really no room in their hearts for Him. This is simply because in their own eyes they are good people, and so works become their substitute for faith, and therefore a life with the Lord Jesus. These and more, are ways the enemy uses to deceive such souls to believe that they are Christians.

THE TWO NATURES

Consider therefore the kindness and sternness of
God: sternness to those who fell, but kindness to
you, provided that you continue in his kindness.
Otherwise, you also will be cut off. [23]And if they
do not persist in unbelief, they will be grafted in, for
God is able to graft them in again. Rom. 11:22-23

This so-called believing and trusting is only a mental assent to
God's Word and nothing else, which comes and goes according to
their feelings. Yet by activities such as being a faithful churchgoer,
giving their services to the church and paying their tithes, they are
deceived to believe the lie that they too are sincerely believing, and
therefore their false sense of spirituality is real to them.

Then, there are those who follow this similar pattern of works to
demonstrate spirituality, although they may never have read God's
Word, much less to know what it says. They might only "pray"
when they have a problem or a need, and they might not even
know what repentance is. Yet being "spiritual" and having others
see them that way, means everything to them —"spiritual," meaning,
they are accepted in the church as Christians, and as a result they
are giving their service to the church. This means everything to
them. The more they do the more spiritual they feel they are. This
gives them a sense of belonging and a sense of acceptation among

Christians in general, as well as those in the church which they are attending. To them, all this translates to be a life in Christ.

> No, but the sacrifices of pagans are offered to demons, not to God, and I do not want you to be participants with demons. [21]You cannot drink the cup of the Lord and the cup of demons too; you cannot have a part in both the Lord's table and the table of demons. [22]Are we trying to arouse the Lord's jealousy? Are we stronger than he? 1 Cor. 10:20-22

What this is saying to us is how deceitful the sinful nature is, or rather, how deceitful the enemy behind the old nature is. It shows us the extent to which he will go to deceive and convince you, that through all these self-efforts, you are really believing in the Lord Jesus. Therefore, you are a Christian, and you are on your way to heaven. In this way, the enemy is then able to keep you from truly believing the Lord Jesus, or even seeing that you have a need to believe Him. This is the real purpose for all these deceits of the enemy, through the old nature.

When we are born of God, we are given a new life. The old has gone and the new has come.

THE TWO NATURES

For Christ's love compels us, because we are convinced that one died for all, and therefore all died.
[15]And he died for all, that those who live should no
longer live for themselves but for him who died for
them and was raised again. [16]So from now on we
regard no one from a worldly point of view. Though
we once regarded Christ in this way, we do so no
longer. [17]Therefore, if anyone is in Christ, he is a
new creation; the old has gone, the new has come!
2 Cor. 5:14-17

If we believe God's Word, it will then become our reality, and
therefore the Lord Jesus and His Word will now be our reference
point. This means that we should now begin to pray and trust the
beloved Lord Jesus to keep us conscious, so that we will no longer
refer to the old life, using the understandings and experiences we
had back there to formulate and make decisions in our new life. If
we depend on those old beliefs, experiences and understandings,
this will be a sure way for the old sinful nature to continue having
its way in what we call our "new life." Therefore, all that we can
do after this takes place, is to pretend that we are living according
to the new life.

THE TWO NATURES

When this is so, if there is a new life, that new life has no chance of coming into its own, because it is dominated by the old mentality governed through the sinful nature by the devil, with its old beliefs, plans, desires, agenda, experiences, abilities, know-how, thoughts, pursuits, etc. Therefore, all your choices will be according to the old carnal mentality – the sinful nature with a false little dash of the new mixed in, in accordance with head knowledge of God's Word, as if putting a new patch on an old garment, or pouring new wine into old wineskins.

> He told them this parable: "No one tears a patch from a new garment and sews it on an old one. If he does, he will have torn the new garment, and the patch from the new will not match the old. [37]And no one pours new wine into old wineskins. If he does, the new wine will burst the skins, the wine will run out and the wineskins will be ruined. [38]No, new wine must be poured into new wineskins. [39]And no one after drinking old wine wants the new, for he says, 'The old is better.' " Luke 5:36-39

You can then begin to understand why so many Christians know only a carnal life. They therefore live out what they call their Christian life, carnally, according to their sinful nature, which the

THE TWO NATURES

Scripture warns us not to do, for it says if we do, we will die. The old life should be viewed in such a way so as to keep us from ever again going back to it. In other words, we should be distancing ourselves further and further from it each day, so that in a short time, it begins to become strange, where you are able to say, "What a fool I was to have believed all those lies to which I was subjected." This is why the Word of God calls the wisdom of the world foolishness. And from the spiritual point of view, that is all that it is – foolishness – yet that is how we have lived, and how many continue to live to this day.

When we come to Christ, all of our old reference points should begin to come to an end. Yes, I say that they should begin to come to an end, because in reality that old life as far as we are concerned is ended. Yet, it is only a choice away until it is finally put to death by the Holy Spirit. Therefore, our old way of believing, desiring, thinking, choosing and acting, along with our reference points, should immediately begin to come to an end when we come to Christ, as the mind is being renewed, or is being transformed, beginning with our beliefs. And yes, I know it won't all happen at once; nevertheless this needs to be embraced, and to begin right away. The quicker the better, because it takes time.

THE TWO NATURES

We need to pray and ask our Lord Jesus to help us with this transformation. Therefore, whenever we are conscious of using the old life as our reference point from which to speak or make decisions, we must immediately realize that this is wrong, and put an end to it in dependency on the Lord Jesus. Ask Him to help you; He is always willing, if you are sincere. For when we do not, the old life will continue, and in a little while it will be as if we were never given a new life, and this is how most Christians live. Everything will be as it was in the old life – boring and miserable and being tormented with the same old beliefs, desires, selfish ambitions, plans, condemnation, choices, etc. This is why you will hear Christians say they are struggling, or that the Christian life is hard and boring, and if they had known that this is what Christianity was all about, they would not have bothered to become a Christian. All this tells you that they have been deceived, and so they have no idea what a life in Christ is all about.

All of these problems are due to those persons not taking God's Word seriously, and due to a lack of sincere commitment and proper teaching. Souls are simply not taught these things, and so they suffer great loss. To avoid this problem, when you come to Christ, you are to immediately begin to learn of Him in His Word, for the Lord Jesus has told us to come to Him and learn from Him. Those who obey His Word and do this, will immediately begin making

choices according to His Word, and will also begin there to participate in His divine nature, while at the same time, continue submitting themselves to be sanctified by the Holy Spirit.

> "Come to me, all you who are weary and burdened,
> and I will give you rest. [29]Take my yoke upon you
> and learn from me, for I am gentle and humble in
> heart, and you will find rest for your souls. [30]For my
> yoke is easy and my burden is light." Matt. 11:28-30

This is to immediately begin the process of turning from the sinful
nature, to the renewing of our minds from the old way of believing,
desiring, thinking, choosing and processing, to the new way of the
Spirit by participating in the divine nature. This is in keeping with
who we now are – children of God. Therefore, our reference point,
along with the knowledge, the understanding, the choices we make
and everything else, will begin to be formulated based on God's
Word. This will then begin to lock out the old life with its agenda
to have its own way, go its own way, and do its own will, and so
to continue sinning against God.

The ways of the sinful nature must now begin to come to their end
through the sanctifying work of the Holy Spirit. At the same time,
the new life must be fed all that it needs to grow more and more

each day – in grace, in truth, in faith, in obedience, in knowledge and in surrendering the life to the Lord Jesus more and more each day, thereby becoming more like our Lord Jesus in nature, every moment of every day.

A good place to begin to choose, is to believe and to be in agreement with God's Word, and also to be sure to be in truth and sincerity – first with your God and Lord, then with those that you deal with. Begin to deny yourself and stop lying, stop making excuses for your sins, stop justifying yourself, while trusting your Lord every step of the way to help you to do this. As you do, keep praying, and trust your Lord to open up new areas of truth for you to enter each day, and He will as you put in practice believing and trusting Him for these things. The following Scriptures will help to confirm what I have been saying.

> You were taught, with regard to your former way of life, to put off your old self, which is being corrupted by its deceitful desires; [23]to be made new in the attitude of your minds; [24]and to put on the new self, created to be like God in true righteousness and holiness. Eph. 4:22-24

THE TWO NATURES

Therefore, I urge you, brothers, in view of God's mercy, to offer your bodies as living sacrifices, holy and pleasing to God – this is your spiritual act of worship. [2]Do not conform any longer to the pattern of this world, but be transformed by the renewing of your mind. Then you will be able to test and approve what God's will is – his good, pleasing and perfect will. Rom. 12:1-2

Do not lie to each other, since you have taken off your old self with its practices [10]and have put on the new self, which is being renewed in knowledge in the image of its Creator. Col. 3:9-10

Now, brothers, I want to remind you of the gospel I preached to you, which you received and on which you have taken your stand. [2]By this gospel you are saved, if you hold firmly to the word I preached to you. Otherwise, you have believed in vain. 1 Cor. 15:1-2

Once you were alienated from God and were enemies in your minds because of your evil behavior. [22]But now he has reconciled you by Christ's

THE TWO NATURES

physical body through death to present you holy in his sight, without blemish and free from accusation – [23]if you continue in your faith, established and firm, not moved from the hope held out in the gospel. This is the gospel that you heard and that has been proclaimed to every creature under heaven, and of which I, Paul, have become a servant. Col. 1:21-23

Therefore, rid yourselves of all malice and all deceit, hypocrisy, envy, and slander of every kind. [2]Like newborn babies, crave pure spiritual milk, so that by it you may grow up in your salvation, [3]now that you have tasted that the Lord is good. 1 Peter 2:1-3

But we ought always to thank God for you, brothers loved by the Lord, because from the beginning God chose you to be saved through the sanctifying work of the Spirit and through belief in the truth. [14]He called you to this through our gospel, that you might share in the glory of our Lord Jesus Christ. [15]So then, brothers, stand firm and hold to the teachings we passed on to you, whether by word of mouth or by letter. 2 Thess. 2:13-15

THE TWO NATURES

And we also thank God continually because, when you received the word of God, which you heard from us, you accepted it not as the word of men, but as it actually is, the word of God, which is at work in you who believe. 1 Thess. 2:13

"Now I commit you to God and to the word of his grace, which can build you up and give you an inheritance among all those who are sanctified. Acts 20:32

Therefore, get rid of all moral filth and the evil that is so prevalent and humbly accept the word planted in you, which can save you. James 1:21

Be imitators of God, therefore, as dearly loved children ²and live a life of love, just as Christ loved us and gave himself up for us as a fragrant offering and sacrifice to God. Eph. 5:1-2

Your boasting is not good. Don't you know that a little yeast works through the whole batch of dough? ⁷Get rid of the old yeast that you may be a new batch without yeast – as you really are. For Christ, our

Passover lamb, has been sacrificed. ⁸Therefore let us keep the Festival, not with the old yeast, the yeast of malice and wickedness, but with bread without yeast, the bread of sincerity and truth. 1 Cor. 5:6-8

To the Jews who had believed him, Jesus said, "If you hold to my teaching, you are really my disciples. ³²Then you will know the truth, and the truth will set you free." John 8:31-32

Watch out that you do not lose what you have worked for, but that you may be rewarded fully. ⁹Anyone who runs ahead and does not continue in the teaching of Christ does not have God; whoever continues in the teaching has both the Father and the Son. 2 John 1:8-9

"If, while we seek to be justified in Christ, it becomes evident that we ourselves are sinners, does that mean that Christ promotes sin? Absolutely not! ¹⁸If I rebuild what I destroyed, I prove that I am a law-breaker. ¹⁹For through the law I died to the law so that I might live for God. ²⁰I have been crucified with Christ and I no longer live, but Christ lives in

me. The life I live in the body, I live by faith in the
Son of God, who loved me and gave himself for
me. Gal. 2:17-20

"Now fear the LORD and serve him with all faithfulness. Throw away the gods your forefathers wor-
shiped beyond the River and in Egypt, and serve
the LORD. [15]But if serving the LORD seems undesirable to you, then choose for yourselves this day
whom you will serve, whether the gods your forefathers served beyond the River, or the gods of the
Amorites, in whose land you are living. But as for
me and my household, we will serve the LORD."
Josh. 24:14-15

There is no trick that the enemy, through the sinful nature, will not
use against you to keep you deceived to believe that you are truly
believing, and that you are trusting in the Lord Jesus, and therefore
convince you that you are a good Christian. And oh, how through
your emotions, backed up with your mental assent, you can be
deceived to feel and actually believe that you really love the Lord
Jesus, when in fact your interests are not about Him. The enemy
does all this with one intent, and that is to keep you from seeing
your true state of unbelief, and therefore your true need for the Lord

Jesus. This is so that you will remain in that state, and never truly repent and turn to sincerely believe in the Lord Jesus.

I cannot emphasize this enough, because it is such a common trick which the enemy uses through the old nature. This trick is so common, that it is accepted and believed by everyone I know. Consequently, they are deceived to remain in that place, where they are always accusing the blessed God and Lord for all their misery and problems. In this way, they will never have to face and acknowledge the real cause of their problems. To them, everything that goes wrong in their lives has nothing to do with their choices. No, it is all God's fault, and it will always be that way. As a result, the enemy uses them to hold resentment in their hearts against God, and even hate towards Him. By so doing, he keeps them far from God.

When there is a sincere believing in the Lord Jesus, there is no lapse in that believing. It is constant, for you are always believing. Regardless of the difficulties that come your way, they never stop you from believing. Rather, they will challenge your faith, which should result in your believing even more. Therefore, when you believe, whether you experience problems or good times, you will always turn to your Lord, looking to Him for either the solution to your problems, or to share the good news, the good times or things with Him. Why? Because you believe, and therefore you trust and love your Lord Jesus, you are able to receive from Him those things that come your way, whether good or bad.

For instance, Job's wife said to him;

> ..."Are you still holding on to your integrity? Curse God and die!" [10]He replied, "You are talking like a foolish woman. Shall we accept good from God, and not trouble?" In all this, Job did not sin in what he said. Job 2:9-10

This is sincere faith in action, as seen in Job's life.

When your believing is not sincere, and you experience good times or good things in your life; many share these times and things with others, rather than with the Lord Jesus. Then there are some who tend to pull inward when they face problems, shutting out their difficulties and hiding from them. Some will look to themselves for the solution to these problems, instead of looking to the Lord Jesus, while living in misery and blaming God for them.

THE TWO NATURES

See to it that no one misses the grace of God and that no bitter root grows up to cause trouble and defile many. Heb. 12:15

Your daily priority should always be to make sure that you are sincerely believing and trusting the Lord Jesus. How do you know that you are sincerely believing Him? Here is the test. When you are able to simply, without reasoning or hesitation, let go your life and all that would come against you to preoccupy your mind, and at a moment's notice turn to your Lord and trust them all to Him and rest, where you are no longer carrying the weight and burden of your life, or being preoccupied with it or the problems thereof, even though you are still feeling in your flesh/body the effect of those things, then you can say, "I believe." Why? Because you were able to trust your Lord and rest all that you are, along with all your problems, including those things that are still opposing you such as your feelings, along with the thoughts that come to preoccupy your mind, etc.. If you are able to take these to your Lord, and rest them in Him, then you are truly believing. This will result in further faith, which brings forth further trust, which translates into deeper rest. This is truly believing. This is faith in action.

This is what the Sovereign LORD, the Holy One of Israel, says: "In repentance and rest is your

THE TWO NATURES

> salvation, in quietness and trust is your strength,
>
> but you would have none of it. Isa. 30:15

Another test that you could carry out to be sure that you are sincerely believing the Lord Jesus, is to examine your responses when you are successful and are happy. Do you enjoy your success and happiness with others in a way that is satisfying to your flesh, and even to show off like so many do? Or, as mentioned before, do you instead, because you believe and are trusting your Lord and receiving guidance from Him, first of all, turn to your Lord and share your success and happiness with Him, receiving them from Him and enjoying them with Him, giving Him thanks for them? Do you choose to enjoy them with Him, rather than to enjoy them carnally, maybe with others and apart from Him? If this is what you do, then you can truly say that, "I believe and therefore I trust the Lord Jesus."

Again, if you have had major losses in your life, and you are able to share these with your Lord and trust Him in the middle of it all, sharing all your griefs, sorrows and disappointments with Him, and receiving from Him the strength you need to stand firm in faith in Him, then you can say that you believe. This is the way we should be living.

THE TWO NATURES

In other words, when you sincerely believe in the Lord Jesus, you should always choose to do everything with your Lord as long as you are conscious to do so, for you know that without Him, you can do nothing. And, if by chance you should act on your own without Him, while being conscious of doing so, you will then know that you are not sincerely believing the Lord Jesus. For some reason or another, you have stopped believing your Lord the way you should, and therefore stopped trusting Him. Maybe you have done so conveniently in order to enjoy some carnal pleasures, or to obtain some favor, position or possessions that you know are not in keeping with God's will for you. Believe me, this is a common practice in the church.

> For if Joshua had given them rest, God would not have spoken later about another day. ⁹There remains, then, a Sabbath-rest for the people of God; ¹⁰for anyone who enters God's rest also rests from his own work, just as God did from his. ¹¹Let us, therefore, make every effort to enter that rest, so that no one will fall by following their example of disobedience. Heb. 4:8-11

I will repeat: Our emphasis should be to believe our God and Lord every day, and throughout the entire day, as long as He keeps us

conscious. When we are not conscious, we are to trust the Lord
Jesus with that too, as well as for whatever happens during that
period of unconsciousness. But as long as we are conscious, we
should remain actively trusting the Lord Jesus, and so remain in
Him. We are to trust Him with our whole life and everything that is
happening then, and will ever happen in our lives. This is without
exception, whether we are conscious or unconscious.

> If anyone does not remain in me, he is like a branch
> that is thrown away and withers; such branches are
> picked up, thrown into the fire and burned. John 15:6

How many times have Christians left the Lord Jesus to go off and
join their old carnal nature, and there choose to do their own will,
while ignoring the Lord's will? This happens every day and every
night. Yet, they never even stop to give it so much as a thought,
much less to acknowledge that they have done something wrong to
be repented of. Nevertheless, be assured that after they have done
their will, and things do not turn out the way they would like, they
will, for sure blame God for it, and accuse Him harshly.

For these many reasons, you will hear some Christians say that
they have lost the joy they once had. And of course they would
have, for as long as they have joined their old nature they are the

THE TWO NATURES

old man, and the old man has never had, nor will ever have the joy of the Lord in him. So then, how could he have lost what he never had? No! The joy of the Lord will only remain with us while we remain in Him, participating in the divine nature. This is just as the Scripture has said:

> Nehemiah said, "Go and enjoy choice food and sweet drinks, and send some to those who have nothing prepared. This day is sacred to our Lord. Do not grieve, for the joy of the Lord is your strength." Neh. 8:10

> Grace and peace be yours in abundance through the knowledge of God and of Jesus our Lord. 2 Peter 1:2

Your joy is being in your Lord. When you are separated from Him, which is always by your own choice, you will indeed have no joy, and this is the reality in which we must walk. "Thank You dearest beloved Lord Jesus."

As I have said before, to doubt the Lord Jesus is not a given, and God's children should never doubt Him. I have constantly heard Bible teachers, preachers and laity alike, say that every Christian doubts God at some time or another. They have even gone as far

as to say that there is no child of God who has never, at some time
or another, doubted God. However, for me this is not the reality,
nevertheless, I do understand because of the darkness that is over
the church. Yet, I have never doubted God, not even once for a
second, in over thirty-nine years since the Lord Jesus has called
me, and He is just now permitting me to see why – I have never left
Him to again join the old sinful nature, and therefore I could not
have doubted Him, for doubt is of the carnal sinful nature. "Thank
You beloved Lord Jesus, for it is You who have kept me in You,
believing and trusting You to keep me in all areas of this life, and
in all things. Thank You again."

You see, doubt is of the sinful nature. Whenever and for whatever reason you end up joining the old nature, even for a short
moment, doubt will be there waiting for you. Sometimes it could
be as simple as a slight uncertainty or hesitation that gradually turns
into unbelief/doubt because you have given it room, or it could
even be a heavy state of disinterest, distrust, uncertainty, skepti-
cism or suspicion, along with all the other evil, selfish, ugly, negative things pushed by the devil on God's children, through that evil
sinful nature. The moment then that you join the old sinful nature in
agreeing with anything that it brings, or that resides there, you will
again be in danger of becoming all that that nature is. Therefore,
you will be capable of committing all the sins that you were once

accustomed to committing when you lived by that nature. The only reason why most do not go this far is because of God's grace.

> With eyes full of adultery, they never stop sinning;
> they seduce the unstable; they are experts in greed
> – an accursed brood! [15]They have left the straight
> way and wandered off to follow the way of Balaam
> son of Beor, who loved the wages of wickedness.
> 2 Peter 2:14-15

However, the moment that you, by God's grace, turn from the old nature in repentance, back to your Lord, and again choose to believe His Word and hold to it, you will once again choose to participate in the divine nature, and you will again desire all the virtues that you once had embraced in the new nature; that is, if God grants you repentance. There, you will again choose to believe God and His Word. As a result, you will choose to embrace faith, love for God, desire for God, admiration for God, truth, righteousness, purity, godliness, truthfulness, faithfulness, honesty, peace, hope, contentment, gratitude, thanksgiving, appreciation, giving rather than only receiving for selfish gain, etc. All these are waiting for you, as you choose to once again participate in the divine nature, and by God's grace, embrace these virtues to be your life. Remember, it is only by God's grace that we are enabled to leave that old nature; without grace, we could not.

All these virtues and more are God's gifts to all who will choose to believe, and therefore embrace the divine nature in His Word. This is why our beloved Lord Jesus tells us to remain in Him, and to participate in the divine nature. For when we do we are further inspired by faith, and are enabled by the blessed Holy Spirit to love our God and Lord even more, and so we are at peace with Him and therefore with ourselves. We are happy, we are full of hope, we love the truth, we want the things of God, and we want our God and Lord. He gives us grace to enable us to want all this, and to walk with Him and in them, as we hold to His Word and choose to participate in the divine nature. This is God's chosen will for us. These are benefits waiting there for all who will embrace them and take them, for they are given to us there in His Word.

The divine nature of which I speak is God's nature, which is clearly revealed and laid out in His Word. For example: God is inestimably good, God is love, God is holy, God is righteous, God is just, God is truth, God is humble, God is meek, God is merciful, God is gracious, God is kind, God is forgiving, God is giving, God is patient, God is long-suffering and God is faithful. God is always doing that which is inestimably good – choosing for others, giving of Himself, lifting up all people, especially the poor and lowly, choosing for the highest good of all, even for those who hate Him, curse Him and despitefully use Him, and He blesses them too. These are a small part of God's nature – who God is.

> Every good and perfect gift is from above, coming down from the Father of the heavenly lights, who does not change like shifting shadows. James 1:17

> He is the image of the invisible God, the firstborn over all creation. [16]For by him all things were created: things in heaven and on earth, visible and invisible, whether thrones or powers or rulers or authorities; all things were created by him and for him. [17]He is before all things, and in him all things hold together. [18]And he is the head of the body, the church; he is the beginning and the firstborn from among the dead, so that in everything he might have the supremacy. [19]For God was pleased to have all his fullness dwell in him, [20]and through him to reconcile to himself all things, whether things on earth or things in heaven, by making peace through his blood, shed on the cross. Col. 1:15-20

THE TWO NATURES

We must pay more careful attention, therefore, to
what we have heard, so that we do not drift away.
²For if the message spoken by angels was binding,
and every violation and disobedience received its
just punishment, ³how shall we escape if we ignore
such a great salvation? This salvation, which was
first announced by the Lord, was confirmed to us
by those who heard him. Heb. 2:1-3

God is also trustworthy, and therefore He can be trusted. He is sincere, honest, dependable, generous, and He suffers long with us. He
gave Himself to lift up others. This is just a small part of the nature
of God – who God is. In His great love and mercy towards us, He
has made us His children in the spirit, and He has commanded us
to be holy as He is holy, that is to say, becoming like Him in nature.
To the natural mind, this seems to be out of this world and far
beyond us, but God says no, it is not out of this world, and neither
is it beyond us. In reality, it is as close as choosing to believe His
Word in your heart, and choosing to come into agreement with it,
knowing that this is the truth, and it is God's will for us.

Now what I am commanding you today is not too
difficult for you or beyond your reach. ¹²It is not
up in heaven, so that you have to ask, "Who will

ascend into heaven to get it and proclaim it to us so we may obey it?" [13]Nor is it beyond the sea, so that you have to ask, "Who will cross the sea to get it and proclaim it to us so we may obey it?" [14]No, the word is very near you; it is in your mouth and in your heart so you may obey it [15]See, I set before you today life and prosperity, death and destruction. [16]For I command you today to love the LORD your God, to walk in his ways, and to keep his commands, decrees and laws; then you will live and increase, and the LORD your God will bless you in the land you are entering to possess. [17]But if your heart turns away and you are not obedient, and if you are drawn away to bow down to other gods and worship them, [18]I declare to you this day that you will certainly be destroyed. You will not live long in the land you are crossing the Jordan to enter and possess. [19]This day I call heaven and earth as witnesses against you that I have set before you life and death, blessings and curses. Now choose life, so that you and your children may live [20]and that you may love the LORD your God, listen to his voice, and hold fast to him. For the LORD is your life, and he will give you many years in the land he swore

THE TWO NATURES

to give to your fathers, Abraham, Isaac and Jacob.

Deut. 30:11-20

God has bowed down low, and has brought His divine nature down to earth where you and I live to reveal it to us through His Word, where we can come in touch with it. It is as if He has set the most elaborate and elegant table, with the most exquisite, abundant and delicious meals that could ever be offered and served. Then, He invited us to come and sit at His massive and elegant table to feast on His Word. He said: Whoever will, may come and partake at My table. I want you all to be clothed with My righteousness, My nature, and to be as I am in love and in true holiness and righteousness, in truth and sincerity, in mercy and justice, in submission and obedience, in faithfulness and giving, etc., as manifested in and through the Lord Jesus, for you are my children.

Simon Peter, a servant and apostle of Jesus Christ,
To those who through the righteousness of our God
and Savior Jesus Christ have received a faith as precious as ours: [2]Grace and peace be yours in abundance through the knowledge of God and of Jesus our Lord. [3]His divine power has given us everything we need for life and godliness through our knowledge of him who called us by his own glory and

THE TWO NATURES

goodness. ⁴Through these he has given us his very great and precious promises, so that through them you may participate in the divine nature and escape the corruption in the world caused by evil desires. ⁵For this very reason, make every effort to add to your faith goodness; and to goodness, knowledge; ⁶and to knowledge, self-control; and to self-control, perseverance; and to perseverance, godliness; ⁷and to godliness, brotherly kindness; and to brotherly kindness, love. ⁸For if you possess these qualities in increasing measure, they will keep you from being ineffective and unproductive in your knowledge of our Lord Jesus Christ. ⁹But if anyone does not have them, he is nearsighted and blind, and has forgotten that he has been cleansed from his past sins. ¹⁰Therefore, my brothers, be all the more eager to make your calling and election sure. For if you do these things, you will never fall, ¹¹and you will receive a rich welcome into the eternal kingdom of our Lord and Savior Jesus Christ. 2 Peter 1:1-11

Be imitators of God, therefore, as dearly loved children Eph. 5:1

THE TWO NATURES

> Do not lie to each other, since you have taken off
> your old self with its practices [10]and have put on the
> new self, which is being renewed in knowledge in
> the image of its Creator. Col 3:9-10

> You were taught, with regard to your former way
> of life, to put off your old self, which is being cor-
> rupted by its deceitful desires; [23]to be made new in
> the attitude of your minds; [24]and to put on the new
> self, created to be like God in true righteousness and
> holiness. Eph. 4:22-24

This is the result of participating in His divine nature, taking it to
be yours, as laid out in His Word, while putting off the old through
the sanctifying work of the Holy Spirit.

To be like God in nature, we must first believe His Word/Truth,
obey it and conform to it, so that it becomes our lives. It is for us to
choose to come into agreement with His Word, and to adopt what
it reveals there of God's nature to be our nature. For instance, the
Word reveals that God is truth, and so truth and sincerity are His
nature. Therefore, we too must choose to be truthful and sincere
in all that we believe, desire, think, choose, say and do, and we are
to pray for this.

THE TWO NATURES

God's Word also reveals that God is inestimably good, and God is love. This is also telling us that to be like God in nature, we too are to love and do that which is good and right in His sight, with His help. It further tells us that God is holy, and because He is holy, He wants us, His children, also to be holy as He is. This means, first of all, that we are to have a pure heart – first towards God, and then towards others, just as He has towards us. We are also to choose that which is good and pure – first towards God and then towards others, as He does towards us. In this we must know that in everything God has called us to do, He has given us the grace to do it. Therefore, in all that we are to do, we must do them in faith, trusting the Lord Jesus every step of the way.

To be like God in nature, we are to choose to be pure and sincere in our beliefs, desires, intentions or motivations, thoughts, choices, words and actions – first of all towards God, and then towards others.

The Word of God also says that God is longsuffering, God is patient and God is kind. Likewise, we too are to be longsuffering, patient and kind, to be like Him in nature. It also says that God is just, and so He also wants us to be just. Because God is humble and forgiving, He wants us to walk in humility, and to forgive one another. Also, because He is the God of truth and He tells no lies,

He therefore wants us to embrace truth, love truth, walk in truth and sincerity, and likewise to tell no lies. God wants His children to walk in integrity.

Our beloved Lord Jesus warns us against lying, because lies, deceit, pretense, falsehood, justification and unnecessary self-defense are all about a selfish and prideful self-life. These are signs that you are walking in pride. So, when you practice these things, you are actually participating in the sinful nature – the nature of the devil, from which the Lord Jesus has delivered us. In such a state, you are walking with the devil, carrying out his will, for pride is of the nature of the devil, while humility is of the nature of God. This is why He calls us away from those things that represent a life of pride, to those things that represent a life of humility, which are of His nature.

> During the days of Jesus' life on earth, he offered
> up prayers and petitions with loud cries and tears to
> the one who could save him from death, and he was
> heard because of his reverent submission. [8]Although
> he was a son, he learned obedience from what he
> suffered [9]and, once made perfect, he became the
> source of eternal salvation for all who obey him

THE TWO NATURES

[10]and was designated by God to be high priest in the order of Melchizedek. Heb. 5:7-10

While lies, deceit, pretense, falsehood, pride, etc. are manifestations of a heart of selfishness, and therefore the nature of the devil; truth and sincerity, honesty and humility on the other hand, represent and manifest a heart of purity, and therefore the nature of God, which He has called us to participate in. Now, you must choose to speak the truth from a sincere heart, even though it exposes and maybe even humiliates you, which truth tends to do at times. Yet, because you have chosen to become like your God and Lord, through your willful participation in His divine nature in dependency on Him, you will now deny your flesh to tell the truth in sincerity, to be honest, to walk in humility, in submission, obedience and faithfulness to your God and Lord, etc. This is an example of what it means to participate in the divine nature. You cannot walk according to the divine nature without denying your flesh, and therefore the sinful nature.

> Since, then, you have been raised with Christ, set your hearts on things above, where Christ is seated at the right hand of God. [2]Set your minds on things above, not on earthly things. [3]For you died, and your life is now hidden with Christ in God. [4]When

THE TWO NATURES

Christ, who is your life, appears, then you also will appear with him in glory. [5]Put to death, therefore, whatever belongs to your earthly nature: sexual immorality, impurity, lust, evil desires and greed, which is idolatry. [6]Because of these, the wrath of God is coming. [7]You used to walk in these ways, in the life you once lived. [8]But now you must rid yourselves of all such things as these: anger, rage, malice, slander, and filthy language from your lips. [9]Do not lie to each other, since you have taken off your old self with its practices [10]and have put on the new self, which is being renewed in knowledge in the image of its Creator. [11]Here there is no Greek or Jew, circumcised or uncircumcised, barbarian, Scythian, slave or free, but Christ is all, and is in all. [12]Therefore, as God's chosen people, holy and dearly loved, clothe yourselves with compassion, kindness, humility, gentleness and patience. [13]Bear with each other and forgive whatever grievances you may have against one another. Forgive as the Lord forgave you. [14]And over all these virtues put on love, which binds them all together in perfect unity. [15]Let the peace of Christ rule in your hearts, since as members of one body you were called to peace.

THE TWO NATURES

And be thankful. [16]Let the word of Christ dwell in you richly as you teach and admonish one another with all wisdom, and as you sing psalms, hymns and spiritual songs with gratitude in your hearts to God. [17]And whatever you do, whether in word or deed, do it all in the name of the Lord Jesus, giving thanks to God the Father through him. Col. 3:1-17

To turn from the sinful nature, we must turn from those things that the Bible reveals to be representative of that nature – those things it reveals to be wrong – to be sin, along with all that is of that old sinful nature. We must turn from those things which God has warned us of in His Word not to do, because they are contrary to His divine nature. To participate then in the divine nature, we are to simply deny our flesh of those things that the Lord Jesus has commanded us not to do, and in turn, do those things that are of His nature and will that He has commanded us to do. These are all clearly laid out for us there in His Word.

Be imitators of God, therefore, as dearly loved children [2]and live a life of love, just as Christ loved us and gave himself up for us as a fragrant offering and sacrifice to God. [3]But among you there must not be even a hint of sexual immorality, or of any

THE TWO NATURES

kind of impurity, or of greed, because these are improper for God's holy people. ⁴Nor should there be obscenity, foolish talk or coarse joking, which are out of place, but rather thanksgiving. ⁵For of this you can be sure: No immoral, impure or greedy person – such a man is an idolater – has any inheritance in the kingdom of Christ and of God. ⁶Let no one deceive you with empty words, for because of such things God's wrath comes on those who are disobedient. ⁷Therefore do not be partners with them. ⁸For you were once darkness, but now you are light in the Lord. Live as children of light ⁹(for the fruit of the light consists in all goodness, righteousness and truth) ¹⁰and find out what pleases the Lord. ¹¹Have nothing to do with the fruitless deeds of darkness, but rather expose them. ¹²For it is shameful even to mention what the disobedient do in secret. ¹³But everything exposed by the light becomes visible, ¹⁴for it is light that makes everything visible. This is why it is said: "Wake up, O sleeper, rise from the dead, and Christ will shine on you." ¹⁵Be very careful, then, how you live – not as unwise but as wise, ¹⁶making the most of every opportunity, because the days are evil. Eph. 5:1-16

THE TWO NATURES

You should know that when you are in your sinful nature, there is misery, doubt, uncertainty, fear, selfish ambitions, dishonesty, lies, deceit, justification, jealousy, dissatisfaction, greed, envy, hate, resentment, selfishness, etc. Here, truth is never desired, and neither is there any sincere desire to be with the Lord Jesus. His Word and prayer are now boring to you, and you will want to get away from them as far as you can.

There is also lust, and all kinds of sexual desires, perversion and immorality in that old nature. The moment that you join up with your old nature, you will again be participating in all these things, for they are part of that nature.

> It is God's will that you should be sanctified: that you should avoid sexual immorality; [4]that each of you should learn to control his own body in a way that is holy and honorable, [5]not in passionate lust like the heathen, who do not know God; [6]and that in this matter no one should wrong his brother or take advantage of him. The Lord will punish men for all such sins, as we have already told you and warned you. [7]For God did not call us to be impure, but to live a holy life. [8]Therefore, he who rejects

THE TWO NATURES

this instruction does not reject man but God, who

gives you his Holy Spirit. 1 Thess. 4:3-8

As you can see, the Lord Jesus did not free us to then force us to remain in Him. In His own words, He tells us, **"If you remain in me, I will remain in you,"** meaning that we are free to choose which of the two natures we will live by. The nature we choose will then become our life, be it the divine or the sinful. This is why His Word tells us to participate, which is a voluntary choice and act of our will, because we want to. The beloved Lord Jesus tells us that whoever will, may come. This means if we do not want to, we will not participate in it.

If you are inclined to follow your desires, thoughts and feelings wherever they choose to lead, then you must understand that by so doing, you will be carried off into all kinds of sin. You must therefore deny yourself of those desires, thoughts and feelings that will lead you into sin, and so separate you from your God and Lord. For instance, you must take a firm stand against fantasies, denying yourself of their seductive power and the pleasures they bring, and see them for what they are – part of the old sinful nature, which is loaded down in sin. There, in the world of fantasy, you can go and be entertained as often as you want, but you must understand that these are pleasurism that are totally unacceptable to the Lord our God. Therefore they are sin against your blessed God and Lord.

> We want each of you to show this same diligence
> to the very end, in order to make your hope sure.
> [12]We do not want you to become lazy, but to imitate
> those who through faith and patience inherit what
> has been promised. Heb. 6:11-12

We must also choose to keep our minds active with the things of the Lord Jesus, especially those of His Word and nature, and not the things that the devil, through the old carnal nature, uses to tie us up so as to carry us off from our Lord.

> Therefore, prepare your minds for action; be self –
> controlled; set your hope fully on the grace to be
> given you when Jesus Christ is revealed. [14]As obe-
> dient children, do not conform to the evil desires
> you had when you lived in ignorance. [15]But just as
> he who called you is holy, so be holy in all you
> do; [16]for it is written: "Be holy, because I am holy."
> 1 Peter 1:13-16

THE TWO NATURES

We have all heard it said some time or another, that persons have fallen into sin. I pray that you will now understand that whenever you hear such comments, you know that what has actually happened is that such persons have turned from their Lord, back to their old carnal sinful nature, where they are then capable of committing all kinds of sins. If it were not for God's protecting grace, there would be no limit to the dimension of sins that would be committed at such times. Neither could anyone turn back from that nature to the Lord Jesus, without the guidance of the Holy Spirit, all as a result of the power that was manifested on Calvary's Cross that broke the chains asunder, and set the captives/prisoners free to choose by the grace given us there.

I do pray that all of us will understand that without God's grace, we would not be able to have one good thought, nor would we even be able to respond in a positive way to God's Word. Neither would we have a desire to remain in the Lord Jesus. None of this is possible, apart from His grace. Without the precious grace of the beloved Lord Jesus, all that we would be able to do is to sin. This is so because without God's grace continually being poured out on us, we would only be able to go in one direction, and that is, into further and deeper darkness/sin, being further corrupted, thereby putting a greater distance between us and our God and Lord, all because of the demonic nature by which we walk in that old life. This is our legacy from our ancestors, Adam and Eve.

So yes, even when we have returned to the old carnal sinful nature, and there sinning violently against our beloved God and Lord, even then He continues to protect us, by keeping us from sinning beyond the point of no return. Even there, His pursuit of us continues. If He does not protect us there, we would not be able to return to Him. Thanks to the beloved Lord Jesus that He never stops protecting us, for if He did, our hearts would be hardened beyond measure.

We must therefore stop to acknowledge, and so give thanks to this wonderful, loving, merciful, kind, generous, patient and forgiving God, to whom we belong. If He does not keep and protect us every step of the way, enabling us at each step, by His precious grace, to choose towards Him, all of us, I mean 100% of us, would never be able to choose against the old sinful nature, where the devil had us locked away in that dark dungeon of sin, so that we would never see the light of our Lord Jesus. Indeed, we would never be able to leave that old nature if He did not intervene to help us at every point to return to Him. This is called protecting grace – God's inestimable goodness. Still, many do not – this is called freewill.

THE TWO NATURES

Yes, as our beloved Lord Jesus said, "Apart from me you can do nothing." This is a precious truth, for indeed, we can do nothing, and I mean nothing spiritually, outside of the Lord Jesus. We can do nothing to move ourselves towards the Kingdom of God; neither can we do anything to move ourselves forward in the Kingdom of God. We can do none of this without our dearest and beloved Lord Jesus, and the continuous leading of His blessed Holy Spirit, imputing life in us continually – keeping us, inspiring us, teaching us, correcting us, helping us in all things, and leading us in His truth to straighten out all our crooked ways, which are many, and turning us from sin. This is called sanctification. "Thank You, beloved Lord Jesus."

> As is written in the book of the words of Isaiah the prophet: "A voice of one calling in the desert, 'Prepare the way for the Lord, make straight paths for him. [5]Every valley shall be filled in, every mountain and hill made low. The crooked roads shall become straight, the rough ways smooth. [6]And all mankind will see God's salvation.'" Luke 3:4-6

Even in our darkest moments, our beloved Lord is there, bringing circumstances to bear in our lives to move us to choose in agreement with Him, so that He can cleanse us and bring about changes

THE TWO NATURES

in our lives. He works in and through all the difficulties we experience to reveal His love for us, and so to persuade us to come home
to Him – our great God, Lord and Father.

> They preached the good news in that city and won
> a large number of disciples. Then they returned to
> Lystra, Iconium and Antioch, [22]strengthening the
> disciples and encouraging them to remain true to
> the faith. "We must go through many hardships to
> enter the kingdom of God," they said. Acts 14:21-22

No matter how tough things may seem, don't ever think or believe
that your God has abandoned you, for He never will. Therefore, if
you have not turned to Him, or if you have turned away from Him,
it is not His fault. Rather, it is because of your own selfishness and
stubbornness in continuing to pursue the desires and ways of the
old sinful nature, and for this you have abandoned your Lord and
His ways for your life. Yes, He has said that He will never leave
you or forsake you, but you are always free to walk away from Him
anytime you choose.

> You were running a good race. Who cut in on you
> and kept you from obeying the truth? [8]That kind of
> persuasion does not come from the one who calls

THE TWO NATURES

you. ⁹"A little yeast works through the whole batch
of dough." Gal. 5:7-9

Let us be absolutely certain of this: it will always be you who has
opposed, resisted, and in the end, rejected your God and Lord. You
will therefore go to hell because of your decision to live for the
satisfaction and pleasures of your soul and therefore your flesh,
following the ways of your carnal sinful nature, in full agreement
with the devil. In this regard, there will be no passing the buck;
there will be no excuses, no justification, no denial, or no standing
on your doctrinal beliefs to justify yourself. No! There will be no
saying that Abraham is your father, or that you are circumcised, or
you have paid your tithe, etc., to escape the truth of God's Word.
There will also be no escaping the consequences of your choices
through pretending that you did not understand, or that you are
innocent because you did not know what was happening.

None of these false reasons will help you to escape your responsibility for not holding firmly to God's Word so that you could continue living according to your sinful nature, while at the same time
justifying yourself through your many excuses. I pray that our God
and Lord will continue to have mercy on us, for: "Oh God, we have
practiced wickedness against You. May You come soon to cleanse
us – Your body/the church. Thank You beloved Lord Jesus."

THE TWO NATURES

"The Redeemer will come to Zion, to those in Jacob who repent of their sins," declares the LORD. Isa. 59:20

I must mention here, that some of the other things that frequently cause souls to turn away from participating in the divine nature, to again return to their old carnal nature (apart from those who have turned away because they have rejected the way of the Lord Jesus), are stress and emotional problems. When souls are deceived to strive to be the best among their brethren or their peers, doing their best to out-perform others and to be number one, the best, or the greatest, these are practices which cause stress and emotional problems. They spring from selfish ambitions, pushed by that chosen, prideful lifestyle of the sinful nature. In the process, these souls sin a lot against their Lord to achieve their goals.

When souls pursue such goals and it is then proven that they cannot succeed, at this point some withdraw and accuse the Lord Jesus for blessing others and not them. On the other hand, you will find that even those who have succeeded and have out-performed others, do not let up in their striving. Rather, they just keep on going, because now that they have achieved their goal of being number one in those areas, they have to hold on to that place, which causes them to be under even more stress. Accusations against God usually follow such pursuits and achievements, or the lack thereof, because of the pressure to sustain that place, or the disappointment of not achieving it. By agreeing with and embracing such accusations, these souls are driven deeper into sin, and further away from their Lord.

When they were first tempted by the enemy with the desire to be the best, it seemed so attractive to them at that time that they willingly ignored the warning of the blessed Holy Spirit to turn from such sins. In their pursuit to be the best, or to be number one among all, they repeatedly ignored the prompting of the Holy Spirit, and He simply allowed them to go and have their own way.

These souls did not turn from the Lord Jesus to join their old sinful nature at the time when these accusations against their Lord began. No! They first left their Lord, and ceased to participate in the divine nature (that is if they ever began) long before that. This happened at the point when they first decided in their hearts, in agreement with the enemy, to pursue their carnal desires and selfish ambitions and interests, along with being the best among their brethren. In that pursuit, they have simply forgotten who they really are in the Lord Jesus, or they simply elevated the natural over the spiritual, and so have permitted darkness to continue overtaking them, to the point where they no longer have any interest in the things of the Spirit.

But my righteous one will live by faith. And if
he shrinks back, I will not be pleased with him."
[39]But we are not of those who shrink back and are
destroyed, but of those who believe and are saved.
Heb. 10:38-39

Indeed, at this point, you could not offer the things of the Lord
Jesus to such souls, for these have now become totally unattractive
and undesirable to them. The blessed Holy Spirit has to now work
through circumstances to put stumbling blocks in their path, to turn
them away from such carnal pursuits; making them empty, unful-
filling and unattractive, in order for them to turn away from them.

So, while pouring out grace on these souls, the Holy Spirit enlightens
and encourages them to again turn back to their Lord and God, by
renouncing those carnal pursuits and putting their trust in the Lord
Jesus, so that they can again participate in the divine nature. If the
blessed Holy Spirit does not do this for us, it will not be done, for
there is no other who can help us in this way. "We give You thanks,
dearest, beloved Lord Jesus for Your patience and gentle long-suffering with us, and for Your guidance and forgiveness of our sins."

It is for freedom that Christ has set us free. Stand
firm, then, and do not let yourselves be burdened

THE TWO NATURES

again by a yoke of slavery. [2]Mark my words! I, Paul, tell you that if you let yourselves be circumcised, Christ will be of no value to you at all. [3]Again I declare to every man who lets himself be circumcised that he is obligated to obey the whole law. [4]You who are trying to be justified by law have been alienated from Christ; you have fallen away from grace. Gal. 5:1-4

As we can see, none of us, not even one of us, has any chance of ever walking with the Lord Jesus, without the wonderful God, Counselor and Teacher – the blessed Holy Spirit. He alone knows the spiritual path, and therefore, only He can lead us on that path. That is the only way we are able to again leave the prison of the old sinful nature, and escape the trap of the enemy.

As the Holy Spirit brings us light to get us to deal with those areas where we are having problems with sin, He will have us come face to face with those sins to get us to acknowledge that, "Yes Lord, I have committed those sins." With this acknowledgement, we are to repent of them so that we can be cleansed of them. If however, we have refused to acknowledge them and repent of them, we will not be cleansed. He will not force us to do anything we do not want to do.

THE TWO NATURES

The ongoing sanctifying work of the Holy Spirit requires our willing and willful participation. There must be truth, sincerity of heart and humility. Then, there must be acknowledgement, repentance and prayer for the cleansing needed in our souls in those particular areas. This is coming into agreement and conformity with our Lord about those things that need to be done in our lives.

This now brings us into agreement/conformity with our Lord over the cleansing to be done in us. This then allows the Holy Spirit to now begin His work to sanctify/cleanse us, and after, to apply death to those areas that are presently in focus or being dealt with. The Holy Spirit will not force us to be cleansed. This is why each time He is about to cleanse us in any area, He will first bring our sins before us to get us to face and acknowledge them. If we are willing and ready to turn from them, we will gladly acknowledge those sins, repent of them and then pray, asking the Lord Jesus to cleanse us of them. Why? Because we do not want to continue sinning against our Lord. Therefore, we will be earnest in prayer; we will continue to pray and trust the Holy Spirit to do His work of sanctifying/cleansing us.

We must remember that this is an ongoing work of sanctification, which the Holy Spirit wants to do in us even more than we want it done. However, He first seeks to bring us into conformity with His will through prayer, so that He can do His work in us without our murmuring and accusing Him. In other words, without any further resistance on our part. Such an attitude makes it clear that indeed, we are finished with sin. The blessed Holy Spirit will now do His work of cleansing/sanctifying us.

When the devil brings our sins to us, he brings them to keep us tied up, to provoke us, to get us to be preoccupied, to weigh us down with worry and guilt, to condemn us, and to make us feel bad. He also brings them to cause us anxiety, and to afflict us with fear and worry to get us to accuse God for the problems he, the devil, has afflicted us with. In this, he is very successful, because many souls fall prey to these tricks of his.

On the other hand, when the Holy Spirit brings your sins before you, He brings them for you to acknowledge them and repent so that He can cleanse you of them and lift you up, to free you from the ways of the sinful nature, the bondage of sin, and the trap of the enemy. This is to remove darkness from your life, and to bring truth, sincerity and humility; to give you light, enlightenment, further peace, contentment, rest and a closer walk with your Lord Jesus, etc. There is no comparison between the two. The Holy Spirit brings your sins, which He sees bogging you down, to free you from them because He loves you, and He wants you to be free so that you can be close to Him. The devil, on the other hand, brings them because he hates you, and he wants to condemn you and to keep you feeling bad about yourself. The devil also wants to get you to beat up on yourself, and to continue using you to accuse God for the problems he is weighing you down with.

I must also mention that many souls want a life with the Lord Jesus based on a false premise of who they are, and we cannot do that. To have a life in the Lord Jesus, you must choose to accept yourself for who you are internally and externally. In this way, you can stop hiding and escaping the reality of who you are, and come to the Lord Jesus as you are, and present to Him the problems that you are facing with sin. You can do this, instead of hiding from them as if you are not the person who has those problems, but rather someone else. You cannot do this and get help from the Lord Jesus, for that is dishonesty, it is falsehood, and so it is sin. You can only come to the Lord Jesus in truth and sincerity of heart.

As you come before the Lord Jesus, you must face the sins that are in your life, as they are. There must be no deceit, no lies, no false-hood, no pretense, and no escaping who you really are, and the sins you are hiding from, as you come before your Lord Jesus. In other words, do not pretend that you are a better person than you really are or were in your sinful nature, or that you are above doing the things you have done, or are still doing, as if you are without sin, or that you are above committing the sins that you have, and maybe still are committing, and now are hiding behind a mask of, "better than that" to give a different image of yourself, which is falsehood and deceit – sin.

The problem here is many souls hate everything about themselves. They are not satisfied to be who they are. They believe that God should have made them "perfect," and because they are not, they reject everything about themselves, while blaming the Lord for making them the way they are. These people are big in their own eyes and very important, and so nothing that is done for them is ever enough – it is never big enough or good enough. They are always deserving of more, and so not even Salvation is enough.

There are still those who hate themselves for all the bad things they have done. Therefore, they do not want to accept that they are the person who did those bad things/sin, and so they escape them within. They do not like the way they are, and so they escape that too, to enter into a state of denial, refusing to accept that this is who they really are, to instead live a false life of self-righteousness in a state of innocence, practicing self-goodness. This is the life that they choose to present before the Lord Jesus, but the Holy Spirit cannot sanctify a false life. So, if you come before the Lord Jesus in falsehood, He cannot help you. You need to come as you are – a real person with real sins, to be able to get real help.

Mental and physical tiredness are also reasons why some repossess their carnal nature. Once deceived by the enemy that they should not suffer these types of discomforts because they are Christians, they then embrace these beliefs and are overcome emotionally by them. They then immediately take control of their lives and turn their backs on their Lord; that is if they had ever sincerely yielded their life to the Lord Jesus in the first place. Others, when faced with such problems, will also take control of their lives, to again fall into distress, depression and self-pity. They then begin to treat themselves through different means; some by taking pills or by going to the doctor. I am not saying that they should not go to the doctor, or take medication. What I am saying is the first step taken should always be to look to the Lord Jesus for the solution to all their problems, for they might not be what they seem to be. Yet, many run ahead and seek professional help, or talk to their friends, or simply withdraw into a state of self-pity. There are even those who believe that they can reason their problems away, and so they try to, believing that they can overcome them in this way. But they never turn to the Lord Jesus and take their problems to Him, which should have been their first thought, choice and act.

THE TWO NATURES

What they need to do, is to turn to the Lord Jesus and surrender their problems and needs to Him, trusting Him and Him alone to deliver them, or provide for their needs, which at least should be the first step taken. Instead, they first run to all these other sources for help. These are signs of lack of trust in their Lord and God, because, when you trust the Lord Jesus, your first response is always to Him. However, when you have problems, and you do not first turn to your Lord, this is a sign that you do not trust Him to do those things that He wants to do for you, according to His will for your life.

I find that when our first response is to the Lord Jesus, believing that He has the answer to the problems, He will resolve them in one way or another. This is either by immediate deliverance, or by receiving from the Lord Jesus, understanding of what He is saying through these kinds of problems – if indeed He is saying anything. If we trust Him, and I stress, if we trust Him to do so, He will give us the understanding to resolve our problems in order for us to move on from there.

Most of the time, these kinds of problems are caused by the lack of sincerity in our walk with our Lord. They are also caused by out-right dissatisfaction and disobedience, lies and deceit, unforgive-ness, and at times outright rebellion and hostility towards our God and Lord, and even against family, friends, co-workers, etc. I have noticed time after time, that once individuals face and sincerely repent of these sins as the Lord reveals them, these afflictions disappear, as if they were never there.

When we are faced with afflictions of any kind, our first response should be, "My Lord, I am having this problem. Are You saying something to me through this? Am I in sin? If I am, please show me so that I can repent, for I choose not to hold sin in my heart against You or anyone else any longer. I also choose to yield this affliction to You, and I trust You to do with it as You see fit, according to Your perfect will for my life. Yet my Lord, You know what I would like in this matter, and that is to be free from this tension, stress, distress, depression, sickness and pain (or whatever you might be going through. What is important here is sincerity of heart with your Lord). So, I do ask You to deliver or to heal me of this affliction, according to Your will. If You are using it to reveal sin in my heart that otherwise I would not be willing to face, please reveal that too, if You so will, so that I can repent, and with Your help turn from them. Thy will be done, Oh Lord."

Of course, our request to be delivered or healed must be according to God's will. Why? Because many times, God cannot get our attention so that He can deal with areas of our lives that must be dealt with. Therefore, He permits afflictions in our lives simply to slow us down, or to stop us in our tracks to get our attention so that we will look to Him. This is why when we look to the Lord Jesus, and trust Him with the problems that we are experiencing, they are resolved. However, this is only after He has dealt with us in those areas that He needs to, for our continual cleansing/sanctification. Sometimes, we are simply being tested.

When we look to the Lord Jesus and trust Him with our problems, He is then able to open our eyes to other areas of our lives where there are problems, which He has been trying to resolve all along. When He opens our eyes to these problems, we are simply to be honest with our Lord about them, and yield them to Him in repentance, just as they are, without adding to them or subtracting from them. Most souls however, approach their Lord in dishonesty, and therefore receive no response or help from Him, for God does not respond to dishonesty or our demands.

We do know that when we are under any kind of affliction, the one thing we want more than anything else is to be free from it. At the same time however, we need to be conscious of who we are in the Lord Jesus, so that we will not choose to have our own way. Rather, we will choose to trust the Lord Jesus for Him to have His way in the matter. If He gives us the faith to trust Him in the matter for its resolution, without taking a pill or going to the doctor, then fine. But if He impresses us to take a pill or go to the doctor, we will obey Him and do so, because what we want above all else is, "Thy will be done Oh Lord." In this same way, we should handle all emotional problems and all other types of afflictions and sicknesses, and indeed all our problems and needs. However, if you are not in that place where your life is totally surrendered to the Lord Jesus, where your trust resides in Him and in Him alone, then maybe your first step needs to be to go to the doctor, as is now the case for most souls in the church today.

We need to be fully aware that our beloved Lord Jesus uses all of these things to test our hearts, for us to see how very little we are trusting Him with the life. It should therefore be obvious when these things come upon us, that maybe our faith is being tested. Yet, many tend not even to notice, much less to acknowledge and accept what these problems are revealing, and that is how little they trust the beloved Lord Jesus.

> Remain in me, and I will remain in you. No branch can bear fruit by itself; it must remain in the vine. Neither can you bear fruit unless you remain in me. John 15:4

THE TWO NATURES

To remain in the beloved Lord Jesus, you must believe in Him in such a way that you can transfer all your trust from yourself to Him. In so doing, you no longer look to yourself for the answers, responses or solutions to your life situations, circumstances or problems. Rather, you look to your Lord, and therefore put your trust in Him for the answer to them, and rest.

Remaining in Him simply means to put all your trust in the Lord Jesus on a continual basis, to the point where whenever or wherever a situation arises in your life, regardless of how good or how bad it may be, your first and continual response will be, "Lord Jesus, what must I do in or with this situation?" or better yet, "What do You want me to do, if anything, about what has happened or is happening? I trust it all into Your hands for Your solution to this problem."

I have mentioned that your first and continual response in every problem or situation that faces you, must be to your Lord Jesus. This simply means that even if your Lord were to direct you to go to the doctor or some other source for the solution to your problem, you are still to look to your Lord to continually guide those who will be helping you throughout the whole process. Indeed, this is the way you should live on a daily, ongoing basis with your Lord. However, be sure that your trust is placed in the Lord Jesus and in no other. This takes sincere faith from a sincere heart that truly believes.

> Trust in the LORD with all your heart and lean not on your own understanding; ⁶in all your ways acknowledge him, and he will make your paths straight. ⁷Do not be wise in your own eyes; fear the LORD and shun evil. ⁸This will bring health to your body and nourishment to your bones. Prov. 3:5-8

When frightened, many souls immediately take charge of their lives, trusting in themselves to handle the situation, rather than to instantly look to their Lord Jesus from their heart and say, "Lord Jesus, please help me. Please take charge of this situation." This should be the natural response of all God's children. The reason why this is not so, is because most are not faithful to their Lord. Therefore, when they are faced with difficulties, they do not then have the confidence that they would have had if they had been faithful to their Lord.

You see, faith, love, submission, obedience and faithfulness to our God and Lord results in a state of ever increasing confidence before Him. Unfaithfulness on the other hand, brings forth a state of uncertainty and timidity, which is demonstrated by a lack of confidence, trust and even shame before our God and Lord. In other words, being sincere and faithful in our walk with our God and Lord, results in a closeness and an ever deepening trust, and a continual bonding with Him, which translates into even greater faith and greater confidence and embrace of Him.

I will put it still another way: When you walk in sin, do not believe that you will have confidence before the Lord Jesus, for you will not. This is because sin separates you from God. Also, because you know that you have not been faithful to the Lord Jesus, this will then cause you to be uncertain of His reaction towards you. So, instead of approaching your Lord in confidence that is of sincere faith, you approach Him in uncertainty, in timidity and in fear, because you know in your heart that you have not been sincere, and therefore, you have been unfaithful to your Lord.

However, when you walk uprightly before your Lord Jesus in truth and sincerity, and in ever increasing faith and faithfulness, this leads to an ever increasing closeness with Him. This will then inspire you to be even more open before the Lord Jesus, where you will feel freer to trust Him more, and to carry out His will from the heart. This ongoing confidence will only increase as you grow in further trust and faithfulness, which leads to further closeness to your Lord.

Therefore, since we have a great high priest who
has gone through the heavens, Jesus the Son of God,
let us hold firmly to the faith we profess. [15]For we
do not have a high priest who is unable to sympa-
thize with our weaknesses, but we have one who
has been tempted in every way, just as we are – yet
was without sin. [16]Let us then approach the throne
of grace with confidence, so that we may receive
mercy and find grace to help us in our time of need.
Heb. 4:14-16

What all of this is saying, is if you are walking confidently before
your God and Lord, and for example, something negative suddenly
happens to you, your response will automatically be, "Lord Jesus,
help me." On the other hand, if you are not walking confidently
before your Lord, and something happens that causes you to be
afraid or otherwise, your response will always be to take control
of the life and the situation to protect yourself from that which is
before you, as if you are capable in yourself to manage the different
situations and circumstances that arise before you.

Such souls will forever be in and out of their Lord Jesus. Why?
Because when they face crisis situations, they do not trust the Lord
Jesus enough to allow Him to have control over their lives, as they

know that they are unfaithful to Him. In that state of deceit, they are led to believe that they can, or should handle these matters themselves, so as to achieve the outcome that they desire. In other words, they do not, and will not trust the Lord Jesus with the results that they desire to have in the particular situation, and for that matter, across their lives. They believe that if they do, they will not get that which they desire to have. Such souls cannot walk confidently with their Lord, for their trust is mostly in themselves.

I must note here that any and everything can, and will be used by the unfaithful as reasons to turn from their Lord. These could even be as simple as not being satisfied with something in their lives, which could be dissatisfaction with their food, clothes, car, home, job, neighbors, neighborhood, wife, husband, children, career, business, boss, salary, money, transportation or because of the things they hear or see on T.V.

Any and everything that you are not satisfied with, can, and will be used as a source of murmuration. If they are not acknowledged and repented of, within a short time the enemy will use them to lead you off and keep you separated from your Lord, and you may not even realize that this is happening.

When your priority is no longer your Lord, but rather these various issues with which you are caught up, and with which you are dissatisfied, the enemy will use them to lead you off. They will then have your full attention and interest, and so they will loom large before you, becoming your primary interest, and then to become your focus.

When such things happen, you will leave your Lord for your new interest, which is self-satisfaction, among other things. Nevertheless, at this point, if you respond to the Holy Spirit's wooing and humble your heart, acknowledge your sins in these areas and repent of them, you will find that you are back with your Lord. Therefore, those things that had held you bound and had you pursuing them, will no longer be your pursuit.

On the other hand, if you choose to follow those other interests and continue in your self-seeking ways, further darkness will overtake you. Your heart will also be further hardened, and all your pursuits will be as they were before – of the old nature, because that is where all such interests reside. Indeed, we can, on a continual basis, know where our interest lies through our beliefs, desires, the plans in our hearts, along with our thoughts. In other words, where our treasure is, there our hearts will be also.

THE TWO NATURES

In reality, the enemy can and will use the simplest thing that you can think of to carry you off. In other words, the enemy will use anything that you are interested in, or anything that holds your interest outside of the Lord Jesus, to tie you up and carry you off.

> See to it, brothers, that none of you has a sinful, unbelieving heart that turns away from the living God. [13]But encourage one another daily, as long as it is called Today, so that none of you may be hardened by sin's deceitfulness. [14]We have come to share in Christ if we hold firmly till the end the confidence we had at first. [15]As has just been said: "Today, if you hear his voice, do not harden your hearts as you did in the rebellion." Heb. 3:12-15

Another easy way that you will be carried off from your Lord is when you want something, and you are determined to have it, no matter what. You can be sure that from the very moment that you chose to agree with such demands, you have already been carried off from your Lord. This will now become your pursuit, because you did not first take into consideration God's will for your life.

> We have much to say about this, but it is hard to explain because you are slow to learn. [12]In fact,

THE TWO NATURES

though by this time you ought to be teachers, you
need someone to teach you the elementary truths
of God's word all over again. You need milk, not
solid food! [13]Anyone who lives on milk, being still
an infant, is not acquainted with the teaching about
righteousness. [14]But solid food is for the mature,
who by constant use have trained themselves to dis-
tinguish good from evil. Heb. 5:11-14

Over the years, I have watched Christian politicians as they cam-
paigned for office, who seemed to be okay when they first started.
However, as the campaign picked up steam and the opposing candidates appeared to be getting too close for comfort, or were overtaking them, you could easily see the immediate change that came
over the Christian candidates as they walked away from their Lord
and took control, believing that this would ensure that they would
come out the winner. By so doing, they stopped trusting the Lord
Jesus for the result, and therefore stopped participating in the divine
nature, turning to the old sinful nature for the solution, out of fear
that they might lose. However, what they did not realize is they
had turned away from their Lord to the enemy for the help that
they needed.

THE TWO NATURES

This is easy to discern, because as they turn away from their Lord, they become like their opponent; promising things that they know they cannot deliver. They begin to deceive, to lie, to justify, to defend and to cover themselves from all directions. Their tone and everything else about them is changed, and you can now easily see and hear the sinful nature in action, for he or she will now do anything to win.

> "Enter through the narrow gate. For wide is the gate and broad is the road that leads to destruction, and many enter through it. [14]But small is the gate and narrow the road that leads to life, and only a few find it. [15]"Watch out for false prophets. They come to you in sheep's clothing, but inwardly they are ferocious wolves. [16]By their fruit you will recognize them. Do people pick grapes from thornbushes, or figs from thistles? [17]Likewise every good tree bears good fruit, but a bad tree bears bad fruit. [18]A good tree cannot bear bad fruit, and a bad tree cannot bear good fruit. [19]Every tree that does not bear good fruit is cut down and thrown into the fire. [20]Thus, by their fruit you will recognize them. Matt. 7:13-20

THE TWO NATURES

With this turn of events, they now justify their positions or lack thereof, and make lots of false statements and promises, etc. In some cases, it seemed as if, in reality, there was no limit to where they would go to win. For when you turn from your Lord to gain a worldly position that really means nothing in the end, there may be no limit to where you will go to achieve this.

The real problem with all of this is it gives a very bad impression of Christians to the world, and leaves a bad taste in the mouth of those who listen to such persons. This turns them away from ever having an interest in the Lord Jesus. By such conduct, the candidates have served themselves, but they did not serve their Lord. Rather, they ran their campaign at the cost of Christ, especially when the church, in its state of blindness, jumps on the bandwagon to support them.

This is my recommendation to Christians who would, in the future, choose to seek political office: Please, if you cannot trust your Lord Jesus to give you that office, if that is His will for you, then don't seek it. Should you choose to seek any office against this advice, then please do not use the name of our Lord Jesus to do so. Do not proclaim that you are a Christian, to later go off in your own strength – sinful nature, demonstrating to the world that your choices and actions represent true Christianity, when they are far from it. When you do these things, you will only bring shame to

THE TWO NATURES

the body of Christ. By these carnal choices, flip-flops, etc., you will only bring reproach to the name of the Lord Jesus, and diminish Christianity in the eyes of those who listen to you, especially those of the world.

> "If, while we seek to be justified in Christ, it becomes evident that we ourselves are sinners, does that mean that Christ promotes sin? Absolutely not! [18]If I rebuild what I destroyed, I prove that I am a law-breaker. Gal. 2:17-18

You see, the Christian candidate should have approached his or her candidacy with the full knowledge that this was God's will for him or her, if in fact that was so. Then, if it was God's will, when the other candidate seemed to be overtaking them, their attitude would have been, "Thy will be done Lord Jesus. If it is Your will for me to enter that office, I will enter it, and if it is not, I won't, and nothing can change that." With such belief, attitude and faith in their Lord Jesus, they could easily rest and continue in Him, being at peace, regardless of what was going on, or the future outcome of the election, because it is God's will and only God's will they want, and not their own. This is a life of faith in Christ Jesus our Lord.

THE TWO NATURES

But no! What usually happens is the candidate becomes afraid of losing, and because they so desperately want the office they are seeking, regardless of whether or not it is God's will for them, they no longer trust the Lord Jesus for His will to be done, and so to direct and control things for them. Instead, they take control, and by doing so they are back in their old carnal nature, looking to themself and to others around them for the direction they are to take to secure their victory. From there on, it is easy to see the change which comes over that candidate. They now become just as the other – doing whatever it takes to win.

In reality, by returning to their carnal nature, they have now become like the other candidate; both functioning in their carnal natures, with their priority being to win at all cost. They will now lie, deceive and promise all kinds of things that they know they cannot deliver, for their first priority is no longer their life in the Spirit with the Lord Jesus. They therefore give no consideration to God's Word or will, or for that matter, participating in the divine nature – none whatsoever.

At this point, the things of the Spirit seem even foolish to them. What is now important and of greater value to them is their pursuit to win the election. If they win, they might repent at that time and turn back to the Lord Jesus, and then again, they might not. All this depends on how much they are caught up with the office they are seeking to hold.

For many, even after they have gained the office they sought, they continue in their old sinful nature, doing the things they do according to that same old fallen nature. On the other hand, if they lose, they might either acknowledge their sins and repent, or they might accuse the Lord Jesus for not giving them victory. If their choice is the latter, they then enter into a deeper state of rebellion, and out-rightly reject the Lord Jesus and His ways. These, and so much more, happen on a daily basis in the church.

> My dear children, for whom I am again in the pains
> of childbirth until Christ is formed in you, [20]how I
> wish I could be with you now and change my tone,
> because I am perplexed about you! Gal. 4:19-20

In these and other ways, we have hurt the heart of our Father in heaven and the Lord Jesus profoundly and continually over these millenniums. "Thank You beloved Lord Jesus, for Your great mercy and patience with us."

> Everyone who sins breaks the law; in fact, sin is
> lawlessness. [5]But you know that he appeared so that

he might take away our sins. And in him is no sin. ⁶No one who lives in him keeps on sinning. No one who continues to sin has either seen him or known him. ⁷Dear children, do not let anyone lead you astray. He who does what is right is righteous, just as he is righteous. ⁸He who does what is sinful is of the devil, because the devil has been sinning from the beginning. The reason the Son of God appeared was to destroy the devil's work. ⁹No one who is born of God will continue to sin, because God's seed remains in him; he cannot go on sinning, because he has been born of God. ¹⁰This is how we know who the children of God are and who the children of the devil are: Anyone who does not do what is right is not a child of God; nor is anyone who does not love his brother. 1 John 3:4-10

Remember, these writings have declared that it is only as you have remained believing, and therefore trusting in the Lord Jesus, that you are able to remain in Him. As long as you remain in the Lord Jesus, you will not sin deliberately against Him. Indeed, you will not, because when you are in Him, your desires are towards Him, but this does not mean that you will not sin, but it will not be deliberate – at least we pray so. When you are in the Lord Jesus,

THE TWO NATURES

your desire is for godliness – to walk uprightly in His ways, so that you will not sin deliberately against Him. This is the way it is supposed to be.

However, the moment that you pick up the issues of your life, instead of trusting them to the beloved Lord Jesus, you are back in your old sinful nature. By picking up those old issues, which should have been left laid down with your Lord, and remained so, your desires now will only be to carry them and work them out all by yourself. By so doing, you have made the statement that you do not trust the Lord Jesus.

It says in verse 6 of 1 John Chapter 3; **"No one who lives in him keeps on sinning. No one who continues to sin has either seen him or known him."** This speaks directly to when one would choose to go back into their carnal nature. In that nature there is no embracing of God, because there is no faith there. Therefore, in that nature, one cannot know God in a way so as to put their trust in Him. Remember, the demons also believe that there is one God, but not in the way that we do, and that knowledge causes them to shudder.

> You believe that there is one God. Good! Even the
> demons believe that – and shudder. James 2:19

THE TWO NATURES

Back in 1 John Chapter 3, verse 7, it says, **"Dear children, do not let anyone lead you astray. He who does what is right is righteous, just as he is righteous."** This speaks of the soul who is remaining in the Lord Jesus, and who is living according to the divine nature by participating in it.

Verse 8 states, **"He who does what is sinful is of the devil, because the devil has been sinning from the beginning. The reason the Son of God appeared was to destroy the devil's work."** This Scripture is also dealing with the soul, since the Scriptures are written to believers. This speaks to the fact that when you choose to leave the Lord Jesus to again join your old sinful nature, you are once again in subjection and obedience to the devil there, for he is the lord of that nature. That is the precise reason why when you are in that nature the heart is so rebellious, and you are then able to commit such outrageous acts against your God and Lord. This is the reality, although you were in the Lord Jesus just a short while before.

This verse also speaks to us of the origination of sin, which was planned by the devil to deceive Adam and Eve. It also speaks to the continuation of sin, which is also maintained and pushed by the same devil, through the sinful nature, and therefore in and through us when we are in agreement with him and what he is doing.

THE TWO NATURES

Verse 9 states, **"No one who is born of God will continue to sin, because God's seed remains in him; he cannot go on sinning, because he has been born of God."** This verse speaks to our spirit that is born of God (John Chapter 1, verses 12 to 13) and is sealed with the Holy Spirit (Ephesians Chapter 1, verses 13 to 14). I need not go any further with this theme here, since I have already written about it extensively in the book, "From Darkness to His Marvelous Light."

We can see clearly now that the new man who sincerely believes God's Word, who puts his trust in Him, and is fully participating in the divine nature, does not want to sin. This is so because when you are participating in the new nature, your desires are towards the Lord Jesus, and your full intention is to take on His nature of love, truth, purity, holiness, righteousness, etc. In fact, when you are walking according to the divine nature, you cannot have enough of the Lord Jesus. Your beliefs and trust are sincere towards Him, because this is what you want above everything else. Therefore, there is love and faith in your heart to continue yielding up your all to Him. This is what you want, and this is what you do.

When you are participating in the divine nature, your desires are to be submissive, obedient and faithful to the Lord Jesus. There is also genuine love for Him in your heart, and there is hope to be home with Him in eternity. This is your desire and hope. These are all there as you participate in His divine nature, as laid out in His Word.

These are all precious gifts from your heavenly Father and Lord, which you do not have to work up or earn. They are given to those who will choose to hold to His Word and remain in Him, participating in the divine nature, and they all come through knowledge of our Lord, through His Word. This inspires you to continue in the Lord Jesus, loving Him and drawing closer and closer to Him each day. "Thank You, Lord Jesus."

Yes, these precious promises and gifts are all there waiting for us in His Word when we choose to believe, trust and to be satisfied in the Lord Jesus, remaining faithful to Him, and participating in the divine nature. However, the moment you choose to join your old sinful nature, they are all gone, as if they were never there. All of a sudden, you have become a stranger to that which you had loved and wanted a short while ago.

> It is for freedom that Christ has set us free. Stand firm, then, and do not let yourselves be burdened again by a yoke of slavery. [2]Mark my words! I, Paul, tell you that if you let yourselves be circumcised, Christ will be of no value to you at all. [3]Again I

THE TWO NATURES

> declare to every man who lets himself be circum-
> cised that he is obligated to obey the whole law.
> [4]You who are trying to be justified by law have been
> alienated from Christ; you have fallen away from
> grace. [5]But by faith we eagerly await through the
> Spirit the righteousness for which we hope. [6]For
> in Christ Jesus neither circumcision nor uncircum-
> cision has any value. The only thing that counts
> is faith expressing itself through love. [7]You were
> running a good race. Who cut in on you and kept
> you from obeying the truth? [8]That kind of persua-
> sion does not come from the one who calls you.
> [9]"A little yeast works through the whole batch of
> dough." Gal. 5:1-9

I believe this Scripture sums up perfectly what I have been saying.
Here we see that if they let themselves be circumcised, this was
to again join the old nature, because doing so was contrary to the
new way of grace, and therefore contrary to remaining in Christ.
This meant having their own way, doing their own thing, which is
the way of the old man and the devil.

When you have tried to be justified by anything other than by faith
in Christ, indeed you have fallen from grace and are alienated from

Christ. That is why Paul says in verse 1 of Galatians Chapter 5, **"It is for freedom that Christ has set us free. Stand firm, then, and do not let yourselves be burdened again by a yoke of slavery."** In other words, do not give room to the old ways of believing, thinking and acting by giving in to the sinful nature and its ways. Rather, stand firm in the Word of the Lord Jesus Christ, holding to it, walking according to it; while at the same time remain participating in the divine nature. In so doing, you will remain in your Lord, being content in Him and in what He offers, rather than believing the lie of the devil through the old man – the sinful nature, to again be carried off by him.

> Formerly, when you did not know God, you were slaves to those who by nature are not gods. [9]But now that you know God – or rather are known by God – how is it that you are turning back to those weak and miserable principles? Do you wish to be enslaved by them all over again? [10]You are observing special days and months and seasons and years! [11]I fear for you, that somehow I have wasted my efforts on you. Gal. 4:8-11

What Paul is saying here, is those who are continually turning from participating in the divine nature to indulge in the old sinful nature, will have problems embracing the new nature to be theirs, and so become accustomed to walking in it. Maybe it is better said, that by continually denying and abandoning a life in Christ, such persons will never become accustomed to walking in the new ways of the Spirit, participating in the divine nature that is laid out in God's Word.

> You, my brothers, were called to be free. But do not use your freedom to indulge the sinful nature; rather, serve one another in love. [14]The entire law is summed up in a single command: "Love your neighbor as yourself." [15]If you keep on biting and devouring each other, watch out or you will be destroyed by each other. [16]So I say, live by the Spirit, and you will not gratify the desires of the sinful nature. [17]For the sinful nature desires what is contrary to the Spirit, and the Spirit what is contrary to the sinful nature. They are in conflict with each other, so that you do not do what you want. [18]But if you are led by the Spirit, you are not under law. [19]The acts of the sinful nature are obvious: sexual immorality, impurity and debauchery; [20]idolatry and witchcraft; hatred, discord, jealousy, fits of rage, selfish ambition, dissensions, factions [21]and

envy; drunkenness, orgies, and the like. I warn you, as I did before, that those who live like this will not inherit the kingdom of God. ²²But the fruit of the Spirit is love, joy, peace, patience, kindness, goodness, faithfulness, ²³gentleness and self-control. Against such things there is no law. ²⁴Those who belong to Christ Jesus have crucified the sinful nature with its passions and desires. ²⁵Since we live by the Spirit, let us keep in step with the Spirit. ²⁶Let us not become conceited, provoking and envying each other. Gal. 5:13-26

THE WAYS OF THE SINFUL NATURE

The devil is the mind and force behind the sinful nature, who causes the bombardment of negative thoughts/sin to fill the mind, which at times leads the soul off into every selfish desire, ambition, greed, immorality, sensual pleasure and craving that are contrary to the knowledge of God. This is to feed its enormous appetite as manifested through the flesh, while always continuing its pursuit for more.

Through these pursuits, the soul and therefore the flesh/body is held prisoner to all the evil selfish beliefs, desires, reasoning, plans, thoughts, choices and actions that are imposed upon it by the deceit of the enemy, through the sinful nature. This deceit is very captivating. Once you receive this continuous bombardment of evil and submit to it, many fall under it and succumb to its seduction. This evil keeps feeding on itself and therefore multiplies. In the process, you will embrace every other evil that comes your way, and will be in full agreement with it to further satisfy your lust and selfish greed.

This kind of seduction leads to further indulgence in sin, which also feeds on itself. Our sole purpose now is to satisfy self. This is what we as human beings, have sunk to under the dominion of the demonic sinful nature, through the flesh.

When we allow the sinful nature to have its own way in anything, and not oppose it and deny ourselves as the Lord Jesus instructs us to do, it will continue subjecting the soul and therefore the flesh even more, holding them prisoner to a life of sin to continue opposing God and rejecting His Word as foolishness – all by our agreement and choice. This is allowed to happen because we have not taken seriously our life in Christ, and so to deny ourselves. This means denying the sinful nature from going its own way and having its way. However, because we do not, it will continue to have its own way.

THE TWO NATURES

We therefore conclude that the way of the sinful nature is one of only following after its own will, its own instinct and its own interests in order to have its own way in everything, serving its master the devil, and carrying out his will through our soul/body.

The sinful nature demands to have the right to fulfill its own filthy, selfish and self-seeking ways, desires, interests and agenda, without any interference or intervention from God or from man. The sinful nature demands to always have the right to fill the heart and mind of man with all the filthy, evil and wicked thoughts, impressions, fantasies, impulses, desires, reasoning, rights and demands it chooses. It also demands the right and freedom to indulge in, and to enjoy without hindrance, its sexual cravings and even immorality, to its heart's desire and content.

The sinful nature, which is of the devil, demands the right to lie, walk in deceit, to deceive others and to live a dishonest life so that it can always justify itself, and therefore be innocent. It wants to be seen as innocent in its own eyes and before others. It cherishes believing itself to be innocent, so that it can continue believing that it is good, and therefore has no need for the Lord Jesus. So then, lies, deceit, murder, theft, assault, slander, bearing false witness, adultery, fornication, jealousy, envy, robbery, offending others (but it must not be offended), etc., are its way of life.

THE TWO NATURES

The sinful nature judges others hypocritically. It judges them falsely and brings false accusations against them. It is also suspicious of others. It demands to influence those around it to follow in its ways. It demands the right to go its own selfish way and to do its own thing, following its greed, cravings and selfish ambitions. It believes that it deserves to have all that it desires, and indeed, when it does not, it accuses the very God who it does not want to acknowledge otherwise.

Yes, the sinful nature demands the right to possess all it believes that it should have, and when it cannot, it murmurs. It lives in a state of discontent and dissatisfaction, and no matter how much it has, it is never satisfied. It is always lying on God and judging Him falsely and harshly, while accusing Him seems to be its past time, for it takes pleasure in doing so.

The sinful nature is a God-hater. Why? Because the devil hates God. It does not believe God, nor will it trust Him – indeed it cannot. Therefore, unbelief, lies, deceit and arrogance are its motto. It afflicts anxiety, fear and doubt on the mind. Uncertainty, misery, worry, torment, hiding and covering itself from its Creator, and therefore from the light and the truth, mark its ways. These are the ways of its master, and so it afflicts those things on the mind and body to control it.

The sinful nature only seeks after its own; it is uncaring, unloving and uninterested in others. Arguments and fights are its ways, and despite all this, it continues to believe the deceit that it is good. It therefore demands the right to feel good, to be comfortable, to have an easy life, etc., and when it does not, it blames God for its misery. It is unrepentant, hateful, resentful, a hater of truth, insincere, dishonest, disloyal, unfaithful, unrighteous, unholy, malicious, etc. This is who it is, for this is who its master is.

When coming to Christ, this is the life we are to bring and surrender to the Lord Jesus, and not the false, innocent one that does not exist, as so many are doing. This very morning (because of the conversation), I asked a Christian who came by if they were ever a sinner. The answer was, "I don't remember, sir." This person does not believe that they have sinned, or that they are a sinner saved by grace. This is also the attitude of part of the church.

These and much more are the ways of the sinful nature, and they are prevalent in the church.

> Therefore, rid yourselves of all malice and all deceit,
> hypocrisy, envy, and slander of every kind. ²Like
> newborn babies, crave pure spiritual milk, so that by
> it you may grow up in your salvation, 1 Peter 2:1-2

THE TWO NATURES

Put to death, therefore, whatever belongs to your earthly nature: sexual immorality, impurity, lust, evil desires and greed, which is idolatry. [6]Because of these, the wrath of God is coming. [7]You used to walk in these ways, in the life you once lived. [8]But now you must rid yourselves of all such things as these: anger, rage, malice, slander, and filthy language from your lips. [9]Do not lie to each other, since you have taken off your old self with its practices [10]and have put on the new self, which is being renewed in knowledge in the image of its Creator. Col. 3:5-10

…And so he condemned sin in sinful man, [4]in order that the righteous requirements of the law might be fully met in us, who do not live according to the sinful nature but according to the Spirit. [5]Those who live according to the sinful nature have their minds set on what that nature desires; but those who live in accordance with the Spirit have their minds set on what the Spirit desires. Rom. 8:3b-5

THE TWO NATURES

THE WAYS OF THE DIVINE NATURE

The ways of the divine nature are the ways of God. They are in line with the narrow way spoken of by the beloved Lord Jesus in the Scriptures. They are the ways of inestimable goodness, love, truth, righteousness, holiness, purity, justice, forgiveness, giving; lifting up the poor and needy, the downcast, the outcast, the helpless; feeding the hungry, looking after the sick, etc. For us, they are also the way of mercy and grace, where faith becomes a way of life, and where God is believed, trusted, looked to and depended on continually for all that we believe, desire, think, choose, say and do. In the divine nature, there is hope always, because the knowledge of God's Word/His truth, is believed and is exalted highly in the heart, and is always there before us to guide us, and it is held to dearly. As a consequence, there is love for God and love for our fellowmen.

In the ways of the divine nature there is obedience, as revealed in the Lord Jesus; first of all to God and His Word, and therefore to all authority. This obedience leads to the acknowledgement of a need to submit ourselves from the heart to our Lord Jesus, and then submit to all other authority as required, and then to one another, in line with God's Word.

The way of the divine nature is denying ourselves of all that is of the old way of life – the ways of the sinful nature and therefore the flesh, no longer obeying its beliefs, desires, thoughts, its impressions and its impulses to carry out or to pursue that which feels good, or it feels it should do or have. The divine nature is the way of sincerity, honesty and humility. It is a surrendered life that is led by the Lord Jesus. Its ways are upright, pure and unselfish, because this is the way of its Lord, and in it, you seek to do the things you do, to please and honor your Lord and God.

The attitude of the divine nature is one of thankfulness, satisfaction, contentment, gratitude and fulfillment, as you walk before your Lord with a heart full of appreciation, thanksgiving and worship, and with lips uttering truth and praise to our God and Lord, from a pure, grateful and sincere heart.

When you walk according to the divine nature, you do not talk back or reason with your God and Lord. Rather, you choose to bow continually, saying yes to Him, because you are submissive, obedient and loyal to your Lord Jesus, while being faithful and trustworthy in your walk before Him. You therefore give yourself first to your Lord, and then to others, according to the will of the Lord Jesus. The way of the divine nature therefore, is love, self-denial and serving others, without emphasizing it. Paul says, **"sorrowful, yet**

always rejoicing; poor, yet making many rich; having nothing, and yet possessing everything." (2 Cor. 6:10)

The way of the divine nature is also the way of being satisfied in your Lord, and being contented in His ways and with His provisions for your life, along with your circumstances – in the difficulties, the suffering, the sickness, the afflictions, the temptations, and in the death of loved ones, etc. It is always being grateful and thankful to your blessed Father for who He is – the great God Almighty and Lord, Giver of life and everything else. Here, you will always remember with great delight and satisfaction, the great blessings the beloved Lord Jesus has blessed us with, beginning with Himself, His Sacrificial Atonement on Calvary's Cross – giving His precious life to redeem ours, and to give us life and life eternal. He has blessed us with the privilege of being the children of God. Then, He further invites us to participate in His divine nature, with the intent and desire for us to be holy as He is holy, according to the light we have. "Thank You dearly beloved Lord Jesus."

The way of the divine nature is one of truth, faith, trust, rest and peace. We are blessed with these blessed virtues because everything that we had claimed to be ours is now laid down and surrendered to our Lord and God. And because all is now the Lord's, all the weight, pressure, fears, anxiety and worries are gone with them, for He took them. We are no longer under these anxieties, weights and pressures, for we are no longer carrying the life. Therefore, the soul is now freed from what it possessed, and therefore free from being possessed by them, along with the desire to have and to possess more. Everything is now the Lord's, for the life has been surrendered in its totality to Him, and we now walk in His peace.

This is why the way of the divine nature carries with it internal liberty, and there is therefore a lightness about it. This is so because there is always openness in every area of that life, as you walk before your God and Lord. You have nothing covered, nothing hidden and nothing to hide. There are no secret sins to protect, for all has been opened before the Lord Jesus, and surrendered to Him through acknowledgement and repentance, and a willful choice of the heart to be transparent about your life before the Lord Jesus continually, and to keep it transparent. When you live this way, there is no guilt or condemnation. There are no worries, no anxiety, no weight and no fears. You no longer have to be hiding, justifying or defending yourself, for there is no longer anything to defend, because now, the light of the Lord Jesus has entered your life and is shining bright within your heart.

To be able to walk consistently in the divine nature, it is necessary to walk openly, truthfully, sincerely and honestly before your

Lord, with yourself, and with your fellow man; always ready to acknowledge your sins and quick to repent of them. This is all a part of the surrendered, submissive life, where obedience that is of faith is uttermost. These are some of the ways of the divine nature.

The way of the divine nature is led by faith and knowledge – knowledge of God's truth/His Word, standing firmly on it and holding firmly to it. It is the way of truth, so that truth will always be in your heart, and at the same time on your lips to honor your Lord, regardless of the consequences.

In the way of the divine nature, it does not matter whether or not you feel good in the flesh; whether the life in the natural is hard or easy; whether it is good or bad, comfortable or uncomfortable; whether or not there is sickness or health, or problems with family, friends, co-workers, etc. It also does not matter whether the work is hard or easy; whether you are being persecuted, ridiculed, rejected, mocked, laughed at or not; whether or not you are alone in some far off land, facing all kinds of difficulties, or whether there is something being gained or lost. It does not matter whether or not the flesh feels that it wants to have its own way; whether or not it feels it does not have the things it wants or even needs; whether or not it feels that it should have more liberty and therefore more rights;

whether or not it feels that it should have more money and possessions; whether or not it is under constant afflictions, etc.

In the divine nature these feelings must not, and cannot be the
deciding factor by which your decisions are made and carried out,
be they positive or negative. No, they cannot be, because if the negative things mentioned are what govern your decisions and actions,
then you must understand that the enemy, through the sinful nature,
is still in charge of your life, and not the Lord Jesus.

In the divine nature, the decisions that are made and the acts that
follow them must be based on the clear knowledge of God's Word,
according to His perfect will and timing for us in those moments.
Therefore, the motivation and desire of the heart is to do the things
that are to be done, in a way that is in line with God's Word, and
therefore His will, so that it will be pleasing in the sight of our God
and Lord. These are some of the ways of the divine nature, and
therefore the ways of our lives.

However, the negative things that were mentioned previously, can
and indeed will come to tempt you and seduce you to take them.
When this happens, you are to acknowledge them to be what they
are – they are of the sinful nature and are sin. Therefore, since you
no longer live according to that old nature, you are to proclaim it,

along with proclaiming who you now are, which is a born-again child of God, who now lives according to God's divine nature, and only according to His divine nature. Proclaim it and emphasize it, and if you truly believe, the temptation will go, and at times immediately. Always look to your Lord and ask Him for the help you need in all situations. Hold firmly to what He did for you on Calvary's Cross, believing it to be the basis and reality of your life and liberty, and for everything else that you believe and do in the Lord Jesus. For without it, there would be no basis for anything that we believe, hold to, or do.

To be able to live faithfully with your Lord according to the new nature, you must be totally finished with the old way of life – the old sinful nature, and so be willing to deny your flesh. If you are not finished with it, it goes without saying that you will not deny it. Rather, you will always indulge it and go back there to visit, as is the reality in so many cases.

Many have lived out what they call their entire "Christian" lives in the old nature. One thing that is very clear, is death is promised to everyone who lives according to the sinful nature.

> Do not be deceived: God cannot be mocked. A man
> reaps what he sows. [8]The one who sows to please

THE TWO NATURES

his sinful nature, from that nature will reap destruc-

tion; the one who sows to please the Spirit, from

the Spirit will reap eternal life. ⁹Let us not become

weary in doing good, for at the proper time we will

reap a harvest if we do not give up. Gal. 6:7-9

God in His great mercy has called us to Himself, and poured out grace on us to enable us to choose good over evil and right instead of wrong. Therefore, I do not see that we can have any excuses to continue escaping the Lord Jesus, to again join our old nature to practice evil. We need to look hard at our choices to be sure where they will lead us, whether to life eternal with our God, Lord and Father in heaven, or to death and destruction in hell, where we will have no one to blame but ourselves.

See, I am setting before you today a blessing and

a curse – ²⁷the blessing if you obey the commands

of the LORD your God that I am giving you today;

²⁸the curse if you disobey the commands of the

LORD your God and turn from the way that I com-

mand you today by following other gods, which you

have not known. Deut. 11:26-28

THE TWO NATURES

I know of people who turn from their Lord because of how they see, judge and perceive people's actions and responses towards them. I also know of people who even turn from the Lord Jesus because of what they believe people think or say about them. The devil uses all this and more to tie up Christians in their old sinful nature, worrying about what others think about them, or how they see them. At times, these things seem so real to them that they are unable to see or to go beyond them. This is why it is so wise to be sure of your true position in the Lord Jesus, so that you remain there in Him, and not give room to the enemy by following the desires and thoughts he brings your way.

You can also leave your Lord and the divine nature by getting caught up in being overly joyful, happy and glad carnally, because things have been going very well for you. Self and its carnal happiness can become your focus, and in this, you forget what should really be important to you. Also, once you have turned back to your sinful carnal nature, all those things that made you so pleased and happy while you were in your Lord Jesus, participating in the divine nature, now become a burden to you and so you hide from them.

> Once you were alienated from God and were ene-
> mies in your minds because of your evil behavior.

THE TWO NATURES

²²But now he has reconciled you by Christ's physical body through death to present you holy in his
sight, without blemish and free from accusation –
²³if you continue in your faith, established and firm,
not moved from the hope held out in the gospel.
This is the gospel that you heard and that has been
proclaimed to every creature under heaven, and of
which I, Paul, have become a servant. Col. 1:21-23

As you read the Scriptures, one thing will become very clear to you,
and that is the old sinful nature never changes. Therefore, every
time that you turn back to the old sinful nature, you will find there
the same desires, the same sinning against God. The same old
sinful desires, thoughts and pursuits will be there waiting for you.

So I tell you this, and insist on it in the Lord, that
you must no longer live as the Gentiles do, in the
futility of their thinking. ¹⁸They are darkened in
their understanding and separated from the life of
God because of the ignorance that is in them due to
the hardening of their hearts. ¹⁹Having lost all sensitivity, they have given themselves over to sensuality so as to indulge in every kind of impurity, with
a continual lust for more. ²⁰You, however, did not

come to know Christ that way. [21]Surely you heard of him and were taught in him in accordance with the truth that is in Jesus. [22]You were taught, with regard to your former way of life, to put off your old self, which is being corrupted by its deceitful desires; [23]to be made new in the attitude of your minds; [24]and to put on the new self, created to be like God in true righteousness and holiness. [25]Therefore each of you must put off falsehood and speak truthfully to his neighbor, for we are all members of one body. [26]"In your anger do not sin": Do not let the sun go down while you are still angry, [27]and do not give the devil a foothold. [28]He who has been stealing must steal no longer, but must work, doing something useful with his own hands, that he may have something to share with those in need. [29]Do not let any unwholesome talk come out of your mouths, but only what is helpful for building others up according to their needs, that it may benefit those who listen. [30]And do not grieve the Holy Spirit of God, with whom you were sealed for the day of redemption. [31]Get rid of all bitterness, rage and anger, brawling and slander, along with every form of malice. [32]Be kind and

THE TWO NATURES

> compassionate to one another, forgiving each other,
>
> just as in Christ God forgave you. Eph. 4:17-32

The old nature cannot change. It will remain the same forever – being God's enemy, and unless the Holy Spirit is allowed to apply death to it through the sanctifying process, it will continue to reign over the soul and therefore the flesh, to keep it in sin against God. This is why you will hear Christians say at times that they are not changing, though they want to be changed. According to them, they desire to be changed, but what really is the truth, because their choices speak loudly to the contrary.

We can only be changed when we sincerely want to be changed. Then and only then, will we make the tough decision by faith that is necessary against our flesh and the ways of the world, to sincerely submit our lives in obedience to our Lord Jesus. The decision to be made is to be finished with sin, and therefore with the ways of the sinful nature, which are manifested through the flesh. If this is so, we are to be sure to submit ourselves according to God's Word, to the Holy Spirit for His sanctifying work to begin in us so that we can be cleansed of all that contaminates us. In the process, we are then to willfully choose to deny our flesh of its old ways, so as to remain faithfully in our Lord Jesus, embracing the divine nature by participating in it and in it alone. We must want it, we must pray for it, and therefore with appreciation and thanksgiving, choose to be satisfied and to be contented there forever. When this happens, there will be permanent changes in that life and continual changes from then on.

> But we ought always to thank God for you, brothers loved by the Lord, because from the beginning God chose you to be saved through the sanctifying work of the Spirit and through belief in the truth. [14]He called you to this through our gospel, that you might share in the glory of our Lord Jesus Christ. [15]So then, brothers, stand firm and hold to the teachings we passed on to you, whether by word of mouth or by letter. 2 Thess. 2:13-15

> It is God's will that you should be sanctified: that you should avoid sexual immorality; [4]that each of you should learn to control his own body in a way that is holy and honorable, [5]not in passionate lust like the heathen, who do not know God; [6]and that in this matter no one should wrong his brother or take advantage of him. The Lord will punish men for all such sins, as we have already told you and warned you. [7]For God did not call us to be impure,

THE TWO NATURES

but to live a holy life. [8]Therefore, he who rejects this instruction does not reject man but God, who gives you his Holy Spirit. 1 Thess. 4:3-8

May God himself, the God of peace, sanctify you through and through. May your whole spirit, soul and body be kept blameless at the coming of our Lord Jesus Christ. [24]The one who calls you is faithful and he will do it. 1 Thess. 5:23-24

"Now I commit you to God and to the word of his grace, which can build you up and give you an inheritance among all those who are sanctified. Acts 20:32

who have been chosen according to the foreknowledge of God the Father, through the sanctifying work of the Spirit, for obedience to Jesus Christ and sprinkling by his blood: Grace and peace be yours in abundance. 1 Peter 1:2

Therefore, get rid of all moral filth and the evil that is so prevalent and humbly accept the word planted in you, which can save you. James 1:21

THE TWO NATURES

Sanctify them by the truth; your word is truth. John 17:17

For the grace of God that brings salvation has appeared to all men. [12]It teaches us to say "No" to ungodliness and worldly passions, and to live self–controlled, upright and godly lives in this present age, [13]while we wait for the blessed hope—the glorious appearing of our great God and Savior, Jesus Christ, [14]who gave himself for us to redeem us from all wickedness and to purify for himself a people that are his very own, eager to do what is good. Titus 2:11-14

But God demonstrates his own love for us in this: While we were still sinners, Christ died for us. [9]Since we have now been justified by his blood, how much more shall we be saved from God's wrath through him! [10]For if, when we were God's enemies, we were reconciled to him through the death of his Son, how much more, having been reconciled, shall we be saved through his life! Rom. 5:8-10

THE TWO NATURES

We are therefore Christ's ambassadors, as though
God were making his appeal through us. We implore
you on Christ's behalf: Be reconciled to God. [21]God
made him who had no sin to be sin for us, so that
in him we might become the righteousness of God.
2 Cor. 5:20-21

Dear friends, now we are children of God, and what
we will be has not yet been made known. But we
know that when he appears, we shall be like him,
for we shall see him as he is. [3]Everyone who has
this hope in him purifies himself, just as he is pure.
1 John 3:2-3

Do not lie to each other, since you have taken off
your old self with its practices [10]and have put on the
new self, which is being renewed in knowledge in
the image of its Creator. Col. 3:9-10

You were taught, with regard to your former way
of life, to put off your old self, which is being corrupted by its deceitful desires; [23]to be made new in
the attitude of your minds; [24]and to put on the new
self, created to be like God in true righteousness

THE TWO NATURES

and holiness. [25]Therefore each of you must put off falsehood and speak truthfully to his neighbor, for we are all members of one body. Eph. 4:22-25

Now, brothers, I want to remind you of the gospel I preached to you, which you received and on which you have taken your stand. [2]By this gospel you are saved, if you hold firmly to the word I preached to you. Otherwise, you have believed in vain. 1 Cor. 15:1-2

Since we have these promises, dear friends, let us purify ourselves from everything that contaminates body and spirit, perfecting holiness out of reverence for God. 2 Cor. 7:1

Therefore, I urge you, brothers, in view of God's mercy, to offer your bodies as living sacrifices, holy and pleasing to God – this is your spiritual act of worship. [2]Do not conform any longer to the pattern of this world, but be transformed by the renewing of your mind. Then you will be able to test and approve what God's will is – his good, pleasing and perfect will. Rom. 12:1-2

THE TWO NATURES

And we, who with unveiled faces all reflect the Lord's glory, are being transformed into his likeness with ever-increasing glory, which comes from the Lord, who is the Spirit. 2 Cor. 3:18

For we are to God the aroma of Christ among those who are being saved and those who are perishing. [16]To the one we are the smell of death; to the other, the fragrance of life. And who is equal to such a task? 2 Cor. 2:15-16

Therefore we do not lose heart. Though outwardly we are wasting away, yet inwardly we are being renewed day by day. [17]For our light and momentary troubles are achieving for us an eternal glory that far outweighs them all. [18]So we fix our eyes not on what is seen, but on what is unseen. For what is seen is temporary, but what is unseen is eternal. 2 Cor. 4:16-18

Then Jesus said to his disciples, "If anyone would come after me, he must deny himself and take up his cross and follow me. [25]For whoever wants to save his life will lose it, but whoever loses his life for me will find it. [26]What good will it be for a man if he gains the whole world, yet forfeits his soul? Or what can a man give in exchange for his soul? Matt.16:24-26

"Enter through the narrow gate. For wide is the gate and broad is the road that leads to destruction, and many enter through it. [14]But small is the gate and narrow the road that leads to life, and only a few find it. Matt. 7:13-14

Those who belong to Christ Jesus have crucified the sinful nature with its passions and desires. [25]Since we live by the Spirit, let us keep in step with the Spirit. [26]Let us not become conceited, provoking and envying each other. Gal. 5:24-26

But you, man of God, flee from all this, and pursue righteousness, godliness, faith, love, endurance and gentleness. [12]Fight the good fight of the faith. Take hold of the eternal life to which you were called when you made your good confession in the presence of many witnesses. 1 Tim. 6:11-12

THE TWO NATURES

Therefore, rid yourselves of all malice and all deceit, hypocrisy, envy, and slander of every kind. ²Like newborn babies, crave pure spiritual milk, so that by it you may grow up in your salvation, ³now that you have tasted that the Lord is good. 1 Peter 2:1-3

And we also thank God continually because, when you received the word of God, which you heard from us, you accepted it not as the word of men, but as it actually is, the word of God, which is at work in you who believe. 1 Thess. 2:13

Your boasting is not good. Don't you know that a little yeast works through the whole batch of dough? ⁷Get rid of the old yeast that you may be a new batch without yeast—as you really are. For Christ, our Passover lamb, has been sacrificed. ⁸Therefore let us keep the Festival, not with the old yeast, the yeast of malice and wickedness, but with bread without yeast, the bread of sincerity and truth. 1 Cor. 5:6-8

We always carry around in our body the death of Jesus, so that the life of Jesus may also be revealed in our body. ¹¹For we who are alive are always being

THE TWO NATURES

given over to death for Jesus' sake, so that his life may be revealed in our mortal body. 2 Cor. 4:10-11

A man is not a Jew if he is only one outwardly, nor is circumcision merely outward and physical. [29]No, a man is a Jew if he is one inwardly; and circumcision is circumcision of the heart, by the Spirit, not by the written code. Such a man's praise is not from men, but from God. Rom. 2:28-29

TAKING SALVATION FOR GRANTED

Over the years, I have worked with several souls, and have led many of them to the Lord Jesus. As I observed them, I have noticed a radical initial transformation in each life. However, I have also noticed that the appreciation, the thanksgiving and the joy that this transformation brings, does not last. This has concerned me for these many years, until the beloved Lord Jesus opened my eyes to the fact that Salvation for our souls is in reality ongoing, in the sense that our souls are being cleansed of the ways of the sinful nature by the Holy Spirit, to enable us to grow up in our Salvation and come to maturity. In that sense, we (meaning our souls) are being saved through the sanctifying work of the Holy Spirit, from the ways of the sinful nature. This takes place as we come to knowledge of God's Word, if we believe it and choose to agree with it, and there choose to go on further with the Lord Jesus, trusting Him and obeying His Word, and thereby continuing in Him. As we do, we are being cleansed through the sanctifying work of the Holy Spirit; being purified and transformed, and therefore being saved from the ways of the sinful nature, as we continue on that road. But continue we must – if we want to be changed.

Let us give you a little background into what we have being dealing with. We must understand that the work of atonement by the Lord Jesus on Calvary's Cross was a finished work – period, for both spirit and soul, but the spirit received the fullness of that finished work once for all time immediately upon coming to Christ, for we were given a new spirit. This is in line with Hebrews Chapter 10, verse 10. But that same finished work has only begun to be brought home to our souls and therefore our bodies through the sanctifying work of the Holy Spirit, as we surrender and acknowledge our need to be cleansed. This work of the Holy Spirit must continue to be applied until we are free from the corruption of the sinful nature, to then live a holy life before God.

> But just as he who called you is holy, so be holy in all you do; [16]for it is written: "Be holy, because I am holy." 1 Peter 1:15-16

THE TWO NATURES

Yet to all who received him, to those who believed

in his name, he gave the right to become children

of God – [13]children born not of natural descent, nor

of human decision or a husband's will, but born of

God. John 1: 12-13

This finished work of the Lord Jesus will not only be a reality in His body on Calvary's Cross and in our spirit, but it will also be a reality in our very soul, manifesting in and through our body, as it is being cleansed of the ways of the sinful nature, and that sinful nature is being put to death area by area through the sanctifying work of the Holy Spirit. As this happens, the finished work is becoming a reality in our souls and therefore our bodies, and in our daily lives and experiences.

But if Christ is in you, your body is dead because of

sin, yet your spirit is alive because of righteousness.

[11]And if the Spirit of him who raised Jesus from the

dead is living in you, he who raised Christ from

the dead will also give life to your mortal bodies

through his Spirit, who lives in you. Rom. 8:10-11

We always carry around in our body the death of

Jesus, so that the life of Jesus may also be revealed

in our body. [11]For we who are alive are always being given over to death for Jesus' sake, so that his life may be revealed in our mortal body. 2 Cor. 4:10-11

I know your deeds, that you are neither cold nor hot. I wish you were either one or the other! [16]So, because you are lukewarm – neither hot nor cold – I am about to spit you out of my mouth. [17]You say, 'I am rich; I have acquired wealth and do not need a thing.' But you do not realize that you are wretched, pitiful, poor, blind and naked. [18]I counsel you to buy from me gold refined in the fire, so you can become rich; and white clothes to wear, so you can cover your shameful nakedness; and salve to put on your eyes, so you can see. [19]Those whom I love I rebuke and discipline. So be earnest, and repent. [20]Here I am! I stand at the door and knock. If anyone hears my voice and opens the door, I will come in and eat with him, and he with me. Rev. 3:15-20

However, many chose not to go on to be sanctified, for after coming to the knowledge of the requirements of God's Word, they rejected it because it did not conform to their carnal ways of believing and thinking, which they did not choose to turn from and die to. It therefore continued to be their way of life although it is of the sinful nature, and so they rejected the ways of the Lord Jesus, and turned from Him. This is a common, everyday happening in the church.

> Then he told them many things in parables, saying: "A farmer went out to sow his seed. ⁴As he was scattering the seed, some fell along the path, and the birds came and ate it up. ⁵Some fell on rocky places, where it did not have much soil. It sprang up quickly, because the soil was shallow. ⁶But when the sun came up, the plants were scorched, and they withered because they had no root. ⁷Other seed fell among thorns, which grew up and choked the plants. ⁸Still other seed fell on good soil, where it produced a crop—a hundred, sixty or thirty times what was sown. ⁹He who has ears, let him hear." Matt. 13:3-9

As we come to knowledge of God's Word, and come into agreement with it, and therefore choose to continue in our Lord Jesus based on His Word, the Holy Spirit uses His Word to transform or renew our minds from the old, wayward beliefs and thinking. The Holy Spirit cleanses us of the old way of life while leading us into the new, through His sanctifying or cleansing process. This happens as we choose to continue in the Word of the Lord Jesus, trusting in Him, while at the same time participating in the divine nature.

I am now understanding that most of those transformations I spoke about do not last, because when some souls are transformed, their focus is on the "feel good" aspect of the transformation, instead of their life in the Spirit with their Lord Jesus. They become light and happy, and many take this for granted and begin to enjoy their new-found happiness in a carnal way. This now becomes their focus instead of taking growing up in their Salvation, and therefore their transformation, in a serious way, and begin to study God's Word to learn what a life in the Lord Jesus is all about. This is so that they can begin to live it, and therefore come to know their Lord, His will, His ways and His requirements for their lives. As a result of this lack, within a short time their new-found state of feeling good begins to diminish, as it usually does, and again they blame the Lord Jesus for their lack of feeling good and their discontent.

> "Listen then to what the parable of the sower means: [19]When anyone hears the message about the kingdom and does not understand it, the evil one comes and snatches away what was sown in his heart. This is the seed sown along the path. [20]The one who received the seed that fell on rocky places

THE TWO NATURES

is the man who hears the word and at once receives it with joy. [21]But since he has no root, he lasts only a short time. When trouble or persecution comes because of the word, he quickly falls away. [22]The one who received the seed that fell among the thorns is the man who hears the word, but the worries of this life and the deceitfulness of wealth choke it, making it unfruitful. [23]But the one who received the seed that fell on good soil is the man who hears the word and understands it. He produces a crop, yielding a hundred, sixty or thirty times what was sown." Matt. 13:18-23

As this happens, those souls become disappointed and disillusioned with what they call a life in Christ, and so become discouraged. At this point, they are turned off from the things of the Lord Jesus, saying that Salvation is not what they had expected it to be. And they are right, for Salvation is not about feelings or a life of carnal happiness. What we are looking at is the fact that these problems are common with many souls, and are ongoing in the church. This happens for lack of commitment and teaching.

This takes place especially when you use God's saving grace to satisfy and serve your flesh, and to honor yourself; using Salvation to show off and to lift up yourself in pride. Rather than honoring the beloved Lord Jesus with that which He has blessed you with – a life in Him, instead you chose to use God's grace to you to feel good. When you listen to and follow the thoughts of the enemy in this way, he will now become your instructor. As you follow his leading, pride now becomes even more evident, and now you choose to please yourself even more. Soon, condemnation and fear take charge, because, according to the enemy, you must now cover yourself with spiritual pride so that no one will know that you have fallen back into your sinful nature, and are once again living according to it. For if they do, you will lose favor in their eyes because you will no longer be seen as that wonderful, transformed, spiritual person you are supposed to be, or were a while ago. A life of pretense and falsehood will now ensue.

Having bought into all these lies that the enemy has fed you and deceived you to believe, they will now become your new reality, and you are now going to act out a spiritual life. In order to cover yourself further, you will now seek to control the life, all under the deceit of the enemy, and you will now begin to pretend that the state of transformation you had before is still with you. So now the push is on to act happy, spiritual and godly, all in deceit, and in your own strength.

This is hard work. Anyone who has done this can tell you that indeed, this is misery, because you have to be on your guard at all times, and when you forget "your line" and blow it, the pattern is to beat up on yourself and fall under condemnation, because the standard under which you are now living is of that old nature, which is all about a self-righteous life. Here the enemy, after condemning you by putting before you how badly you have blown it, then begins to convince you that your problems are all God's fault, and it is because He does not love you or He does not want to help you or He is playing games with you, or He has deceived you, etc. These are some of the usual tricks of the enemy, which are all lies. This is how he portrays God before many souls and plays with their mind, to once again have them reject the Lord Jesus, so that he can make them his captive again.

Once you have bought into these lies, anger and then resentment and frustration follow, and you now enter into a full state of rebellion against God, because according to the enemy's lie that you have embraced – this is all God's fault. All the evil in which you have joined the enemy, and have come into agreement with him in, will now begin to manifest itself in and through you, against the Lord Jesus. In addition, all the old patterns of sins that you should have submitted yourself to be cleansed of will now come home to roost. This is because you did not spend your time surrendering yourself to the Holy Spirit to be cleansed, but instead, you spent your time glorying over how good you felt in your flesh, how successful you are, and so you were not cleansed because you were too busy with yourself.

> Jesus told them another parable: "The kingdom of heaven is like a man who sowed good seed in his field. [25]But while everyone was sleeping, his enemy came and sowed weeds among the wheat, and went away. [26]When the wheat sprouted and formed heads, then the weeds also appeared. [27]"The owner's servants came to him and said, `Sir, didn't you sow good seed in your field? Where then did the weeds come from?' [28]" `An enemy did this,' he replied. "The servants asked him, `Do you want us to go and pull them up?' Matt.13:24-28

As a result, you will now begin to see deep hostility, resentment, hate and even bitterness, against the very God whom you had proclaimed to have loved just a short time ago. This occurs all because you used the gift of Salvation that the Lord Jesus blessed you with to feel good about yourself in your flesh and to show off, instead of being serious about a life in the Lord Jesus, and therefore remain in

Him, learning from Him in His Word, growing in faith, knowledge, in obedience and faithfulness, etc.

> For this very reason, make every effort to add to your faith goodness; and to goodness, knowledge; [6]and to knowledge, self–control; and to self–control, perseverance; and to perseverance, godliness; [7]and to godliness, brotherly kindness; and to brotherly kindness, love. [8]For if you possess these qualities in increasing measure, they will keep you from being ineffective and unproductive in your knowledge of our Lord Jesus Christ. 2 Peter 1:5-8

There are those who believe that they should always feel good and happy, especially now that they are saved, and when they do not, they murmur against the Lord Jesus. They further believe that they should have no bad feelings, no sickness, no personal problems, much less problems with their circumstances or with finances or with others. Therefore, when problems arise, which they will, such persons rise up in anger and rebellion against the Lord Jesus. They withdraw from the Lord Jesus, believing that they deserve better than they are receiving from Him, because they are deceived to believe they have given up much in order to come to the Lord Jesus, while getting little or nothing in return. Such souls put no value at all on Salvation. Rather, their value is in the ways of the sinful nature, the natural, their flesh, the world, and on how they feel and understand these things.

> Trust in the LORD with all your heart and lean not on your own understanding; [6]in all your ways acknowledge him, and he will make your paths straight. [7]Do not be wise in your own eyes; fear the LORD and shun evil. [8]This will bring health to your body and nourishment to your bones. Prov. 3:5-8

There are also those who believe that now that they are saved, their future in heaven is secure. All this is according to how they feel, and not according to knowledge. They now have eternal life, according to their interpretation of Scripture, and they will use these Scriptures to keep themselves feeling secure. They now see themselves as free to live their lives according to how they feel in their flesh, and never according to the Word of God, without ever realizing that they have chosen to go the way of the sinful nature. This is the danger when God's Word is taken for granted and ignored.

The way of the feelings is the way of the sinful nature. Therefore, once you have been deceived to go the way of your feelings, you have again joined your sinful nature, and are now being led by the enemy. Your heart will now be full of demands before God; for once again it is the great self who is reigning. Such souls now see themselves as deserving more than ever, for they believe that they have given up everything to come to the Lord Jesus. Therefore, because they see themselves as having sacrificed so much, they believe that the Lord Jesus owes them. In fact, the Lord Jesus now owes them such a great debt, that He can never do enough to fulfill all that they demand of Him to pay this debt. Indeed, every prayer they "pray" are prayers of demand for that which they believe the Lord Jesus owes them and should do for them, and this must be done immediately, for they deserve it.

Their state is one of rigid arrogance before the Lord Jesus, because they believe that since they deserve and have asked, it must be given them immediately. This is the carnal man. This is the man who has fallen back into his carnal sinful nature. This is what Paul calls, "fallen from grace."

If anything, even the minutest thing, should occur in the lives of such souls that is not pleasing to them, they immediately rise up in rebellion and in accusation to the Lord Jesus. This is so because their demand and expectation is that the Lord Jesus must make everything smooth, peaceful, perfect, easy, pleasant and wonderful for them. This is all according to their will and the ways of their sinful nature in which they are walking, while deceived to believe that they are with the Lord Jesus.

In these beliefs, such persons tolerate no discomfort. In this mindset, they also believe that they deserve Salvation, along with all the promises that are in God's Word. This is all coming out of a heart that believes that God owes them a lot. Even hearing their name mentioned offends them. They believe that no one should ever mention their name in their absence, without their knowing beforehand what is going to be said. They are highly exalted, full of themselves, and therefore full of arrogance.

Such a heart can never get enough. Nothing will ever be enough to satisfy such souls. Who will ever believe that such a heart could have once known the Lord Jesus, and proclaimed love for Him? No one will, and I could not blame them, for I too did not believe these things were possible, until the blessed Lord Jesus revealed them to me, through the very lives of those He placed with me, and through other souls.

The unfortunate end result of all this, is that once you have returned to your sinful nature, the joy of the Lord Jesus, the joy of being saved and being His little child, the joy of coming to know and to love Him who is our Father, the joy of knowing His love, His tender embrace, the confidence that we have through faith in Him, the peace and the security one experiences upon receiving Salvation, are all eroded by these carnal beliefs, expectations and demands.

I saw on the news, just a week ago, the leader of an atheist organization being interviewed. He was once a pastor. I was surprised to see and to hear such things as was said by him and his wife. This man's anger against the Lord was very real, as revealed through his expression and his words. He proclaimed religion and their God, to be the reason for all the killings and problems in the world throughout history. Religion and their God are to be blamed, he said. His wife was with him, and she was equally angry, if not more so, against God.

How could such a thing happen, having been a pastor in a Baptist church? It happened because, at a point, through sickness or other problems, some pressure or disappointment or another, he was deceived to believe a lie of the enemy that says it is all God's fault, and so turned back to his sinful nature. There, he was once again trapped by the enemy, to carry out his will against God. These things are happening every day in the church. Think of the thousands of pastors who have abandoned their ministries every year – and on and on it goes. However, it seems to me that no one wants to believe, and therefore examine why these things are happening. This goes on simply because their doctrines do not permit them to believe that such things can happen, and so for them they don't.

> Blessed is the man who does not fall away on account of me." Luke 7:23

CHAPTER 3

THE WORKS OF SATAN

I t has now been ten years since the Lord Jesus moved me to write, and although He has kept before me this which I am about to write, I have delayed doing so because the reality of this subject has been too difficult for me to face, as it has always seemed too unlikely, too unreal and too foreign to me. I believe this is because when I first came to the Lord Jesus, the church that I first attended and became a part of, along with the few other churches that I visited on occasion, the Christian radio and television programs that I listened to, and all the Christians that I knew, all believed and taught dogmatically, that Christians could not be possessed by demons.

> Those who oppose him he must gently instruct,
> in the hope that God will grant them repentance

THE TWO NATURES

leading them to a knowledge of the truth, [26]and that they will come to their senses and escape from the trap of the devil, who has taken them captive to do his will. 2 Tim. 2:25-26

This Scripture is speaking of Christians taken captive by satan because of their opposition to the way the Holy Spirit was leading them. Maybe they did not want to give up the old ways. This is a common happening in the church, which usually ends up with persons running from the Lord Jesus to avoid laying down the life to Him. I myself have had continual opposition from Christians, so yes, the devil does take Christians captive when they live according to their sinful nature, ignoring God's Word and seeking to carry out their own will and agenda. When you do this, you become a prime target for the enemy to carry you off.

So, as the Holy Spirit says: "Today, if you hear his voice, [8]do not harden your hearts as you did in the rebellion, during the time of testing in the desert, [9]where your fathers tested and tried me and for forty years saw what I did. [10]That is why I was angry with that generation, and I said, 'Their hearts are always going astray, and they have not known my ways.' [11]So I declared on oath in my anger, 'They shall never enter my rest.' " ¹²See to it, brothers, that none of you has a sinful, unbelieving heart that turns away from the living God. ¹³But encourage one another daily, as long as it is called Today, so that none of you may be hardened by sin's deceitfulness. ¹⁴We have come to share in Christ if we hold firmly till the end the confidence we had at first. ¹⁵As has just been said: "Today, if you hear his voice, do not harden your hearts as you did in the rebellion." Heb. 3:7-15

I easily believed and embraced this doctrine, and for years this was my reality. I became as dogmatic as they were, and so no one could convince me otherwise. My belief was: if the Lord Jesus is in you, demons could not occupy that body. Therefore my question always was – how could anyone believe that the Lord Jesus and demons could be in the same body? I held this belief firmly in my heart, and it was difficult for me to let it go because it seemed right and logical to me.

But over the years, the Lord Jesus has been slowly but surely breaking down the barriers of these beliefs that I held. He has made it clear to me several times in many ways, that no, He does not occupy our body, per se, but rather our spirit, because that is the

THE TWO NATURES

only place in us that is pure and holy because it has been born of God, and is sealed with the Holy Spirit, and no demons can occupy that place once you are born-again.

> Yet to all who received him, to those who believed in his name, he gave the right to become children of God – [13]children born not of natural descent, nor of human decision or a husband's will, but born of God. John 1:12-13

> And you also were included in Christ when you heard the word of truth, the gospel of your salvation. Having believed, you were marked in him with a seal, the promised Holy Spirit, [14]who is a deposit guaranteeing our inheritance until the redemption of those who are God's possession—to the praise of his glory. Eph. 1:13-14

Our spirit then, becomes the place of abode for the Holy Spirit. Our soul was redeemed, to then be purified through the sanctifying work of the Holy Spirit. Therefore, there is no hallowed ground there for the Lord Jesus and the Holy Spirit to reside, for there the ways of the sinful nature are still embraced until we have come to knowledge of it in God's Word, and have chosen in obedience to the Lord Jesus, to deny it and reject its ways with His help. As we do this, the Holy Spirit is cleansing it and applying the death of the Lord Jesus on Calvary's Cross to it, area by area, through His sanctifying work. For this reason, He said we are to deny ourselves.

The denial of self the Lord Jesus is speaking of here, is to deny the ways of the sinful nature that keep us sinning. Until the Holy Spirit brings death area by area to the sinful nature, diminishing its power through His cleansing/sanctifying work of the soul, it is still alive and functioning, and where the sinful nature is there are demons attached to it. This means that there are demons attached to every sinful nature as that nature is of the enemy, and since every human has one from the time of the fall, this means that there are demons assigned by satan to every human being, be they Christians or not. In the same way, angels are assigned to each and every child of God.

Becoming a Christian does not change this, because the sinful nature is still active. It is only as the Holy Spirit cleanses/sanctifies the soul and therefore the body, area by area over time, and applies death to those areas of the sinful nature that He has cleansed, will it continue to diminish; losing its power to influence the soul and therefore the body to sin. This is if the soul continues in the Lord

THE TWO NATURES

Jesus, and embraces the sanctifying work of the Holy Spirit for Him to continue His cleansing.

I have noticed over the years, that each and every Christian that I had to minister to, had hosts of demons which the Lord Jesus led me to cast out, and only then were they free to make choices in those areas where they had been bound. (Obviously the Lord Jesus has several ways in which He delivers us.) The students that I am working with are a good example of this truth. Each of the students who have been set free from the bondage of satan's grip on their lives through the sinful nature, were set free through the deliverance that the Lord Jesus permitted to come into their lives, along with the choices they had to make to turn from sin. The Lord brought to my mind David, who was incited by satan to take a census of the fighting men of Israel (1 Chron. 21:1).

> Satan rose up against Israel and incited David to take a census of Israel. 1Chron, 21:1

Then there was Peter, who satan used by speaking through him to appeal to the flesh of the Lord Jesus, and the Lord Jesus told satan, who was speaking through Peter, **"Get behind me, Satan!..."** (Matthew 16:23). Moses' brother Aaron was used by satan in the desert during the absence of Moses, to make a calf for the people to worship, etc. (Exodus 32:1-9).

> Why is my language not clear to you? Because you are unable to hear what I say. [44]You belong to your father, the devil, and you want to carry out your father's desire. He was a murderer from the beginning, not holding to the truth, for there is no truth in him. When he lies, he speaks his native language, for he is a liar and the father of lies. [45]Yet because I tell the truth, you do not believe me! John 8:43-45

The reason that the Lord Jesus said that you belong to your father the devil, is because the sinful nature that is in us is of the devil. The sinful nature was imposed upon Adam and Eve by the devil through conquest. he conquered them through deceit, and through the sinful nature he is able to have input and great influence in every aspect of human life. This is why in Ephesians Chapter 6, verse 12 it tells us that our struggle is not against flesh and blood.

> For our struggle is not against flesh and blood, but against the rulers, against the authorities, against the powers of this dark world and against the spiritual forces of evil in the heavenly realms. Eph. 6:12

THE TWO NATURES

So instead of Adam being our father, satan took that place through conquest, and became our father. I have several souls who have told me that they heard the devil tell them that they are his, and to a point he is right, because his nature is in us. This further legitimizes his claim. This is why it is so important to know that satan is defeated, and his power and claim over us has been broken by the Lord Jesus on Calvary's Cross, so that we who have believed in the Lord Jesus Christ no longer belong to satan; nor should we be under his power or control any longer, or walk in fear of him and obey him.

> In him you were also circumcised, in the putting off of the sinful nature, not with a circumcision done by the hands of men but with the circumcision done by Christ, [12] having been buried with him in baptism and raised with him through your faith in the power of God, who raised him from the dead. [13]When you were dead in your sins and in the uncircumcision of your sinful nature, God made you alive with Christ. He forgave us all our sins, [14]having canceled the written code, with its regulations, that was against us and that stood opposed to us; he took it away, nailing it to the cross. [15]And having disarmed the powers and authorities, he

THE TWO NATURES

made a public spectacle of them, triumphing over
them by the cross. Col. 2:11-15

However, for those who do not believe and therefore do not embrace
the Lord Jesus, the devil continues to be their father. Therefore,
opposition and denial of God, even of His very existence, His Word
and His ways continue by many. Consequently, theories such as
the big bang, evolution, etc., become their beliefs, and they are
held prisoner to those beliefs by their father the devil, and so their
opposition to God continues. These are also some of the reasons
for the different religious cults around the world, and why God is
so opposed and rejected. The Word, ways and things of God are
being put down, belittled, scoffed at, ridiculed, turned upside down
and trampled on. The Name of the Lord Jesus is being blasphemed
and rejected by a hostile world. Christians in schools, in the military and in public places, government buildings and elsewhere,
cannot use or pray in the Name of the Lord Jesus. Pastors are being
arrested in Britain for preaching areas of God's Word that refers
to homosexuals, because it is seen as "hate speech," and in many
countries the Gospel and the Bible are not permitted at all. Yes,
things have been turned upside down! The things of God have been
placed underfoot, while at the same time the things of satan have
been exalted all over the world, and are being fully embraced by
a world that is deceived as Adam and Eve were. The examples are

before us: Halloween, the demonic movies, the millions of books that are sold each year about witches – training children how to cast spells; their little minds being taken over by demons, and according to the world it's all in fun, while the devil is laughing and seeing us for who we are – fools – to be buying into all this satanic culture.

> We know that anyone born of God does not continue to sin; the one who was born of God keeps him safe, and the evil one cannot harm him. [19]We know that we are children of God, and that the whole world is under the control of the evil one. [20]We know also that the Son of God has come and has given us understanding, so that we may know him who is true. And we are in him who is true— even in his Son Jesus Christ. He is the true God and eternal life. [21]Dear children, keep yourselves from idols. 1 John 5:18-21

satan has been at work ever since the fall to keep us enslaved to him and his ways – sin. his intent is to steal every good thing that God has given us. As the Lord Jesus said, satan comes to steal, kill and to destroy. This is his intent and nothing less will do.

THE TWO NATURES

The thief comes only to steal and kill and destroy;
I have come that they may have life, and have it to
the full. John 10:10

I now begin to see why the Lord Jesus kept me locked away for thirty-six years with the brethen. This was for me to see the demonic activities on a daily basis, both here and those places where He had sent me, only I could not put all this together although I could see it, talk about it, and deal with it in many ways. Yet I did not come to terms with the fact that demons actually live in Christians as well, and fully embrace it, until fifteen or so years had passed. Obviously this is God's doing, because He had to teach me all the ins and outs and fully convince me, for me to act upon it. It took another fifteen years for me to now be able to freely write about it, and I am now ready to boldly take this message to whomever and wherever the Lord Jesus chooses, which I could not even think about doing before.

In a large house there are articles not only of gold and silver, but also of wood and clay; some are for noble purposes and some for ignoble. [21]If a man cleanses himself from the latter, he will be an instrument for noble purposes, made holy, useful to the Master and prepared to do any good work. [22]Flee

THE TWO NATURES

the evil desires of youth, and pursue righteousness,
faith, love and peace, along with those who call on
the Lord out of a pure heart. ²³Don't have anything
to do with foolish and stupid arguments, because
you know they produce quarrels. ²⁴And the Lord's
servant must not quarrel; instead, he must be kind
to everyone, able to teach, not resentful. ²⁵Those
who oppose him he must gently instruct, in the hope
that God will grant them repentance leading them
to a knowledge of the truth, ²⁶and that they will
come to their senses and escape from the trap of
the devil, who has taken them captive to do his will.
2 Tim. 2:20-26

I know that most of the church does not believe that demons possess
Christians. The question then is: How can the church fight against
an enemy that it does not believe exists in its midst, because this is
the problem. Obviously it cannot. For this reason, the Lord Jesus
has used me over these many years in the lives of many persons,
and through these experiences of which I have written about in
some of the books, and through the revelation of the accusation that
came through my own thoughts on my way from Mexico City. He
further revealed through the anointing, satan answering, through
my thoughts, the question that I had asked the Lord Jesus. This I

have written about in "Called for the Very Last of Days," Volume 2. We need to think about what the Lord Jesus has said in Matthew Chapter 13, verse 19, concerning the fact that satan could snatch the Word from within the heart of people that received the Word.

> When anyone hears the message about the kingdom
> and does not understand it, the evil one comes and
> snatches away what was sown in his heart. This is
> the seed sown along the path. Matt. 13:19

The Lord Jesus has placed me on the front line of this battle to reveal through me and through all the experiences He has permitted me to go through, the work of satan in our midst. In all these experiences He has permitted me to have or to go through, He was always right there with me, as revealed in several of these writings. The Lord Jesus was sending this message to His church all along, only I did not know until now what He was doing.

All the other souls whom the Lord Jesus has placed before me over all these thirty-six years – every soul I had to deal with – all experienced demonic possession and diversions of all kinds. Diversions such as: while reading their Bible or going to prayer, suddenly diversionary thoughts of all kinds arise from within, causing them to struggle so that they could not read or pray. I myself have

experienced these things. Then arise running thoughts, lack of con-
sciousness, at other times heavy attacks of weariness and sleepi-
ness, where, a moment ago, they were very alert. he also afflicts
them with itching in different parts of their bodies, to keep them
occupied with itching. At different times they are attacked with
desires of all kinds, and carnal pleasures such as: food, shopping,
family, cars, houses, clothing, etc., to lead them off in pursuit of
them; others to frustrate them and cause them to give up.

> We know that anyone born of God does not continue
> to sin; the one who was born of God keeps him safe,
> and the evil one cannot harm him. [19]We know that
> we are children of God, and that the whole world
> is under the control of the evil one. 1 John 5:18-19

When we live according to the sinful nature, we are living contrary
to God's Word and will. This is sinning, and therefore the doors
of our hearts are open to the enemy to lead us wherever he wants.

At other times, the enemy places several things before them for
them to do as priority, so that they would get up from their prayer
or Bible reading to go and do them, if not he hits them with heavy
desires and fantasies. He brings memories from the past with
accompanying emotions, whether positive to exalt you, or negative

THE TWO NATURES

to embarrass you or at other times to condemn you. The devil uses these to tie you up. Feelings of boredom to pray or read your Bible, or heavy, seductive sleep to stop you from reading the Bible; feelings of discomfort and restlessness in your body so that you are unable to focus on your Lord; desires to eat certain things or feelings of hunger; desires to watch television; desires to see or talk to someone; desires to be active, to be busy doing things. The devil will bring feelings of rejection towards the Lord Jesus, and so remove any desire to pray; feelings and thoughts that prayer is hard work – an additional work after all the work you already have to do, so you will avoid praying or pray while murmuring that you have to do this too; feelings of misery, hate, bitterness and resentment towards others. The devil is the cause of arguments and fights, and is the source of discontent, arrogance and pride. The devil will bring reasons to the mind, and will reason with you to convince you that what is happening is not of him. In the midst of these struggles he brings thoughts to your mind that say all your problems are God's fault.

These things that I have mentioned are daily happenings that have been reported to me over and over again. These, plus the physical attacks upon the body – afflictions from A to Z – sicknesses of every kind, so I have to continually be praying for souls; and the Lord Jesus has been graceful to us – He always delivered those souls as we prayed. I myself have been under continual attack over all these years non-stop, and this has continued to this very day. I cannot recall a day that I have not experienced satan attacking me in one way or another, and this, seven days per week for thirty-nine years now.

The enemy is the one who is causing you to struggle, and his intention is to get you to give up and blame God, which many have done. These attacks and afflictions play a big part in all backsliding. He attacks souls with selfish ambition, greed, envy and jealousy; he hypes sexual desires to lead souls to lust and commit adultery. He manipulates your desires and feelings and uses them to lead you off in pursuit of fulfilling those feelings, even to commit adultery and homosexual acts, as we have seen over the years. Many pastors have fallen by such acts. Indeed, our struggle is not against flesh and blood.

> Finally, be strong in the Lord and in his mighty power. [11]Put on the full armor of God so that you can take your stand against the devil's schemes. [12]For our struggle is not against flesh and blood, but against the rulers, against the authorities, against the powers of this dark world and against the spiritual forces of evil in the heavenly realms. Eph. 6:10-12

THE TWO NATURES

The devil pushes and even pressures people to be dishonest and to lie. At times he sets them up in ways so that they feel obligated to lie to save face. At the same time, he hits them with pride to force them into the deceit and lies he has planned for them to fall into. Then when they have, he then hits them with condemnation, to now have them accuse the Lord Jesus for it all. The devil uses everything under the sun that he believes he can use, to tempt us and to get us to take them. The devil is a master of deceit and temptation, he uses it to set us up and trip us up, and in most cases, he is successful.

The devil uses manipulation of the mind to affect our desires, feelings and thoughts, and therefore our choices. Through the manipulation of the mind, the devil can change body temperature, change moods, cause you to have feelings, thoughts and impressions of all kinds, cause you to feel good or bad, have highs and lows, cause sickness and headaches. he can also hit you with discouragement and depression. I have had several reports from different souls who have felt movements within their heads, as if something is moving around within their mind that caused them to have a change of mood, while the mind is flooded with undesirable thoughts. I have seen different aspects of the body swollen as much as half, and other times twice its size suddenly, and as quickly as I rebuked it, it disappeared as if it had never happened. There was also the cut on the young man's hand that vanished as if it never was. This I do not understand, and I am sure we will not understand everything, because they are not all given to be understood. However the things that are given, we must seek to understand them so that we will not remain in ignorance to be used of the enemy against God, ourselves and others.

This that I am sharing is only the tip of the iceberg. I am only scratching the surface of the work of satan against us – the church of the Lord Jesus Christ. This is only the beginning of the opening up of the work of satan against us, the church, that the Lord Jesus is revealing to wake us up, and to get us to open our eyes, come to our senses, and begin to take action in faith with the help of the Holy Spirit, to oppose the work of satan against us by first understanding it.

The Lord Jesus has placed all this before me. There was also the time when satan launched at me with a vengeance, wanting to kill me, but the Lord Jesus kept him from harming me. This attack, along with his many afflictions and many other things that I have not mentioned, simply because they are too numerous to write about.

THE TWO NATURES

The purpose for all this is to wake up the body of the Lord Jesus Christ – the church, to the work of satan in its very midst, through it, against it, and among it. This keeps the church anemic and weak. Let us wake up! I have written about these things in drips and drops throughout some of the books, but I have not before confronted this subject head-on until today, because the Lord Jesus requires it done, and so has moved me in a heavy way to write about this. If He had not, I definitely would not. "Thank You, beloved Lord Jesus for waking up your body, the church, to come to its senses."

CHAPTER 4

A FURTHER VIEW OF THE WORK OF SATAN AGAINST THE CHURCH

J esus told them another parable: "The kingdom of heaven is like a man who sowed good seed in his field. [25]But while everyone was sleeping, his enemy came and sowed weeds among the wheat, and went away. [26]When the wheat sprouted and formed heads, then the weeds also appeared. [27]"The owner's servants came to him and said, 'Sir, didn't you sow good seed in your field? Where then did the weeds come from?' [28] "'An enemy did this,' he replied. "The servants asked him, 'Do you want us to go and pull them up?' [29]"'No,' he answered, 'because while you are pulling the weeds, you may root up the wheat with them. [30]Let both grow together until the harvest. At that time I will tell the harvesters: First collect the weeds and tie them in bundles to be burned; then gather the

THE TWO NATURES

wheat and bring it into my barn.'" ³⁶Then he left the crowd and went into the house. His disciples came to him and said, "Explain to us the parable of the weeds in the field." ³⁷He answered, "The one who sowed the good seed is the Son of Man. ³⁸The field is the world, and the good seed stands for the sons of the kingdom. The weeds are the sons of the evil one, ³⁹and the enemy who sows them is the devil. The harvest is the end of the age, and the harvesters are angels. ⁴⁰ "As the weeds are pulled up and burned in the fire, so it will be at the end of the age. ⁴¹The Son of Man will send out his angels, and they will weed out of his kingdom everything that causes sin and all who do evil. ⁴²They will throw them into the fiery furnace, where there will be weeping and gnashing of teeth. ⁴³Then the righteous will shine like the sun in the kingdom of their Father. He who has ears, let him hear. Matt.13:24-30, 36-43

Another question to be answered is, "Why Christians do stupid, foolish and ungodly things, and at times even break the law in ways that are no different from what the people of the world do?

To understand this question, we must first understand that although we are Christians, we still have a sinful nature, and the sinful nature cannot be saved because it is of the devil, and so demons are attached to that nature by him to carry out his will against us. Their mission is to keep us enticed with the things that are in line

THE TWO NATURES

with the ways of the sinful nature and therefore the world, fulfilling satan's will and desires through the cravings of our souls through our flesh for the pleasure, things and ways of the world, according to the plan of satan for our lives through our sinful nature.

For instance, they will bring impressions and thoughts about things that you might not even want to think about or do, and even when you resist them, they will try to force them on you to keep your mind tied up in them. This is to keep your mind off spiritual things. At times they will bring wild running thoughts to your mind that you do not want, all to wear you down and frustrate you, to in the end, get you to blame the Lord Jesus and accuse Him for your miserable state. They will deceive you to see and even believe that your circumstances are worse than those of all others, and much, much worse than the people of the world, and that God has done this to you because He does not love you, or that He hates you, etc.

They will deceive you to believe that God is to be blamed for all your problems, your disappointments, your misery, dissatisfaction, discontent, the burden that he, the devil, has laid on you, and the weight of life under which you are deceived to be walking. They will cause you to see the things you are to do as huge mountains before you, all to make life difficult, hard and seemingly impossible for you to continue in it, for which they will have you accuse God, to keep you at bay from the Lord Jesus.

They will bring suggestions to your mind to get you to carry them out. They will place images before you to entice you to indulge your flesh to divert you from the things of the Spirit. They will seduce you through fantasies to occupy your mind and keep you busy enjoying those things that are contrary to God's plan for your life, so that you will turn from the things of the Lord Jesus. They will encourage you to be selfish and at other times to be extravagant, wasteful, envious, jealous, covetous, malicious and deceitful, and also to be a man-pleaser, seeking people's favor to be pleasing and acceptable to them so that you can lift yourself up to be "somebody," etc. If you agree with those things, they will hold you prisoner in them to a life of deceit, where you will believe all the lies that they will bring to you. They will fill your thoughts with deceitful, lying reasons and suggestions as to why you should abandon a life in the Lord Jesus and give up, and better yet, don't even bother to start. They will fill your mind with lying judgments and accusations against the Lord Jesus, and against everything truly spiritual.

They will afflict you with pain, sickness and other kinds of afflictions, such as: greed, divisiveness, defensive ways, sneaky suspicious ways, justification, lies, deceit and dishonesty, falsehood and pretense, along with every other kind of illicit and immoral behavior such as: fornication, adultery, sexual immorality and pedophilia – in general sexual greed, etc. They will provoke fights and arguments between families, people, communities and countries to have them destroy each other. They will afflict you with fear, worry, anxiety, uncertainties, misery, rebellion, torment, discouragement and discontent. They will put alternatives before you to divert you from your spiritual pursuit. They can tie you up in a life of lies and dishonesty, where you find yourself lying and deceiving everyone around you, even yourself, if you agree with the lies that they bring to your mind, and also the impressions and feelings. The devil and his demons are able to do all these things because of the sinful nature, for he accomplishes his work through that nature. Again, that is why the Lord Jesus tells us to deny ourselves, meaning the things that come to us through that nature – the things of the flesh and the world that are contrary to His Word and ways.

> Then he said to them all: "If anyone would come after me, he must deny himself and take up his cross daily and follow me. 24For whoever wants to save his life will lose it, but whoever loses his life for me will save it. 25What good is it for a man to gain the whole world, and yet lose or forfeit his very self? Luke 9:23-25

THE TWO NATURES

These are all reasons why we should all gladly submit to be cleansed of the ways of the sinful nature through the sanctifying work of the Holy Spirit, where He cleanses us and puts death to the sinful nature as He cleanses us area by area, freeing us from that nature and its connection to the kingdom of the underworld.

They will pressure you mentally, and in general through your feelings to intimidate you to get you to accept those things that they are pushing on you. They will do whatsoever is necessary to get you to agree with and take the things that they are forcing on you, because the power that they have over you is your believing their lies, and coming into agreement with those lies they are pushing on you. Once you agree with them you are trapped. This is all designed to get you to blame the Lord Jesus for all that is happening to you so that you will reject the Lord Jesus, curse Him and give up. One of their tactics is to pressure you long enough with the things they are attacking you with, to outlast your resistance to them. They are usually very successful in using this tactic against souls.

All this is designed to keep you living according to the sinful nature in sin – separated from the Lord Jesus forever. This is why in 2 Peter Chapter 1, verse 4, we are told to participate in the divine nature in order to escape the corruption of the world caused by evil desires. These evil desires that the Scriptures speak of are of the sinful nature. Again, this is why the Lord Jesus tells us to deny ourselves, meaning we are to deny that which is of the sinful nature. Speaking to young Christians, the Scriptures say in 1 Peter, Chapter 2, verses 1-3:

> Therefore, rid yourselves of all malice and all deceit, hypocrisy, envy, and slander of every kind. [2]Like newborn babies, crave pure spiritual milk, so that by it you may grow up in your salvation, [3]now that you have tasted that the Lord is good. 1 Peter 2:1-3

As the Scriptures say, we are to rid ourselves of all those things, but we are Christians, we are born-again, washed in the blood of the Lord Jesus, born of the Spirit of God. The Lord Jesus tells us that who He set free is free indeed. Aren't we then free from all those things? Some think that we are, and others say at least we should be, but they are both wrong, because they are not taking into account that the sinful nature needs to be reckoned with, because although put to death in the body of the Lord Jesus on Calvary's Cross, it is only now being put to death in us as we come to knowledge of God's Word, believe it and embrace it to be the way of life that we want to live, and therefore begin to choose to live according to it, where the Word of God then becomes our reality and the boundary within which we walk. This has to be accepted by us. When it is, the Word of the Lord Jesus which says, **"So if the Son sets you free, you will be free indeed"** will be our life.

That is why the Scriptures say, **"now that you have tasted that the Lord is good."** And yes, we have tasted the goodness of the Lord Jesus through His Sacrificial Atonement, His forgiving us of our sins and our Salvation, His grace extended to us, His love, mercy and grace etc. For He died a cruel death to save wretches like you and me, and His goodness to us is confirmed and continues to be reaffirmed every day through the grace He has given us, and through His abiding Word, and by His Spirit guiding us, cleansing us and leading us into all truth; into a whole new way of life, etc.

And yes, we want and do choose to crave spiritual milk, because we want to grow up in our Salvation so that we will be able to draw closer to our Lord. We must then learn to deny the work of satan that is against us through the sinful nature, by refusing to further agree with the things that the enemy brings to our minds, and through impressions, etc. The power the enemy has over us is through our beliefs, and therefore our agreement with him in the things that he brings to deceive us.

How do we stop him and the things he brings to pollute our minds to divert us from the things of the Lord Jesus? Simply by believing the Lord Jesus and His Word, hold to it and stand on it, and stop believing satan's lies – he is defeated for he is a liar and the father of lies. Then begin to declare all that he brings to your mind to be of him, the enemy, and see them as the lies that they are, and affirm that you do not want those things in your mind anymore. Anything that comes to your mind that is negative and contrary to the Word of God, is of the devil. You must then oppose them by no longer believing that they are from you, and so stop agreeing with them.

> We demolish arguments and every pretension that
> sets itself up against the knowledge of God, and we
> take captive every thought to make it obedient to
> Christ. 2 Cor. 10:5

In so doing, you will begin, with the help of the Holy Spirit, to start to come out of agreement with all that is of your sinful nature, and therefore the enemy, and start to come into agreement with God's Word, embracing it to be your life. You must then actively choose to participate in His divine nature. The Holy Spirit will immediately begin His sanctifying/cleansing work in you when you do, turning you away from the ways of the sinful nature, by putting to death area by area, the ways of that nature. This then frees you each day more and more to live in the Lord Jesus and for the Lord Jesus, when you choose along with Him, to deny yourself of the ways of the sinful nature, and come into agreement with the Lord Jesus of your need to be sanctified. You are to diligently pray for these things.

> Now that you have purified yourselves by obeying the truth so that you have sincere love for your brothers, love one another deeply, from the heart. ²³For you have been born again, not of perishable seed, but of imperishable, through the living and enduring word of God. 1 Peter 1:22-23

> Dear friends, I urge you, as aliens and strangers in the world, to abstain from sinful desires, which war against your soul. ¹²Live such good lives among the pagans that, though they accuse you of doing wrong, they may see your good deeds and glorify God on the day he visits us. 1 Peter 2:11-12

Christians live sinful, ungodly lives because they have been deceived, and so have submitted to live according to the ways of the sinful nature instead of the divine nature. They therefore do foolish, stupid and ungodly things, and at times they even run afoul of the law. These things are common across the church. In all this, they have sinned, and continue to sin against the Lord Jesus.

THE TWO NATURES

Many continue in this mode, because according to them, they see nothing wrong with it. Others simply take doing such things for granted because they have been doing them for so long, they now mean nothing to them.

> For the grace of God that brings salvation has appeared to all men. [12]It teaches us to say "No" to ungodliness and worldly passions, and to live self-controlled, upright and godly lives in this present age, [13]while we wait for the blessed hope – the glorious appearing of our great God and Savior, Jesus Christ, [14]who gave himself for us to redeem us from all wickedness and to purify for himself a people that are his very own, eager to do what is good. [15]These, then, are the things you should teach. Encourage and rebuke with all authority. Do not let anyone despise you. Titus 2:11-15

SOME OF THE REASONS WHY THE CHURCH IS IN DARKNESS

The principal reason for the darkness the church is in, is the deceptive work of satan that is actively, consistently and continually working against it, which the church is mostly ignorant of.

THE TWO NATURES

The following points are results of this work of satan.

1) From the inception of the church, prideful men have tried to reign over the church of our Lord Jesus Christ. And indeed, since the death of the apostles, men have reigned over the church, and have brought man-made doctrines into it which has distorted the view of their followers to God's truth – His Word. This has continued to this day.

2) God's Word is not held in high esteem and honored by most Christians and believed to be the infallible Word of God – the Truth, the rule and conduct of faith and everything else in the life of a child of God. By this we must live.

3) As a result, love for God is lukewarm, and in too many cases it is only empty words spoken.

4) The guidance of the Holy Spirit is not sought after, nor embraced by most.

5) Erroneous doctrines that mislead God's people. The result is: no sincere submission and obedience or faithfulness from the hearts of many to the Lord Jesus; nor are His Word and will fully embraced, and therefore obeyed.

6) The spirit and soul are not defined and taught by the church because it seems that they are not clearly understood by it. This lack results in much difficulty for God's people.

7) Truth and sincerity of heart are far from the hearts and therefore the lips of many of God's people, therefore having their own way in dishonesty, deceit, pride, falsehood, pretense and self-will, prevail.

8) Most churches do not believe, and therefore do not accept or understand the working of satan against them, neither do most understand the difference between Salvation and Sanctification – being sanctified/the cleansing of the soul – and so satan has a free hand to work havoc in their minds, and in their midst.

9) Because of the lack of faith in the Lord Jesus Christ, psychoanalysis has been given great influence over God's people in several churches. The question is, how could such a theory have such a hold on God's children, when its foundation was laid by an enemy of God? Sigmund Freud was an atheist and a cocaine addict. He is the father of psychoanalysis. His teaching seems to be mostly mental gymnastics to deceive God's people and keep them in a state of

false hope, believing that through such mental manipulation they can get the knowledge they need to fix and change themselves without surrendering to the Lord Jesus Christ. Surrender would enable them to trust their lives, and therefore all their problems to the Lord Jesus – the only One who can fix and change lives. It seems the mission of Freud was to circumvent the work of the Holy Spirit to change the lives of God's people, by having them dependent on this type of analysis, rather than their Lord Jesus. This might be good for the world, but it is definitely not good for God's people. This is darkness over the church.

10) The wickedness, greed and immorality that are common across the church, which satan uses against men and women of God so successfully to bring them down, and therefore to cause discouragement to the body of Christ.

11) Envy, jealousy, competition and resentment are major tools in the hand of the devil, which he uses so destructively to bring division amongst brethren in the church, especially among the leadership.

12) The greed for power; "I deserve"; "I am better than you"; "I should be in that place, not you," so therefore, ignorance,

pride, arrogance, lack of submission and obedience to authority in the church, are tools the devil loves to use to exalt one and to bring down another and to bring division in the church.

13) There is too much political influence in the church, and it misguides and leads many away from the truth of God's Word.

14) There is too much adultery: supposedly men of God committing adultery with the opposite sex, the same sex, and with young boys and girls.

15) Many souls in the church believe that they are walking in humility, in obedience to the Word of God, and are therefore walking with the Lord Jesus. However, in reality, they are walking in pride, highly exalted in their hearts and minds, which is the way of the devil. The Lord Jesus tells us in His Word that unless we humble ourselves as a little child, we will not see or enter the Kingdom of God. This tells us that when we come to the Lord Jesus, we are to deliberately choose to walk in truth and sincerity, and therefore humility. Without these and a heart of faith, we cannot walk with the Lord Jesus. Humility is a requisite to walk with the Lord

Jesus, and pride is required to walk with satan. We have a need to come to knowledge of this truth so that we will be able to choose who we want to walk with, for we are the only ones who can make such a choice.

In a large house there are articles not only of gold and silver, but also of wood and clay; some are for noble purposes and some for ignoble. [21] If a man cleanses himself from the latter, he will be an instrument for noble purposes, made holy, useful to the Master and prepared to do any good work. [22] Flee the evil desires of youth, and pursue righteousness, faith, love and peace, along with those who call on the Lord out of a pure heart. 2 Tim. 2:20-22

As a result of taking a life in Christ for granted, and ignorance of a true life in Christ, plus other neglects not mentioned here, the church is in darkness, and we cannot live the abundant life that the Lord Jesus brought. Yet for most, they believe that they are living it. These few points that are listed are barely touching the surface of the problems that the church faces. This is caused by the lack of acknowledging the deceitful forces of satan that are at work against it.

THE TWO NATURES

Finally, be strong in the Lord and in his mighty
power. [11] Put on the full armor of God so that you
can take your stand against the devil's schemes. [12]
For our struggle is not against flesh and blood, but
against the rulers, against the authorities, against the
powers of this dark world and against the spiritual
forces of evil in the heavenly realms. Eph. 6:11-12

Your eye is the lamp of your body. When your eyes
are good, your whole body also is full of light. But
when they are bad, your body also is full of darkness. [35]See to it, then, that the light within you is not
darkness. [36]Therefore, if your whole body is full of
light, and no part of it dark, it will be completely
lighted, as when the light of a lamp shines on you."
Luke 11:34-36

(This subject continues in more detail in the book, "Called For The
Very Last of Days" Volume 2.)

"Go up and down the streets of Jerusalem, look
around and consider, search through her squares. If
you can find but one person who deals honestly and
seeks the truth, I will forgive this city. [2]Although

THE TWO NATURES

they say, `As surely as the LORD lives,' still they are swearing falsely." [3]O LORD, do not your eyes look for truth? You struck them, but they felt no pain; you crushed them, but they refused correction. They made their faces harder than stone and refused to repent. [4]I thought, "These are only the poor; they are foolish, for they do not know the way of the LORD, the requirements of their God. [5]So I will go to the leaders and speak to them; surely they know the way of the LORD, the requirements of their God." But with one accord they too had broken off the yoke and torn off the bonds. Jer. 5:1-5

THE TWO NATURES

OTHER BOOKS BY
THE AUTHOR

"THE TWO NATURES." THIS IS THE SIXTH BOOK IN THE SERIES "GOD SPEAKS" WHICH TOTALS 14 BOOKS.

BOOKS PUBLISHED BY XULON PUBLISHERS IN THIS SERIES ARE:

GOD SPEAKS – 1 "CALLED FOR THE VERY LAST OF DAYS."
IBSN 978-1-5456-3607-7

This book is the autobiography of the author, and details his calling, separation and anointing by the Lord Jesus with the purpose to prepare and then to give him knowledge and understanding to write this and the books that follow. These books are for the cleansing and preparation of His Church for His Second Coming.

GOD SPEAKS – 2 "CALLED FOR THE VERY LAST OF DAYS – VOLUME 2."
IBSN 978-1-5456-4852-0

This book is the continuation and completion of the first. It gives in depth spiritual knowledge and understandings of the work of the enemy against us, so we are no longer ignorant of his devices. This serves to then bring us into the abundant life that our Lord Jesus brought and is yet to be lived by the Church as a whole. The author also tells of his personal struggles and failures and how he overcame all through faith in and obedience to our Lord Jesus.

GOD SPEAKS – 3 "FREEWILL."
IBSN 978-1-5456-5838-3

This book is fundamental to the believer to have a unshakable walk of faith. Through the Scriptures it shows that Freewill has been given by God, to each and every individual in honor of His prized creation, and the absolute necessity that because of this blessing, responsibility for our each and every choice is what determines whether the believer will have a spiritual life, and to what dimension, versus a carnal, defeated and "dead" life (currently the experience for most of the Church).

THE TWO NATURES

GOD SPEAKS – 4 "THE PROMISED BLESSING TO THE NATIONS."
IBSN 978-1-5456-5843-7

This book gives clear, concise details – all based on the Scriptures that God made and gave no other Promise to bless the nations. It is an easy to read account in TRUTH and gives the reader unshakable knowledge of Who our Lord Jesus is, His purpose and His uniqueness – setting Him apart from all others. Here the answer to the questions as to whether or why we uphold and believe Jesus to be the ONLY WAY, TRUTH and LIFE. The ONLY WAY TO GOD.

GOD SPEAKS – 5 "FAITH AND BELIEVING."
IBSN 978-1-54566-597-8

This Book gives clear guidelines based on the Word of God, how to choose and to put into practice to live by Faith & Believing in God on a daily, moment-by-moment basis. It demystifies Faith – seen by many in the church as "too hard" to live by, and reveals clearly that the opposite is true – that in Faith & Believing we enter into His Peace and Rest – now and for all eternity. This Book is written to give every believer all the knowledge required to lay hold of and to live in Faith & Believing – to erase all the doubts, fears and confusion that so plagues and burdens His Church.

CPSIA information can be obtained
at www.ICGtesting.com
Printed in the USA
FSHW011010100819
60889FS